CORRECT WRITING

Third Edition

Eugenia Butler

University of Georgia

Mary Ann Hickman

Gainesville Junior College

Lalla Overby

Brenau College

D.C. Heath and Company
Lexington, Massachusetts
Toronto

To the Instructor

Correct Writing, Third Edition, is a revision and enlargement of earlier editions. This edition has been updated and revised in the light of universal needs in colleges which now find it necessary to return to the teaching of basic grammar, punctuation, and mechanics before moving on to instruction in composition and rhetoric. The authors have amplified the body of grammatical information to a considerable degree through the addition of definitions of terms and careful explanations of the principles involved in sentence structure. These definitions and explanations come at the earliest mention of a term, so that students will not have to continue their study of a grammatical principle without a clear understanding of what they have already been told. Discussions which may be enlarged upon in other chapters carry convenient cross-references that point the reader to further information available on a given topic.

The format for this edition of *Correct Writing* combines the best features of a handbook of grammar and composition with a workbook of exercises. Wherever possible the exercises have been simplified to make them more than usually illustrative of the grammatical principles involved. The exposition of the various aspects of grammar and sentence structure is presented to the student in as simple terms as possible and is more extensive than that in most other workbooks. Although the discussion of many aspects of grammar is not intended to be exhaustive, information in this present book is thorough enough for a student to grasp and to learn without having constantly to rely on the instructor's further discussion. The Glossary of Faulty Diction is an especially useful feature, and it is accompanied by exercises so that it may be applied in a practical way as well as used as a reference.

The treatment of punctuation is a strong feature of this book, because it serves as a follow-up to the chapters in which the basic principles of sentence structure are discussed. When students reach this lesson on punctuation, they will already have learned most of the rules in the lesson, which can then serve as a review of the subject instead of a listing of arbitrary rules to be memorized. There are, however, some occasions when it seems appropriate simply to cite a rule without attempting theoretical explanations which would defeat the purpose of the text as an elementary handbook for composition. A rule governing punctuation, grammar, or sentence structure may be susceptible to modification or exception, but it is nevertheless useful for being arbitrarily stated. If students do not know that their sentences contain faulty parallelism, for example; they are hardly able at an early stage to explore the subtleties of such constructions.

A central point which should emerge through a student's careful use of this text is that the study of grammar and of sentence elements is of value primarily as a means of improving communication and understanding.

To the Student

This book is a combination textbook, workbook, and reference handbook. It contains a great deal of information in the various chapters that precede the exercises. It is a workbook in which you will be able to write your answers concerning grammatical principles which you have just studied. When you have worked all the exercises as well as the Review and Achievement Tests, you will still have a convenient reference handbook in which you can check points of grammar, usage, punctuation, and mechanics whenever you need to.

Working conscientiously through the chapters and exercises of this book will put you well on your way to a mastery of grammar and usage, which in turn will help you to write and speak accurately and effectively.

Contents

DIAGNOSTIC TEST

A. In the following sentences identify the part of speech of each *italicized* word by writing one of the following numbers in the space at the right:

1 if it is a *noun,*	**5** if it is an *adverb,*
2 if it is a *pronoun,*	**6** if it is a *preposition,*
3 if it is a *verb,*	**7** if it is a *conjunction,*
4 if it is an *adjective,*	**8** if it is an *interjection.*

1. *I* will see you in the morning. _____
2. *While* we were in New York, we saw three plays. _____
3. Horace has *large* hands. _____
4. *Throughout* the term we studied several poets. _____
5. Procrastination is the *thief* of time. _____
6. I have *recently* read a very funny book. _____
7. Does any one thing *spark* your creative powers? _____
8. *Some* of my fondest childhood memories are of trips to the circus. _____
9. One of the most prominent names in American comedy for the past *forty* years is that of Bob Hope. _____
10. Virtually all of the shops close *by* six o'clock. _____
11. A favorable *reaction* to Professor Little's nomination is expected. _____
12. Improved methods of *geological* exploration have led to discoveries of new sources of petroleum. _____
13. *Frequently* his argument is overstated rather than misleading. _____
14. Public attitudes *toward* controversial issues are constantly shifting. _____
15. Biomass is a new *energy* source. _____
16. The old hound *looked* with disdain at the noisy teenagers. _____
17. Tim, get *your* feet off the sofa. _____
18. *Wow!* Did you see that catch? _____
19. We wanted to go *but* had to stay. _____
20. By using coupons, Marie *saved* five dollars. _____
21. The state office buildings *are located* on Capitol Avenue. _____
22. The committee worked diligently on *its* report. _____
23. *How* do you spend your leisure time? _____
24. Chess is a game of intelligence *and* patience. _____
25. When I called *yesterday,* you were out. _____

B. Each of the following sentences either contains an error in grammar or is correct. Indicate the error or the correctness by writing one of the following numbers in the space at the right:

1 if the *case of the pronoun is incorrect,*
2 if the *subject and verb do not agree,*
3 if a *pronoun and its antecedent do not agree,*
4 if an *adjective or an adverb is used incorrectly,*
5 if the *sentence is correct.*

26. The street needs resurfacing bad. _____
27. Neither the players nor the coach were prepared for the game. _____
28. Both my brother and me attended Baylor University. _____
29. I hope you don't mind me doing this. _____
30. Almost everyone wants to do their best. _____
31. Beyond the barn is the apple orchard and the vineyard. _____
32. The swimming team has respect for their coach. _____
33. The boys and girls are real excited about their camping trip. _____
34. Each of the salesmen was given their own copy of the annual report. _____
35. The old Ferguson home sure needs some repairs. _____
36. Everyone is already on board the train except he and Gail. _____
37. The squadron of planes are based at an airfield near Albany. _____
38. According to the fashion editor, dresses will be some shorter next year. _____
39. I am surprised that neither of the restaurants serve breakfast. _____
40. The manager as well as his assistant are attending a seminar in San Francisco. _____
41. Appearing as elegantly as ever, the model strolled down the runway. _____
42. Most of the community knows that it is her who donated the money for the playground. _____
43. The media, of course, said that it would work for open meetings of the city council. _____
44. No one but Dick and I went to the movie this weekend. _____
45. Ask whoever answers the telephone for Mr. Goodman's initials. _____
46. The Douglas fir is one of those trees that is valued as a source of timber. _____
47. Every member of the company understood that their orders came from Captain Townsend. _____
48. I hope that Mrs. Blair offers Dana and I tickets to the tennis match. _____
49. Five dollars are all that I have left in my billfold. _____
50. I feel badly that we do not have room in the car for Isabel. _____

C. Each of the following sentences either contains an error in sentence structure or is correct. Indicate the error or correctness by writing one of the following numbers in the space at the right:

> 1 if the sentence contains a *dangling modifier*,
> 2 if the sentence contains a *misplaced modifier*,
> 3 if the sentence contains a *faulty reference of a pronoun*,
> 4 if the sentence contains *faulty parallelism*,
> 5 if the sentence is *correct*.

51. The air conditioner runs quietly, steadily, and it has certainly improved since Mr. Proxmire worked on it. _____
52. With that forecast one really ought to carry your umbrella. _____
53. I'm going to give Arnold a tennis racket for his birthday, because he really enjoys it. _____
54. After reading the directions, the game was not difficult to play. _____
55. That man works in my office sitting with Emily in the next booth. _____
56. They not only plan to fly to Toronto but also to go by train to Winnipeg. _____
57. Mrs. Yeager told her neighbor that her house could use a good cleaning. _____
58. The house was restored where the nineteenth century musician lived recently. _____
59. Teresa said that she only saw the last fifteen minutes of the news. _____
60. For my birthday I received a subscription to *Seeds*; this was a complete surprise. _____
61. To paint the ceiling, a longer ladder than this one is going to be necessary. _____
62. In all this fog it is difficult to clearly see the top of the Washington Monument. _____
63. When enlarged, the whole family will enjoy the den. _____
64. I do believe that even my hometown is larger than Rachel. _____
65. After consulting Dr. Snyder, Liza decided to take the computer course. _____
66. The center is a tall boy but who can move quickly. _____
67. My desk is piled high with papers, which is a source of embarrassment to me. _____
68. Mr. McRae says that he cannot recommend Flora for a raise because she is lazy, unreliable, and she takes no real interest in her work. _____
69. We are planning to rent a chalet and spend the whole weekend on the slopes, which should be great fun. _____
70. Tootsie told Nell that she had been wrong about the opening date for the antique show. _____
71. My plane's departure was announced just before entering the airport building. _____
72. The young man who was holding the wheel in place carefully tightened each bolt. _____
73. "I only want one more piece of the caramel cake," said Marcia. _____
74. To be certain that the fire is out, it must be thoroughly doused with water. _____
75. While swimming with Sam, the ham salad I had made was eaten by a dog. _____

D. Each of the following sentences contains an error in punctuation or mechanics, or is correct. Indicate the error or the correctness by writing one of the following numbers in the space at the right:

1 if a *comma* has been omitted,
2 if a *semicolon* has been omitted,
3 if an *apostrophe* has been omitted,
4 if *quotation marks* have been omitted,
5 if the sentence is *correct*.

76. After we had eaten the dogs finished up the scraps. _____

77. I will leave home at nine o'clock you probably should leave fifteen minutes earlier. _____

78. Janice Martha and Sara are the girls who have been chosen to attend the meeting in Philadelphia. _____

79. There is a musical show named after Fats Waller's famous song Ain't Misbehavin'. _____

80. I was trying to find my glasses and Mother kept telling me to hurry. _____

81. Jason and Charlie have bought an old Lincoln and plan to turn it into a collectors' piece. _____

82. Its amazing how often I seem to run out of money before payday. _____

83. The slow relentless dripping of the rain made us all feel gloomy. _____

84. Surely Sydney you realize that Kitty is old enough to make her own decisions. _____

85. Let's all try to meet at the same time and place next year, suggested Grady. _____

86. Sitting on its nest, the thrush stared at me with bright, steady eyes. _____

87. When he was a child in New Orleans my father used to visit the French Market every day with his mother. _____

88. Do you know the limerick that begins, A lady with money to fry...? _____

89. You never cross your *t*'s, Mary consequently, they look like *l*'s. _____

90. Wont you reconsider your decision not to join us for dinner, Mrs. Peabody? _____

91. Nathan tried several times to reach Elsie on the telephone but could not get an answer. _____

92. I wish somebody would hide Tim's record of Willie Nelson singing On the Road Again. _____

93. The snow is certainly beautiful however, those icy patches on the walk are treacherous. _____

94. After dinner the Johnsons came over to watch television with us. _____

95. I approve of Frans going back to school, don't you? _____

96. On my way to the drugstore I saw Harry and Dick but they didn't see me. _____

97. Our club now has its own headquarters so please send all correspondence to the new address. _____

98. It's a blessing, sighed Jennie Lou, that we had enough kindling and logs to last through the ice storm. _____

99. When I was in high school I learned Bryant's long poem "Thanatopsis" by heart. _____

100. While she was typing the letter from Nancy arrived. _____

CORRECT WRITING

Third Edition

1

The Parts of Speech

Our own language is one of the most fascinating subjects that we can investigate, and those of us who speak and write English can find pleasure in seeking to understand its various aspects. The concern of this book is Standard English and its use in contemporary writing. The study and description of Standard English, based on the thoughtful use of language by educated people, provide standards for correct writing. Although the English language is flexible and continually changing, it is possible to follow certain principles and to observe certain characteristics of usage which can make grammar a relatively exact study and one which can widen the scope of the individual in a satisfying way.

An understanding of the accurate and effective use of English is important not only for communication but also as a vital element of creative thought. Because words are used in the formulation of conscious thought, precise grammatical usage promotes clear thinking and insures logical and systematic transmission of ideas.

Knowledge of Standard English and its acceptable forms is basic to the education of all college students. Learning grammatical terms is an essential first step toward understanding what is correct and what is incorrect in the writing of standard English prose. The best place to begin this learning of terms is with the various elements that make up a sentence, elements called **parts of speech.** Any word's identification as a part of speech depends upon its usage within a sentence. The names of the eight parts of speech are as follows:

noun	adverb
pronoun	preposition
adjective	conjunction
verb	interjection

1a   Noun

A **noun** (from Latin *nomen*, name) is the name of a person, place, thing, or idea. All nouns are either proper nouns or common nouns. A **proper noun** is the name of a particular person, place, or thing and is spelled with a capital letter:

John F. Kennedy	London, England
California	The Washington Monument
The Vatican	O'Keefe Junior High School

A **common noun** is the name of a class of persons, places, things, or ideas, and is not capitalized:

girl	home	dog	disgust
teacher	park	automobile	friendship
student	street	honesty	poverty

Nouns may also be classified as **individual** or **collective. Collective** nouns name groups of persons, places, or things that function as units:

flock	dozen
jury	the rich
team	club

Finally, nouns may be classified as **concrete** or **abstract.** The **concrete** noun names a person, place, or thing which can be perceived by one of the five senses. It can be seen, felt, smelled, heard, or tasted. Here are some examples of concrete nouns:

door	woman	scream
dress	city	snow
tree	odor	museum

An **abstract** noun is the name of a quality, condition, action, or idea. The following are examples of abstract nouns:

beauty	truth	kindness
fear	loneliness	campaign
dismissal	hatred	courtesy

A noun is said to belong to the **nominative**, the **objective**, or the **possessive case**, depending upon its function within a sentence. Subjects are in the nominative case (The *truck* stopped), objects are in the objective case (He saw the *parade*), and nouns showing possession are in the possessive case (That car is *John's*). As you can see, there is no difference in form between nouns in the nominative and the objective cases. The possessive case, however, changes a noun's form. (See Chapter 11 for a thorough discussion of case.)

A noun may be **singular** or **plural**, forming its plural generally by the addition of *-s* or *-es* to the end of the singular form (*girl, girls; potato, potatoes*).

Nouns, together with pronouns and other words or expressions that function as nouns, are sometimes called **substantives.**

1b Pronoun

A **pronoun** (from Latin *pro,* for, and *nomen,* name) is a word used in place of a noun. A pronoun usually refers to a noun or other substantive already mentioned, which is called its **antecedent** (from Latin *ante,* before, and *cedere,* to go). Most pronouns have antecedents, but some do not.

Pronouns are divided into seven categories:

> PERSONAL PRONOUNS: I, you, he, it, they, etc.
>
> DEMONSTRATIVE PRONOUNS: this, that, these, those
>
> INDEFINITE PRONOUNS: each, anyone, everyone, either, several, some, etc.
>
> INTERROGATIVE PRONOUNS: who, which, what
>
> RELATIVE PRONOUNS: who, which, that
>
> REFLEXIVE PRONOUNS: myself, yourself, herself, themselves, etc.
>
> INTENSIVE PRONOUNS: I *myself,* you *yourself,* she *herself,* they *themselves,* etc.

The personal pronouns have differing forms depending upon whether they are subjects (*I* will help Mr. Curtis) or objects (Gene told *him* the plan) or show possession (The red coat is *hers*). These differences in form, which are seen only in the possessive case of nouns, occur in all three cases (*nominative, objective,* and *possessive*) of pronouns.

Personal pronouns, like nouns, are singular and plural, but their plurals are irregularly formed: I, *we*; she, *they*; it, *they*; etc. The following table shows the various forms of the personal pronouns:

SINGULAR

	Nominative	*Objective*	*Possessive*
1st person	I	me	my, mine
2nd person	you	you	your, yours
3rd person	he, she, it	him, her, it	his, her, hers, its

PLURAL

	Nominative	*Objective*	*Possessive*
1st person	we	us	our, ours
2nd person	you	you	your, yours
3rd person	they	them	their, theirs

1c Adjective

An **adjective** (from Latin *adjectivum,* something that is added) modifies, describes, limits, or adds to the meaning of a noun or pronoun (*strange, lovely, three, French, those*). In other words, adjectives modify substantives. The articles *the, a,* and *an* are adjectives. Nouns in the possessive case (*Martha's* book, the *cat's* whiskers) and some possessive forms of the personal pronouns are used as adjectives:

> my   our
>
> your   your
>
> his, her, its   their

Many demonstrative, indefinite, and interrogative forms may be used as either pronouns or adjectives:

> DEMONSTRATIVE: this, that, these, those
>
> INDEFINITE: each, any, either, neither, some, all, both, every, many, most
>
> INTERROGATIVE: which, what, whose

When one of these words appears before a noun or other substantive, describing it or adding to its meaning (*this* cake, *those* gloves, *any* person, *some* food, *which* dress), it is an adjective. When the word stands in the place of a noun (*Those* are pretty roses), it is, of course, a pronoun.

Adjectives formed from proper nouns are called **proper adjectives** and are spelled with a capital letter **(German, Christian, Biblical, Shakespearean)**.

1d   Verb

A **verb** (from Latin *verbum*, word) is a word used to state or ask something and usually expresses an action (*spoke, tells, ran, argued, fights*) or a state of being (*is, seemed, existed, appears*). As its Latin origin indicates, the verb is *the* word in the sentence, for every sentence must have a verb, either expressed or understood.

TRANSITIVE AND INTRANSITIVE VERBS

A verb is called **transitive** if its action is directed toward some receiver, which may be the object of the verb or even its subject. (*David flew the plane,* or *The plane was flown by David.* Whether *plane* is the subject or object of the verb, the fact remains that David flew the plane, making *plane* in both sentences the receiver of the verb's action.)

NOTE: The term *action* should not be misinterpreted as always involving physical activity. The so-called "action" of a verb may not refer to a physical action at all: Mr. Lee *considered* the plan, Amanda *believed* Frank's story, Louise *wants* a new car. The verbs *considered, believed,* and *wants* are transitive verbs; and their objects *plan, story,* and *car* are receivers of their "action," even though there is no physical action involved.

A verb is called **intransitive** if its action is not directed toward some receiver. (*Lightning strikes. Mother is ill.*) Most verbs may be either transitive or intransitive, simply depending on whether or not a receiver of the verb's action is present in the sentence: *Lightning strikes tall trees* (*strikes* is transitive because *trees* is its object). *Lightning strikes suddenly* (*strikes* is intransitive because no receiver of its action is present).

LINKING VERBS

There is a special group of intransitive verbs which make a statement not by expressing action but by indicating a state of being or a condition. These verbs are called **linking verbs** because their function is to link the subject of a sentence with a noun, pronoun, or other substantive that identifies it or with an adjective that describes it. A subject and a linking verb cannot function together as a complete sentence without the help of the substantive or adjective needed to complete the thought; for example, in the sentence *Dorothy is my sister* the word *sister* is necessary to complete the sentence, and it identifies *Dorothy*, the subject. In the sentence *Dorothy is vigorous* the word *vigorous* is necessary, and it describes the subject.

The most common linking verb is the verb *to be* in all its forms, but any verb that expresses a state of being and is followed by a noun or an adjective that identifies or describes the subject is a linking verb. Following is a list of some of the most commonly used linking verbs:

appear	grow	seem	taste*
become	look	smell	
feel	remain	sound	

You will notice that those verbs referring to states of being perceived through the five "senses" are included in the list: *look, feel, smell, sound,* and *taste.* (Sally *looks* happy, I *feel* chilly, The coffee *smells* good, The ticking of the clock *sounded* loud, The plum pudding *tastes* spicy.)

ACTIVE AND PASSIVE VOICE

Transitive verbs are said to be in the **active voice** or the **passive voice. Voice** is the form of a verb that indicates whether the subject of the sentence performs the action or is the receiver of the action of the verb. If the subject performs the action, the verb is in the *active voice* (*Andy ate soup for lunch today*). If the subject receives the action, the verb is in the *passive voice* (*Soup was eaten by Andy for lunch today*).

TENSE

Tense is the form a verb takes in order to express the time of an action or a state of being, as in these examples: *Helen walks* (**present tense**); *Helen walked* (**past tense**). These two tenses, present and past, change the verb's simple form to show the time of the verb's action. The other four of the six principal tenses found in English verbs are formed through the use of **auxiliary** (helping) verb forms like the following:

am	is	were	have	had
are	was	will	has	been

The use of these auxiliary verbs creates **verb phrases** (groups of related words that function as single parts of speech). These verb phrases enable the writer to express time and time relationships far beyond those found in the simple present and past forms: She *has gone* to the office; Maggie *will ride* with me; You *must finish* your dinner; He *had expected* to win the prize; I *am planning* a trip.

CONJUGATION OF VERBS

Showing all forms of a verb in all its tenses is called **conjugation.** Any verb may be conjugated if its **principal parts** are known. These are (1) the first person singular, present tense, (2) the first person singular, past tense, (3) the past participle. (The **participle** is a verbal form which must always be accompanied by an auxiliary verb when it is used to create one of the verb tenses.)

---

*These verbs are not exclusively linking verbs; they may also be used in an active sense, possibly having objects, as in the following:

The dog cautiously *smelled* the food in its bowl.
We *looked* everywhere for the lost key.
Sharon *felt* the warmth of the log fire across the room.
Nick *tasted* the chowder and then added salt.

The principal parts of the verb *to call* are (1) *call,* (2) *called,* (3) *called.* The first two of these provide the basic forms of the simple tenses; the third is used with the auxiliary verbs to form verb phrases for the other tenses. The conjugation in the **indicative mood** (that form used for declarative or interrogative sentences) of the verb *to call* is given below:

ACTIVE VOICE

Present Tense

Singular	*Plural*
1. I call	We call
2. You call	You call
3. He, she, it calls	They call

Past Tense

1. I called	We called
2. You called	You called
3. He, she, it called	They called

Future Tense

1. I shall (will) call	We shall (will) call
2. You will call	You will call
3. He, she, it will call	They will call

Present Perfect Tense

1. I have called	We have called
2. You have called	You have called
3. He, she, it has called	They have called

Past Perfect Tense

1. I had called	We had called
2. You had called	You had called
3. He, she, it had called	They had called

Future Perfect Tense

1. I shall (will) have called	We shall (will) have called
2. You will have called	You will have called
3. He, she, it will have called	They will have called

PASSIVE VOICE

Present Tense

1. I am called	We are called
2. You are called	You are called
3. He, she, it is called	They are called

Past Tense

1. I was called	We were called
2. You were called	You were called
3. He, she, it was called	They were called

Future Tense

1. I shall (will) be called	We shall (will) be called
2. You will be called	You will be called
3. He, she, it will be called	They will be called

Present Perfect Tense

1. I have been called	We have been called
2. You have been called	You have been called
3. He, she, it has been called	They have been called

Past Perfect Tense

1. I had been called	We had been called
2. You had been called	You had been called
3. He, she, it had been called	They had been called

Future Perfect Tense

1. I shall (will) have been called	We shall (will) have been called
2. You will have been called	You will have been called
3. He, she, it will have been called	They will have been called

NOTE: You have probably noticed that in the future and future perfect tenses the auxiliary verb *shall* is used in the first persons singular and plural. Traditionally, written English has required this usage, but contemporary grammarians now suggest that the distinction need be made only in formal written English and that *will* may usually be used throughout a conjugation. For emphasis, however, *shall* may occasionally be needed, especially to express strong determination or invitation:

We *shall* overcome!

Shall we dance?

PROGRESSIVE TENSES

To express an action or state in progress either at the time of speaking or at the time spoken of, forms of the auxiliary verb *to be* are combined with the present participle (See Chapter 4, Section C) as follows:

Progressive Present Tense

1. I am calling	We are calling
2. You are calling	You are calling
3. He, she, it is calling	They are calling

Progressive Past Tense

1. I was calling	We were calling
2. You were calling	You were calling
3. He, she, it was calling	They were calling

This process may be continued through the various tenses of the active voice, as indicated below:

> PROGRESSIVE FUTURE TENSE: I shall (will) be calling, etc.
>
> PROGRESSIVE PRESENT PERFECT TENSE: I have been calling, etc.
>
> PROGRESSIVE PAST PERFECT TENSE: I had been calling, etc.
>
> PROGRESSIVE FUTURE PERFECT TENSE: I shall (will) have been calling, etc.

In the passive voice, the progressive is generally used only in the simple present and past tenses:

> PROGRESSIVE PRESENT TENSE: I am being called, etc.
>
> PROGRESSIVE PAST TENSE: I was being called, etc.

In the remaining tenses of the passive voice, the progressive forms—though feasible—become awkward (I shall be being called, I have been being called, etc.).

AUXILIARY VERBS *TO BE* AND *TO HAVE*

As you have seen, the verbs *to be* and *to have* are used to form certain tenses of all verbs. Following are the conjugations of these two auxiliary verbs in the indicative mood, active voice:

The principal parts of *to be* are (1) *am*, (2) *was*, and (3) *been*.

Present Tense	
Singular	*Plural*
1. I am	We are
2. You are	You are
3. He, she, it is	They are

Past Tense	
1. I was	We were
2. You were	You were
3. He, she, it was	They were

Future Tense	
1. I shall (will) be	We shall (will) be
2. You will be	You will be
3. He, she, it will be	They will be

Present Perfect Tense	
1. I have been	We have been
2. You have been	You have been
3. He, she, it has been	They have been

Past Perfect Tense	
1. I had been	We had been
2. You had been	You had been
3. He, she, it had been	They had been

Future Perfect Tense

1. I shall (will) have been	We shall (will) have been
2. You will have been	You will have been
3. He, she, it will have been	They will have been

The principal parts of the verb *to have* are (1) *have,* (2) *had,* and (3) *had.*

Present Tense

Singular	*Plural*
1. I have	We have
2. You have	You have
3. He, she, it has	They have

Past Tense

1. I had	We had
2. You had	You had
3. He, she, it had	They had

Future Tense

1. I shall (will) have	We shall (will) have
2. You will have	You will have
3. He, she, it will have	They will have

Present Perfect Tense

1. I have had	We have had
2. You have had	You have had
3. He, she, it has had	They have had

Past Perfect Tense

1. I had had	We had had
2. You had had	You had had
3. He, she, it had had	They had had

Future Perfect Tense

1. I shall (will) have had	We shall (will) have had
2. You will have had	You will have had
3. He, she, it will have had	They will have had

MOOD

Mood is the form a verb may take to indicate whether it is intended to make a statement, to give a command, or to express a condition contrary to fact. Besides the **indicative** mood shown in the conjugations above, there are the **imperative** and the **subjunctive** moods.

The **imperative** mood is used in giving commands or making requests, as in *TAKE me out to the ball game.* Here *TAKE* is in the imperative mood. The subject of an imperative sentence is *you,* usually understood, but sometimes expressed for the sake of emphasis, as in *You get out of here!*

The **subjunctive** mood is most often used today to express a wish or a condition contrary to fact. In the sentences *I wish I WERE going* and *If I WERE you, I would not go,* the verbs in capitals are in the subjunctive mood.

1e Adverb

An **adverb** (from Latin *ad,* to or toward, and *verbum,* word) usually modifies or adds to the meaning of verbs, adjectives, and other adverbs. Sometimes, however, it may be used to modify or qualify a whole phrase or clause, adding to the meaning of an idea that the sentence expresses. The following sentences illustrate the variety of uses of the adverb:

> He ran *fast.* [*Fast* modifies the verb *ran.*]
>
> The judges considered the contestants *unusually* brilliant. [*Unusually* modifies the adjective *brilliant.*]
>
> She sang *very* loudly. [*Very* modifies the adverb *loudly.*]
>
> The doves were flying *just* outside gun range. [*Just* modifies either the preposition *outside* or the whole prepositional phrase *outside gun range.*]
>
> He had driven carefully *ever* since he was injured. [*Ever* modifies either the conjunction *since* or the whole clause *since he was injured.*]
>
> *Unfortunately,* she has encountered rejection everywhere. [*Unfortunately* modifies the whole idea expressed in the sentence and cannot logically be attached to a single word.]

1f Preposition

A **preposition** (from Latin *prae,* before, and *positum,* placed) is a word placed usually before a substantive, called the *object of the preposition,* to show relationship between that object and some other word in the sentence. The combination of a preposition, its object, and any modifiers of the object is called a **prepositional phrase** (*in the mood, on the porch, of human events, toward the beautiful green lake*). You will see how necessary prepositions are to our language when you realize how often you use most of the ones in the group below, which includes some of the most commonly used prepositions:

about	between	over
above	beyond	past
across	but (meaning *except*)	since
after	by	through
against	concerning	throughout
along	down	to
amid	during	toward
among	except	under
around	for	underneath
at	from	until
before	in	up
behind	into	upon
below	like	with
beneath	of	within
beside	off	without
besides	on	

Ordinarily a preposition precedes its object, as its name indicates. Although a sentence ending with a preposition is frequently unemphatic or clumsy, it is in no way contrary to English usage. *She asked what they were cooked in* is better English than *She asked in what they were cooked.*

1g Conjunction

A **conjunction** (from Latin *conjungere,* to join) is a word used to join words or groups of words. There are two kinds of conjunctions: **coordinating conjunctions** and **subordinating conjunctions.**

COORDINATING CONJUNCTIONS

Coordinating conjunctions join sentence elements of equal rank. In the sentence *She was poor but honest* the conjunction *but* joins the two adjectives *poor* and *honest.* In *She was poor, but she was honest* the conjunction *but* joins the two independent statements *She was poor* and *she was honest.* The common coordinating conjunctions are the following:

> and   but   or   nor   for

Yet in the sense of *but,* and *so* in the sense of *therefore* are also coordinating conjunctions. **Correlative conjunctions,** which are used in pairs (*either . . . or . . . , neither . . . nor . . .*) are coordinating conjunctions also.

SUBORDINATING CONJUNCTIONS

Subordinating conjunctions introduce certain subordinate or dependent elements and join them to the main or independent part of the sentence. In *Jack has gone home because he was tired* the subordinating conjunction *because* subordinates the clause that it is part of and joins it to the main part of the sentence, *Jack has gone home.* There are many subordinating conjunctions. Some common ones are the following:

> after   although   as   before   if   since
> unless   until   when   whether   while

NOTE: Words like *however, therefore, nevertheless, moreover, in fact, consequently, hence,* and *accordingly* are essentially adverbs, not conjunctions; they are sometimes called **conjunctive adverbs.**

1h Interjection

An **interjection** (from Latin *inter,* among or between, and *jectum,* thrown) is an exclamatory word like *oh, ouch, please, why, hey* thrown into a sentence or sometimes used alone. An interjection is always grammatically independent of the rest of the sentence. Adjectives, adverbs, and occasionally other parts of speech become interjections when used as independent exclamations (*good! horrible! fine! what! wait!*).

Exercise 1   NOUNS AND PRONOUNS

Write in the first blank at the right any *italicized* word that is a *noun* and in the second any that is a *pronoun*.

	NOUN	PRONOUN
EXAMPLE: Do *you* have tickets for Saturday's *game*?	*game*	*you*
1. *Fall* is a *beautiful* time of the year.		
2. *Have you* written the research *paper*?		
3. I *telephoned everyone* but *Jeff.*		
4. *Who* is recommending you *for* the *job*?		
5. Now is the *time* to stop *this* nonsense.		
6. Can *we* take *freedom* for granted?		
7. Several of *us* are planning a *trip to* Banff.		
8. *They* will arrive in *Atlanta* tonight from New York.		
9. *I* frequently *forget* the *titles* of books.		
10. *We* missed the last *train* by *five* minutes.		
11. *Sometimes people* do *change.*		
12. Can *you envision* John as *president*?		
13. *Some* of the *guests* will *always* arrive late.		
14. *Who* volunteered to clean up *after* the *party*?		
15. *Both* of the *pilots live* in Oregon.		
16. *Everyone* in the sorority was *invited* to the *luncheon.*		

	NOUN	PRONOUN
17. *Bob* took *them* to the fair.	_____	_____
18. Have *you ever* visited *New York City*?	_____	_____
19. *She* is in Japan on a *scholarship from* the museum.	_____	_____
20. *We* look *forward* to your *visit*.	_____	_____

Exercise 2 | PRONOUNS

In the sentences below identify the *italicized* pronouns by writing one of the following abbreviations in the space at the right:

P for personal,	**Inter** for interrogative,
D for demonstrative,	**Inten** for intensive,
I for indefinite,	**Ref** for reflexive
Rel for relative,	

EXAMPLE: *You* need a new parking permit on your car.   _____P_____

1. I do not understand *that*.   _____

2. Russ *himself* told me the story.   _____

3. *Who* will represent the University of Wisconsin at the meeting?   _____

4. *I* read only five books last quarter.   _____

5. *We* remodeled the family room.   _____

6. The free tickets are for *anyone*.   _____

7. Jessie will ride with *us*.   _____

8. *Each* of us has a secret dream.   _____

9. *Which* is the best route to Highlands, North Carolina?   _____

10. The book, *which* I really enjoyed, was *A Confederacy of Dunces*.   _____

11. No, *that* does not fit you at all.   _____

12. I do not have the key; I lost *it* yesterday.   _____

13. The auctioneer sold *us* two antique vases.   _____

14. Have *you* ever tried to teach a child solitaire?   _____

15. *These* are the only shells we found.   _____

16. You *yourself* can make a significant contribution to our country.   _____

17. *Those* are not the pictures I purchased.   _____

18. You must decide *yourself.*　　　　　　　　　　———

19. *Either* of the answers is correct.　　　　　———

20. Jeff is obviously fond of *himself.*　　　　　———

Exercise 3	ADJECTIVES AND ADVERBS

In the following sentences underline once all the adjectives and words used as adjectives except the articles **a, an,** and **the.** Underline all adverbs twice.

EXAMPLE: The old house stood on a very quiet street.

> *The old house stood on a very quiet street.*

1. The young lady by the door is quite lovely.

2. Can you completely restore this antique chair?

3. Ulysses' dog patiently awaited his master's return from the war.

4. This beautiful canyon provides a spectacular setting for white-water canoeing.

5. In the fall the mountains are a favorite attraction of tour groups.

6. The cemetery loomed in the foreground.

7. The highway was dangerously slippery after the rain.

8. From the back door we eagerly awaited a sight of the eclipse.

9. The little boy sang for his grandmother.

10. The spacious mountain hotel is a peaceful vacation spot.

11. Dark clouds hovered menacingly over the ocean.

12. The morning jogger ran quietly and swiftly through the neighborhood.

13. Behind the tree the hunter waited patiently for dawn.

14. The lantern cast an eerie light.

15. The dresser drawer was completely empty.

16. Finally we decided on a topic for his research paper.

17. The shrill whistle instantly stirred old memories.

18. The ancient truck careened wildly down the road.

19. The young pianist played the Chopin selections brilliantly.

20. Until midnight we decorated for our class reunion.

Exercise 4	VERBS

In the following sentences underline all verbs, and then write them in the first column at the right. In the second column write **A** if the verb is in the active voice, **P** if it is in the passive voice. In the last column write **T** if the verb is transitive, **I** if it is intransitive.

	VERB	A/P	T/I
EXAMPLE: The pilot <u>taxied</u> the plane down the runway.	*taxied*	*A*	*T*
1. The clouds swirled around the mountain top.			
2. The iceberg floated dangerously close to the ship.			
3. A visit to the Johnson Space Center is an educational experience.			
4. Sleep refreshed the weary traveler.			
5. Betsy will play in the chess tournament.			
6. The museum was privately funded by the fishermen in Portland.			
7. We didn't have supper.			
8. Travel broadens one's outlook.			
9. The team demonstrated concentration and discipline.			
10. The average American eats more than ten grams of salt a day.			
11. I really enjoyed Ann Firor Scott's book *The Southern Lady.*			
12. His apartment is around the corner.			

	VERB	A/P	T/I
13. At the end of the book the author offers no solution.	_____	____	____
14. In 1497, Vasco da Gama sailed around the Cape of Good Hope.	_____	____	____
15. Ed's mother has a doctorate in biochemistry.	_____	____	____
16. The new president will probably reorganize the entire college.	_____	____	____
17. John was elected president of his class.	_____	____	____
18. The book contains a wealth of folklore.	_____	____	____
19. For the last two days he has been pruning the boxwood.	_____	____	____
20. Whom has he chosen to represent the University of Maine?	_____	____	____

Exercise 5	PREPOSITIONS

In the following sentences underline all *prepositions,* and then write them in the first column at the right. Write the *objects* of the prepositions in the second column. If a sentence contains no preposition, leave the spaces blank.

	PREP.	OBJECT
EXAMPLE: We invited everyone in our class.	*in*	*class*
1. The hound rested beneath the house.		
2. Everyone answered my lettter except Tom.		
3. She left early with her friends.		
4. I received several comments about his speech.		
5. To his surprise the gas gauge registered empty.		
6. After the concert we ate dinner.		
7. The one-room schoolhouse is a thing of the past.		
8. I catch my morning train at seven-thirty.		
9. Wait here for me.		
10. We heard the children laughing behind the barn.		
11. No license is required for deep-sea and surf fishing.		
12. One's attitude about food changes frequently.		
13. Despite warnings we continue wasting our natural resources.		
14. We will arrive on the night train.		

	PREP.	OBJECT

15. Without her assistance, he cannot complete
    the study.

16. From my window I watch the martins feed
    their young.

17. Last summer we drove through many quiet
    little towns.

18. No one was there except the physician.

19. Which of the movies did the critics pan?

20. A child's attitude toward books reflects the
    parents' attitude.

Exercise 6	CONJUNCTIONS

In the following sentences there are both coordinating and subordinating conjunctions. Underline all conjunctions, and then write them in the first column at the right. In the second column write **C** if the conjunction joins sentence elements of equal rank, **S** if it joins unequal elements.

	CONJ.	C/S
EXAMPLE: Women's shoes are pretty, <u>but</u> they are not comfortable.	*but*	*C*
1. Although the President's advisers acknowledge the problem, few offer a solution.		
2. Neither you nor Bob can afford to miss the next test.		
3. Students soon realize that expanding their vocabulary makes writing less painful.		
4. If we fail to meet the challenges, we will face the consequences.		
5. He missed the train this morning because he had forgotten to set his alarm.		
6. Both the team and the coach are flying to Los Angeles.		
7. Neither Ned nor I am planning to attend the Cotton Bowl game.		
8. When I visit New York, I always see at least one play.		
9. Will walked three miles to town but hitched a ride home.		
10. After Nellie received her doctorate, she decided not to return to teaching.		
11. Soren Kierkegaard, a Danish philosopher, was born in 1813 and died in 1855.		

	CONJ.	C/S

12. Mason was unable to make the trip because he had a soccer game on Friday.   _____ _____

13. Before her family moved to Dallas, she had always lived on a farm.   _____ _____

14. No one enjoys a constant complainer or a Pollyanna.   _____ _____

15. Mountain climbing is exciting but dangerous.   _____ _____

16. He will babysit for you until you finish your shopping.   _____ _____

17. I think that borscht is one of the best soups in the world.   _____ _____

18. As a graduate student he learned to organize his time and his work.   _____ _____

19. If you cannot come, will you send a substitute?   _____ _____

20. The author autographed both Betsy's and my books.   _____ _____

| Exercise 7 | **REVIEW OF PARTS OF SPEECH** |

In the following sentences identify the part of speech of each *italicized* word by writing one of the following abbreviations in the space at the right:

N for noun,	**Adv** for adverb,
V for verb,	**Prep** for preposition,
P for pronoun,	**C** for conjunction,
Adj for adjective,	**I** for interjection.

EXAMPLE: *What!* You aren't going to the game?   _____I_____

1. Did you have *enough* to eat?   _____

2. *After* supper she always takes a walk.   _____

3. *Both* O. Henry *and* Poe practiced the art of the short story.   _____

4. Jane looks exactly *like* her father.   _____

5. *What* are you doing?   _____

6. Despite her *busy* schedule President Elliot always took time to meet with her students.   _____

7. The Crystal Cathedral is *often* called an architectural miracle.   _____

8. Mona's pound cake *tastes* good because she uses real butter.   _____

9. Lisa is a solar designer and *technical* editor for a solar design magazine.   _____

10. *During* the past several years his duties have taken him from Alaska to Africa.   _____

11. Pork is the basic *meat* of typical Sunbelt cookery.   _____

12. Tanzania is *one* of the world's poorest countries.   _____

13. The little girl's question was *quite* innocent.   _____

14. The oldest building in Waterford, Ireland, *was built* by Reginald the Dane in 1003.   _____

15. Observatory research is exciting, *even* to the novice.   _____

16. The only person one cannot fool is *himself.*   _____

25

17. The University's president will address *pertinent* issues in his talk tonight.   _____

18. *When* I was seven, I learned to skate.   _____

19. *No!* I will not vote for her.   _____

20. Her son was *first* in his class at Vanderbilt Medical School.   _____

Exercise 8	REVIEW OF PARTS OF SPEECH

In the following sentences identify the part of speech of each *italicized* word by writing one of the following abbreviations in the space at the right:

N	for noun,	**Adv**	for adverb,
V	for verb,	**Prep**	for preposition,
P	for pronoun,	**C**	for conjunction,
Adj	for adjective,	**I**	for interjection.

EXAMPLE: *Where* did you find your shirt? <u>_Adv_</u>

1. Asbury Park has been a *popular* shore resort since its founding. _____

2. One's attitude *is* often *reflected* in his facial expression. _____

3. Because of the heat, I seldom use my hammock in July *or* August. _____

4. In many ways *biochemistry* is a unique science. _____

5. Each one of *us* wanted to win the contest. _____

6. Reasoning *with* him is impossible. _____

7. One of the objectives of the *Voyager* mission was to gather information about Saturn's satellites. _____

8. Louise was born *in* Strawberry Plains, Tennessee. _____

9. My cousin quit her job as a nurse *and* became a plumber. _____

10. Do these scissors cut *well*? _____

11. Karen and Phil recently took jobs with an *oil* company in Houston. _____

12. Edwin *finds* mathematical abstraction difficult to comprehend. _____

13. Many of *our* greatest leaders had little formal education. _____

14. The author understands *both* children *and* adults. _____

15. Jane loves horses, but she *has* never *ridden* one. _____

16. *Yes!* I did wait forever for the commuter train. _____

17. There are many new *families* in our apartment complex. _____

18. The captain invited a few *of* us to eat at his table. _____

19. The proper disposal of *hazardous* waste is of national concern. _____

20. *We* will meet you in front of the library. _____

2
Recognizing Subjects, Verbs, and Complements

2a   The Sentence

A **sentence** is made up of single parts of speech combined into a pattern which expresses a complete thought. In other words, a sentence is a group of words that expresses a complete though. On the page it begins with a capital letter and ends with a period, question mark, or exclamation mark. In its simplest form this complete statement is an independent clause or a **simple sentence**.

2b   Subject and Predicate

Every simple sentence must have two basic elements: (1) the thing we are talking about, and (2) what we say about it. The thing we are talking about is called the **subject**, and what we say about it is called the **predicate**. The subject is a noun, a pronoun, or some other word or group of words used as a noun. The essential part of the predicate is a verb—a word which tells something about the subject. It tells that the subject *does* something or that something *is true* of the subject. Therefore, a subject and a verb are the fundamental parts of every sentence. In fact, it is possible to express meaning with just these two elements:

> Pilots fly.
> Flowers bloom.

In each example the verb says that the subject does something. The sentences are about pilots and flowers. What does each do? The pilots fly; the flowers bloom.

2c   Finding the Verb

Finding verbs and subjects of verbs in a sentence is the first step in determining whether or not a group of words expresses a complete thought. Therefore, look first for the verb, the most important word in the sentence, and then for its subject.

The verb may sometimes be difficult to find. It may come anywhere in the sentence; for instance, it may precede the subject, as in some interrogative sentences (*Where is my pencil?*). It may consist of a single word or a group of two or more words; it may have other words inserted within the verb phrase; it may be combined with the negative *not* or with a contraction of *not*. To find the verb, look for the word or group of words that expresses an action or a state of being. In the following sentences the verbs are in italics:

> His friend *stood* at his side. [The verb *stood* follows the subject *friend.*]
>
> At his side *stood* his friend. [The verb *stood* precedes the subject *friend.*]
>
> His friend *was standing* at his side. [The verb *was standing* consists of two words.]
>
> His friend *can*not *stand* at his side. [The verb *can* is combined with the negative adverb *not*, which is not part of the verb.]
>
> *Did* his friend *stand* at his side? [The two parts of the verb *did stand* are separated by the subject.]

2d   Finding the Subject

Sometimes finding the subject may also be difficult, for, as we have just seen, the subject does not always come immediately before the verb. Often it comes after the verb; often it is separated from the verb by a modifying element. Always look for the noun or pronoun about which the verb asserts something and disregard intervening elements:

> *Many* of the children *come* to the clinic. [A prepositional phrase comes between the subject and the verb.]
>
> There *are flowers* on the table. [The subject comes after the verb. The word *there* is never a subject; in this sentence it is an *expletive*, an idiomatic introductory word.]
>
> In the room *were* a *cot* and a *chair*. [The subject comes after the verb.]

In an imperative sentence, a sentence expressing a command or a request, the subject *you* is usually implied rather than expressed. Occasionally, however, the subject *you* is expressed:

> Come in out of the rain.
>
> Shut the door!
>
> *You* play goalie.

Either the verb or the subject or both may be **compound**; that is, there may be more than one subject and more than one verb:

> The *boy* and the *girl* played. [Two subjects.]
>
> The boy *worked* and *played*. [Two verbs.]
>
> The *boy* and the *girl worked* and *played*. [Two subjects and two verbs.]

In the first sentence the compound subject is *boy* and *girl*. In the second sentence there is a compound verb, *worked* and *played*. In the third sentence both the subject and the verb are compound.

2e   Complements

Thus far we have discussed two functions of words: that of nouns and pronouns as subjects and that of verbs as predicates.

A third function of words which we must consider is that of completing the verb. Nouns, pronouns, and adjectives are used to complete verbs and are called **complements**. A complement may be a **direct object**, an **indirect object**, a **predicate noun** or **pronoun**, a **predicate adjective**, an **objective complement**, or a **retained object**.

A **direct object** is a noun or noun equivalent which completes the verb and receives the action expressed in the verb:

> The pilot flew the plane. [*Plane* is the direct object of *flew.* Just as the subject answers the question "*who?*" or "*what?*" before the verb (Who flew?), so the direct object answers the question "*whom?*" or "*what?*" after the verb (Flew what?).]

An **indirect object** is a word (or words) denoting the person or thing indirectly affected by the action of a transitive verb. It is the person or thing to which something is given or for which something is done. Such words as *give, offer, grant, lend, teach,* etc., represent the idea of something done for the indirect object:

> We gave *her* the book. [*Her* is the indirect object of *gave.* The indirect object answers the question "*to (for) whom or what?*" after the verb *gave* (Gave to whom?).]

Certain verbs that represent the idea of taking away or withholding something can also have indirect objects:

> The judge *denied him* the opportunity to speak in his own defense.
>
> Father *refused Frances* the use of the car.

A **predicate noun** (also called **predicate nominative**) is a noun or its equivalent which renames or identifies the subject and completes such verbs as *be, seem, become,* and *appear* (called linking verbs):

> The woman is a *doctor.* [The predicate noun *doctor* completes the intransitive verb *is* and renames the subject *woman.*]
>
> My best friends are *she* and her *sister.* [The predicate pronoun *she* and the predicate noun *sister* complete the intransitive verb *are* and rename the subject *friends.*]
>
> Mary has become a *pilot.* [The predicate noun *pilot* completes the intransitive verb *has become* and renames the subject *Mary.*]

A **predicate adjective** is an adjective which completes a linking verb and describes the subject:

> The man seems *angry.* [The predicate adjective *angry* completes the intransitive verb *seems* and describes the subject *man.*]

An **objective complement** is a noun or an adjective which completes the action expressed in the verb and refers to the direct object. If it is a noun, the objective complement is in a sense identical with the direct object; if it is an adjective, it describes or limits the direct object. It occurs commonly after such verbs as *think, call, find, make, consider, choose,* and *believe:*

> Jealousy made Othello a *murderer.* [The objective complement *murderer* completes the transitive verb *made* and renames the direct object *Othello.*]
>
> She thought the day very *disagreeable.* [The objective complement *disagreeable* is an adjective which describes the direct object *day.*]

A **retained object** is a noun or noun equivalent which remains as the object when a verb which has both a direct and an indirect object is put into the passive voice. The other object becomes the subject of such a verb. Although either object may become the subject, the indirect object more commonly takes that position, and the direct object is retained:

> The board granted him a year's leave of absence.
> He was granted a year's leave of absence.

> [In the second sentence the verb has been put into the passive voice, the indirect object of the first sentence has become the subject of the second, and the direct object has been retained.]

> The teacher asked the student a difficult question.
> A difficult question was asked the student.

> [In the second sentence the verb has been put into the passive voice, the direct object of the first sentence has become the subject of the second, and the indirect object has been retained.]

Exercise 9	SUBJECTS AND VERBS

In each of the following sentences underline the subject once and its verb twice. Then write the subject in the first column and the verb in the second column at the right:

	SUBJECT	VERB
EXAMPLE: Bruce has always been afraid of snakes.	Bruce	has been
1. The players are being honored at the banquet.		
2. In the Soviet Union algebra is taught in the sixth and seventh grades.		
3. Every morning about three o'clock the squirrel in the attic drops nuts through the walls.		
4. He is always complaining about something.		
5. Among the treasures displayed in Biltmore House are two paintings by Renoir.		
6. Insulation can reduce energy consumption by as much as fifteen percent.		
7. Not many homes today have parlors.		
8. There is a piece of chocolate cake in the kitchen.		
9. Across the street from us lives Mrs. Stephens' brother.		
10. Between you and me, I did not enjoy his speech.		
11. Subjects and verbs—I am tired of them!		
12. Will you explain these data one more time?		
13. There are over two hundred women college presidents in the United States.		

	SUBJECT	VERB

14. The art of compromise is the foundation of democracy.

15. On winter evenings my father sits by the fire and reads to us.

16. The phrase "Once upon a time" reminds us all of times gone by.

17. Here she comes with that dull cousin of hers.

18. We have rented a house in the country for the month of August.

19. Miss Piggy has great charm.

20. Dan and Laura wallpapered their kitchen.

21. Yesterday was our busiest day.

22. In primitive societies decisions were often made by the witch doctors.

23. The rather lengthy report by Dr. John Rumple-meyer deserves comment.

24. Despite its flaws the new system has worked.

25. The next conference will be held at Cornell University.

Exercise 10 | SUBJECTS AND VERBS

In each of the following sentences underline the subject(s) once and its verb(s) twice. Then copy the subject(s) in the first column and the verb(s) in the second column at the right.

	SUBJECT	VERB
EXAMPLE: He sang and danced in the talent show.	*He*	*sang, danced*

1. Both of my brothers are attending the University of Oregon.

2. Mary and Mike will arrive after supper.

3. The rain is almost over.

4. Either football or baseball dominates fall television.

5. There were no tickets for the play.

6. Did you remember the chess board?

7. Where did they go on vacation?

8. Saturn has a mass twenty-five times that of Earth.

9. My neighbors and I cleaned the vacant lot for the bazaar.

10. I enjoy sales, but I always buy too much.

11. The golf team finished the fall schedule with only one loss.

12. Our neighbors eat dinner around eight o'clock.

13. Both of the children have been invited to visit their aunt in Arizona.

	SUBJECT	VERB
14. The Eiffel Tower in Paris was built by a French engineer.	_____	_____
15. How many research projects do you have this term?	_____	_____
16. While on a tour of Canada, I lost my camera.	_____	_____
17. Emily's plane from Fairbanks will arrive early.	_____	_____
18. Directly across the street was the restaurant.	_____	_____
19. Have you chosen a major?	_____	_____
20. Professor Wright's experiment is a difficult one.	_____	_____

| Exercise 11 | DIRECT OBJECTS AND PREDICATE NOUNS |

In each of the following sentences underline the complement. Then identify the complement by writing in the space at the right one of the following abbreviations:

DO if it is a direct object,
PN if it is a predicate noun.

EXAMPLE: Our Latin professor also teaches French.   __DO__

1. She will someday be a senator.   _____

2. Al is the only one here.   _____

3. The average child watches television four hours a day.   _____

4. Whom did you see at the movie?   _____

5. Philip is a brilliant surgeon.   _____

6. The Southern writer displays a great love of the land.   _____

7. Bad weather delayed our helicopter flight.   _____

8. House plants require various growing conditions.   _____

9. She is my choice for the directorship.   _____

10. We painted the entry hall yellow.   _____

11. A successful dinner is a combination of planning, food, and people. _____

12. Our return trip was a pleasant one.   _____

13. The building at the top of the hill is the Arthur J. Dyer Observatory. _____

14. An author needs several hours each day to write.   _____

15. Professor Alexander's reading list contained a variety of authors. _____

16. I am not a linguist but a student of literature.   _____

17. Our new president is a coal miner's daughter.   _____

18. In the morning you will meet the keynote speaker.   _____

19. Did you understand that question?   _____

20. Someday he will become a great jurist.   _____

Exercise 12 | INDIRECT OBJECTS AND OBJECTIVE COMPLEMENTS

In each of the following sentences identify the *italicized* complement by writing in the space at the right one of the following abbreviations:

> **IO**   if it is an indirect object,
> **OC**   if it is an objective complement.

EXAMPLE: The store offered our *class* a special discount.   *IO*

1. Of course we painted our barn *red.*   _____

2. Can you bring *me* a book from the library?   _____

3. Our company provides its *employees* limited expense accounts.   _____

4. His know-it-all attitude makes him *unpopular* with his classmates.   _____

5. The team considered Carrie the best *player.*   _____

6. The professor is not giving *Mack* a make-up test.   _____

7. Mother ordered *me* a gift from the L. L. Bean Christmas catalog.   _____

8. The Texas Bar Association elected Al *president.*   _____

9. Do you consider the plan *workable?*   _____

10. Sam gave *Bo* and *me* his tickets to the ballet.   _____

11. My friends find him *charming.*   _____

12. Did you lend *Larry* your biology notes?   _____

13. I thought John Updike's latest book extremely *readable.*   _____

14. The coach bought the *team* lunch.   _____

15. Has the committee announced Meredith the *winner?*   _____

16. The bank grudgingly gave the young *man* an automobile loan.   _____

17. The professor never promised *us* an easy course.   _____

18. I will make *you* coffee in the morning.   _____

19. Send the *school* your name and address.   _____

20. The critics called Beverly Sills's performance *brilliant*.   _____

Exercise 13 | COMPLEMENTS

A. In each of the following sentences identify the *italicized* word by writing one of the following abbreviations in the space at the right:

PN if it is a predicate noun,	**IO** if it is an indirect object,
PA if it is a predicate adjective,	**OC** if it is an objective complement.
DO if it is a direct object,	

EXAMPLE: Elliott can never find his *keys*. _DO_

1. Generally speaking, Yorktown was the last real *battle* of the American Revolution. _____

2. Every spring I take long *walks* in the country. _____

3. Will you bring *me* my glasses? _____

4. Everyone thought the interview *informative*. _____

5. Will is a crusty old *friend* of mine. _____

6. Several years ago in Venice I shared a *motorboat-taxi* with a couple from Butte, Montana. _____

7. Tom is extremely *bright*. _____

8. Agricultural research is *vital* to America's future. _____

9. The committee will probably elect James *secretary*. _____

10. Every morning the dog brings *Dad* the paper. _____

11. Our sorority is exploring new *ways* to make money. _____

12. Ellen's field of specialization is *political science*. _____

13. Her tone was unnecessarily *belligerent*. _____

14. His explanations are *simple* and *direct*. _____

15. My brother does not consider Nancy *pretty*. _____

B. Write sixteen sentences, four of which contain direct objects; four, indirect objects; four, predicate nouns; four, predicate adjectives. In the space at the right, write **DO** (direct object), **IO** (indirect object), **PN** (predicate noun), or **PA** (predicate adjective) as the case may be.

1. _____ _____

2. _____ _____

3. _____ _____

4. _____ _____

5. _____ _____

6. _____ _____

7. _____ _____

8. _____ _____

9. _____ _____

10. _____ _____

11. _____ _____

12. _____ _____

13. _____ _____

14. _____ _____

15. _____ _____

16. _____ _____

3

The Sentence Fragment

3a Grammatical Fragments

If you are not careful to have both a subject and a predicate in your sentences and to express a complete thought, you will write sentence fragments instead of complete sentences. Observe, for example, the following:

> A tall, distinguished-looking gentleman standing on the corner in a pouring rain.
>
> Standing on the corner in a pouring rain and shielding himself from the deluge with a a large umbrella.

The first of these groups of words is no more than the subject of a sentence or the object of a verb or preposition. It may be part of such a sentence, for example, as *We noticed a tall, distinguished-looking gentleman standing on the corner in a pouring rain.* The second group is probably a modifier of some kind, the modifier of a subject, for instance: *Standing on the corner in a pouring rain and shielding himself from the deluge with a large umbrella, a tall, distinguished-looking gentleman was waiting for a cab.*

Another type of fragment is seen in the following illustrations:

> Because I had heard all that I wanted to hear and did not intend to be bored any longer.
>
> Who was the outstanding athlete of her class and also the best scholar.
>
> Although he had been well recommended by his former employers.

Each of these groups of words actually has a subject and a predicate, but each is still a fragment because the first word of each is a subordinating element and clearly indicates that the thought is incomplete, that the thought expressed depends upon some other thought. Such fragments are subordinate parts of longer sentences like the following:

> I left the hall because I had heard all that I wanted to hear and did not intend to be bored any longer.

43

The valedictorian was Alice Snodgrass, who was the outstanding athlete of her class and also the best scholar.

He did not get the job although he had been well recommended by his former employers.

3b Permissible Fragments

A sentence fragment is often the result of ignorance or carelessness and is the sign of an immature writer. On the other hand, much correctly spoken and written English contains perfectly proper fragments of sentences. The adverbs *yes* and *no* may stand alone, as may other words and phrases in dialogue (though our chief concern remains written prose). There is nothing wrong, for example, in such fragments as the following:

The sooner, the better.

Anything but that.

Same as before.

Interjections and exclamatory phrases may also stand alone as independent elements. The following fragments are correct:

Ouch!

Tickets, please!

Not so!

3c Stylistic Fragments

There is another kind of fragment of rather common occurrence in the writing of some of the best authors. It is the phrase used for realistic or impressionistic effect, the piling up of words or phrases without any effort to organize them into sentences: "The blue haze of evening was upon the field. Lines of forest with long purple shadows. One cloud along the western sky partly smothering the red." This kind of writing, if it is to be good, is very difficult. Like free verse, it may best be left to the experienced writer. Students should learn to recognize a sentence fragment when they see one. They should use this form sparingly in their own writing. And they should remember two things: first, that the legitimacy of the sentence fragment depends upon whether it is used intentionally or not, and second, that in an elementary course in composition most instructors assume that a sentence fragment is unintended.

Study carefully the following sentence fragments and the accompanying comments:

A large woman of rather determined attitude who says that she wishes to see you to discuss a matter of great importance. [This is a typical fragment unintended by the writer, who seems to have felt that it is a complete sentence because there are a subject and a predicate in each subordinate clause.]

He finally decided to leave school. Because he was utterly bored with his work and was failing all his courses. [Here the second group of words is an unjustifiable fragment. It is a subordinate clause and should be attached to the main clause without a break of any kind.]

There were books everywhere. Books in the living room, books in the bedroom, books even in the kitchen. [The second group of words is a fragment, but it may be defended on grounds of emphasis. Many writers, however, would have used a comma or colon after *everywhere* and made a single sentence.]

| Exercise 14 | THE SENTENCE FRAGMENT |

Indicate in the space at the right by writing **C** or **F** whether the following groups of words are complete sentences or fragments of sentences. Rewrite any fragment, making it a complete sentence.

EXAMPLE: This lamp, which is an antique Chinese porcelain.   _____F_____

   This lamp is an antique Chinese porcelain.

1. Biltmore House, built by George W. Vanderbilt.   _____

2. Putting aside the errors and contradictory statements in the article.   _____

3. The college-survey results indicate a moderate increase in business majors for next year.   _____

4. Is there any evidence that Scholastic Aptitude Test scores are good predictors of creative ability in mathematics?   _____

5. Charles's hypothesis, which has absolutely no known foundation.   _____

6. A telephone, a radio, and good television reception are commonplace in the homes of most Americans.   _____

7. In Alaska telephone and television services are far less common.   ———

8. The importance of the role of science and technology in foreign policy
   cannot be underestimated.   ———

9. As other countries become more proficient in science and technology.   ———

10. The fact that the data came only from people who were employed at the time.   ———

11. Designers are seeking new ways to increase the speed of computers.   ———

12. Irving Stone's life of Charles Darwin is testimony to his ability as a
    biographer.   ———

13. The skills which college-bound students should possess have been listed by
    the faculty.   ———

14. Although most illnesses run their course and are seldom life-threatening.   ———

15. A full, scientific understanding of the origin of the species.   _____

16. *Whose Life Is It, Anyway?,* a story which is told with sensitivity, realism,
and humor.   _____

17. When her father bought her a new puppy named Boogie.   _____

18. Neither the pilot nor his passengers were injured when the plane crashed.   _____

19. The American "jazz age" following World War I found literary expression in
the novels of F. Scott Fitzgerald.   _____

20. The gift which he had wrapped in bright red paper.   _____

21. The longer we had to wait, the angrier we became.   _____

22. We were walking home when it began to rain.   _____

23. Because we knew that Todd was waiting for us. _____

24. Gail, who is an outstanding debater. _____

25. Where the rainbow ends is a pot of gold. _____

Exercise 15 | THE SENTENCE FRAGMENT

Some of the following groups are fragments. Some are fragments and sentences. Some are complete sentences. Rewrite in such a way as to leave no fragments. If the group of words is already a complete sentence, leave it as it is and mark it **C**.

EXAMPLE: After she finished graduate school. She married a law student.

After she finished graduate school, she married a law student.

1. Snacks, as we all know, are a problem.

2. He suggested that we not attend the concert. When I told him the cost of the tickets.

3. Because she came from a family of preachers. Sue was comfortable with preachers.

4. That I must set aside more time for physical exercise. I know that.

5. The strength of great universities lies in the humanities.

6. John Nance Garner who was Vice President. He served under Franklin D. Roosevelt from 1933 to 1941.

7. While playing golf, Anita wrenched her back.

8. The door handle having moved. We waited anxiously to see who would enter the room.

9. My father, a gentle man. He always smoked a pipe after eating.

10. The car ahead of us having suddenly stopped.

11. The young girl who is walking across the street.

12. Although they went skiing last weekend.

13. Kennebunkport, a beautiful seacoast town in Maine.

14. Dr. Jacobs, recognized nationally for his achievements in the field of actuarial science.

15. Quite apparent that he is not the best student in the world.

Exercise 16 | THE SENTENCE FRAGMENT

Complete or revise the following sentence fragments in such a way as to make complete sentences.

EXAMPLE: Having avoided the detour.

        Having avoided the detour, we arrived on time.

1. In spite of all that Roger had done to make the team.

2. After carefully searching the house, John, who suspected robbery.

3. When I had finished reading Percy's new novel, *The Second Coming.*

4. Taking time to survey the bases, Dean, our number one pitcher.

5. The vibrations of the commuter train.

6. After the tests are turned in and graded, Dr. Lauren, who is the department head.

7. After experiencing a day in Houston traffic, Dennis, who is not known for his patience.

8. When the fog lifts around the bay.

9. Mark, a veteran of several colleges and universities.

10. The clock having stopped last night.

4

Verbals

You may sometimes have trouble in recognizing sentence verbs because you may confuse them with certain verb forms which function partly as verbs and partly as other parts of speech. (The *sentence verb* is the verb that states something about the subject, one capable of completing a statement.) These other verb forms are made from verbs but also perform the function of nouns, adjectives, or adverbs. In other words, they constitute a sort of half-verb. They are called **verbals**. The three verbal forms are the **gerund**, the **participle**, and the **infinitive**.

4a Verbals and Sentence Verbs

It is important that you distinguish between the use of a particular verb form as a verbal and its use as a main verb in a sentence. An illustration of the different uses of the verb form *running* will help you to make this distinction:

> *Running* every day is good exercise. [*Running* is a **gerund** and is the subject of the verb *is.*]
>
> *Running* swiftly, he caught the bandit. [*Running* is a **participle** and modifies the pronoun *he.*]
>
> The boy *is running* down the street. [*Is running* is the **sentence verb.** It is formed by using the present participle with the auxiliary verb *is.*]

It must be emphasized that *a verbal cannot take the place of a sentence verb* and that *any group of words containing a verbal but no sentence verb is a sentence fragment:*

> The boy *running* [A sentence fragment.]
>
> *To face* an audience [A sentence fragment.]
>
> The boy *running* up the steps is Charles. [A complete sentence.]
>
> *To face* an audience was a great effort for me. [A complete sentence.]

The following table shows the tenses and voices in which verbals appear:

GERUNDS AND PARTICIPLES

Tense	Active Voice	Passive Voice
Present	doing	being done
Past		done (This form applies only to participles.)
Present Perfect	having done	having been done
Progressive Present Perfect	having been doing	

INFINITIVES

Tense	Active Voice	Passive Voice
Present	to do	to be done
Present Perfect	to have done	to have been done
Progressive Present	to be doing	
Progressive Present Perfect	to have been doing	

4b   The Gerund

A **gerund** is a verbal used as a noun and in its present tense always ends in *-ing.* Like a noun, a gerund is used as a subject, a complement, an object of a preposition, or an appositive. Do not confuse the gerund with the present participle, which has the same form but is used as an adjective:

> *Planning* the work carefully required a great deal of time. [*Planning* is a gerund used as subject of the sentence.]
>
> She was not to blame for *breaking* the vase. [*Breaking* is a gerund used as object of the preposition *for.*]
>
> I appreciated your *taking* time to help me. [*Taking* is a gerund used as direct object of *appreciated.*]
>
> His unselfish act, *giving* Marty his coat, plainly showed Ed's generosity. [*Giving* is a gerund used as the appositive of *act.*]

In the sentences above you will note examples of gerunds functioning as nouns but also taking objects as verbs do. In the first sentence the gerund *planning* is used as the subject of the verb *required. Planning* itself, however, is completed by the object *work* and is modified by the adverb *carefully.* This dual functioning of the gerund is apparent in the other three sentences as well.

It is important to remember a rule concerning the modification of gerunds: Always use the possessive form of a noun or pronoun before a gerund. Because gerunds are nouns, their modifiers, other than the adverbial ones just mentioned, must be adjectival; therefore, the possessive form, which has adjectival function, is the correct modifier:

Mr. Bridges was surprised at *Doug's* offering him the motorboat.

NOT

Mr. Bridges was surprised at Doug offering him the motorboat.

4c The Participle

A **participle** is a verbal used as an adjective. The present participle is formed by adding *-ing* to the verb: *do — doing*. Again, remember not to confuse the gerund and the present participle, which have the same form but do not function similarly. The past participle is formed in various ways. It may· end in *-ed, -d, -t,* or *-n: talk — talked, hear — heard, feel — felt, know — known*. It may also be formed by a change of vowel: *sing — sung*.

> The baby, *wailing* pitifully, refused to be comforted. [*Wailing* is a present participle. It modifies *baby*.]
>
> The *broken* doll can be mended. [*Broken* is a past participle, passive voice. It modifies *doll*.]
>
> An old coat, *faded* and *torn*, was her only possession. [*Faded* and *torn* are past participles, passive voice, modifying *coat*.]
>
> *Having been warned,* the man was sent on his way. [*Having been warned* is the present perfect participle, passive voice. It modifies *man*.]

Like the gerund, the participle may have a complement and adverbial modifiers. In the sentence *Wildly waving a red flag, he ran down the track,* the participle *waving* has the object *flag* and the adverbial modifier *wildly*.

4d The Infinitive

An **infinitive** is a verbal consisting of the simple form of the verb preceded by *to* and used as a noun, an adjective, or an adverb:

> *To err* is human. [*To err* is used as a noun, the subject of *is*.]
>
> He wanted *to go* tomorrow. [*To go* is used as a noun, the object of the verb *wanted*.]
>
> He had few books *to read*. [*To read* is used as an adjective to modify the noun *books*.]
>
> Frank seemed eager *to go*. [*To go* is used as an adverb to modify the adjective *eager*.]
>
> She rode fast *to escape* her pursuers. [*To escape* is used as an adverb to modify the verb *rode*.]

Sometimes the word *to* is omitted:

> Susan helped *carry* the packages. [*To* is understood before the verb *carry*. (*To*) *carry* is used as an adverb to modify the verb *helped*.]

NOTE: An adverbial infinitive can frequently be identified if the phrase "in order" can be placed before it, as in *Katy paid ten dollars* (in order) *to get good seats at the play*.

Like the gerund and the participle, the infinitive may have a complement and adverbial modifiers:

> He did not want *to cut the grass yesterday*. [The infinitive *to cut* has the object *grass* and the adverbial modifier *yesterday*.]

| Exercise 17 | VERBS AND VERBALS |

In the following sentences identify each *italicized* expression by writing on the line at the right:

V if it is a verb,	**Part** if it is a participle,
Ger if it is a gerund,	**Inf** if it is an infinitive.

EXAMPLE: Princeton University Press plans *to publish* the papers of Albert
Einstein.   *Inf*

1. We had *to rethink* our priorities.   _____

2. The cat silently *stalked* the bird.   _____

3. *Remembering* names is difficult for me.   _____

4. During the summer my neighbors *mow* their lawn every Wednesday.   _____

5. Medusa had *hissing* serpents for hair.   _____

6. Mike enjoys *cooking* Chinese dinners.   _____

7. Boyd first became interested in wildlife *painting* several years ago.   _____

8. It seemed prudent for us *to arrive* early.   _____

9. The architect recommended *strengthening* the north wall.   _____

10. Jane's inability *to write* a well-organized theme made her dread English class.   _____

11. The commuter train *having been delayed,* I drove to work.   _____

12. His offering the *arresting* officer a bribe was a mistake.   _____

13. Playing golf was her way of *relieving* tension.   _____

14. Dwight *has been playing* golf for years.   _____

15. Another *pressing* concern of Caroline's is her interview with the admissions committee.   _____

16. Although Henry has shown no signs of *following* in his father's footsteps, I think he will decide to practice law.   _____

17. Both Ruth and I encouraged her *to take* some graduate courses at Marquette.   _____

18. When he stands before a group to speak, his charisma *captures* the audience.   _____

19. Because our train left at seven, we ate a *hurried* breakfast.   _____

20. *Woodburning* stoves are very popular in Maine.   _____

21. Harry is in the business of *finding* and *selling* antiques.   _____

22. Dr. Dixon *read* his own poetry to the class.   _____

23. There is nothing more irritating than *to be patronized.*   _____

24. A freshman's difficulty with science often arises from a lack of *training* in high school.   _____

25. *Set* the candlesticks on the mantel.   _____

Exercise 18 | GERUNDS

In the following sentences underline each gerund. Copy the gerund on the first line at the right. On the second line write

> **S** if the gerund is the subject of the verb,
> **PN** if the gerund is the predicate nominative,
> **DO** if the gerund is the direct object of the verb,
> **OP** if the gerund is the object of the preposition.

	GERUND	USE

EXAMPLE: Allison's continual <u>sneezing</u> is of some concern
to her parents. → *sneezing* — *S*

1. Wishing will not make dreams come true. _____ _____

2. Uncle Dean enjoys walking after supper. _____ _____

3. We are all excited about his playing the leading role in
   Cabaret. _____ _____

4. Icarus' flying too close to the sun caused his death. _____ _____

5. My aunt caught me in the act of taking several cookies
   from the cookie jar. _____ _____

6. Harris always did like playing in the snow. _____ _____

7. The poets say that wisdom comes through suffering. _____ _____

8. Cherie's main concern is maintaining her grades so that
   she can enter pharmacy school. _____ _____

9. Mary Ann has a gift for making people feel good. _____ _____

10. Hearing him rant and rave all day gives me a headache. _____ _____

11. We all want to thank you for participating in our program. _____ _____

12. His only interest is painting. _____ _____

GERUND   USE

13. As soon as soccer practice is over, begin studying for your
    examinations.   _____ _____

14. Writing in a foreign language requires a thorough knowl-
    edge of the language.   _____ _____

15. Henry has always enjoyed rummaging through old trunks.   _____ _____

16. Clyde took flying as an elective.   _____ _____

17. Collecting rocks and leaves is a favorite pastime of little
    children.   _____ _____

18. Too often people in power are more interested in
    protecting themselves than in providing leadership.   _____ _____

19. Making wine is a family tradition in many Italian families. _____ _____

20. Reducing the amount of gasoline that we import will help
    our balance of trade.   _____ _____

21. Rosemary's fear of wasting time made her a "workaholic."   _____ _____

22. Yes, Vernon's favorite sport is fishing.   _____ _____

23. None of us understood his quitting the team.   _____ _____

24. Playing chess requires concentration as well as skill.   _____ _____

25. Our family enjoys decorating the Christmas tree together. _____ _____

Exercise 19 | PARTICIPLES

Underline the participle in each of the following sentences, and then write in the space at the right the word that the participle modifies.

EXAMPLE: Jimmy dislocated his shoulder playing basketball.　　　*Jimmy*

1. She uses dried fruits to make her pies.　　　_____

2. As he opened the door, he heard the telephone ringing.　　　_____

3. I left the book lying on the chair next to the door.　　　_____

4. Most reporters long for a fast-breaking story.　　　_____

5. Norma has been asked to prepare a working paper for our next
    committee meeting.　　　_____

6. The club's driving range is open from 6:30 a.m. until 10:30 p.m.　　　_____

7. Scratching noises on the door frightened us.　　　_____

8. Dunleith, a mansion near Natchez, Mississippi, is probably the
    most photographed house in America.　　　_____

9. For detailed instructions on proper care of your appliances, write
    to the company.　　　_____

10. Advertising claims in television commercials are often obviously
    exaggerated.　　　_____

11. When is the plumber coming to repair our broken pipes?　　　_____

12. Along the winding drive from the Catalina Airport to the town,
    motorists can observe herds of buffalo.　　　_____

13. I always order French fried potatoes with a hamburger.　　　_____

14. When driving through the mountains, watch for falling rocks.　　　_____

15. He is a retired sheriff.   _____

16. The surprising complexity of Saturn's rings will be studied for
     decades.   _____

17. Our president is an unusually dedicated educator.   _____

18. Diane has a well-developed sense of humor.   _____

19. Everyone questioned was considered a suspect.   _____

20. Overshoes help prevent frozen feet.   _____

21. The teen-ager was seen roaming the streets.   _____

22. Careening around a blind curve, the truck caused an accident.   _____

23. The care of children is a fulfilling occupation.   _____

24. The rattling old car did not pass inspection.   _____

25. We all enjoyed the overnight camping trip.   _____

26. In Scotland pouring rain and thick gorse proved formidable obstacles
     for the American golfers.   _____

27. We heard the wind whistling around the house all night.   _____

28. Tim's swollen arm had to be packed in ice.   _____

29. Can you repair this broken clock?   _____

30. The half-eaten cookie was thrown to the floor by the angry child. _____

| Exercise 20 | INFINITIVES |

Underline the infinitive in each of the following sentences, and in the space at the right indicate its use in the sentence by writing **N** for noun, **Adj** for adjective, **Adv** for adverb.

EXAMPLE: He wanted to borrow the wheelbarrow.   *N*

1. Many artists prefer to make preliminary drawings on canvas before beginning with paint and brush. _____

2. To prepare herself for the team, Robbie practiced two hours every day. _____

3. Susan went to buy a dress for the senior prom. _____

4. The books on the table are ready to be shelved. _____

5. Wayne wants to go with us to the movie. _____

6. Many hours are required to teach a dog tricks. _____

7. As I raised my camera to focus, the bird flew away. _____

8. Professor Bourne bought Tracy Kidder's *The Soul of a New Machine* to read. _____

9. He wants to ask only one question. _____

10. We are planning to rewire our house. _____

11. We had hoped to hear that Russ was coming. _____

12. Our class has five novels to read this term. _____

13. The officer suggested a better route to follow. _____

14. Driver education should teach her the proper way to drive. _____

15. His family was eager to meet his fiancée. _____

16. We have tickets to see *Private Lives.* _____

17. Uncle Les gave Ross a check to buy a football. _____

18. During the holidays all she wanted was to sleep.   _____

19. Nora intends to be elected representative from our ward.   _____

20. To see Santa Claus excites small children.   _____

21. To respect my teachers was important to me.   _____

22. The mayor seemed glad to welcome the visitors from Japan.   _____

23. Learning to swim is necessary for toddlers if a pool or lake is near.   _____

24. I was happy to study with a great professor.   _____

25. The woodman did not want to fell the old oak tree.   _____

26. You must try to read Vaillant's study *Adaptation to Life.*   _____

27. Sal doesn't often have an opportunity to sleep until noon.   _____

28. Pat and Jim plan to move to Augusta in February.   _____

29. To argue for the sake of arguing is immature.   _____

30. I hope to call you tomorrow.   _____

Exercise 21 | VERBALS

In the following sentences underline each verbal. On the first line at the right identify the
type of verbal by writing

Ger for gerund, **Part** for participle, **Inf** for infinitive.

On the second line at the right indicate the *use* of the verbal by writing

Adj for adjective,	**PN** for predicate nominative,
Adv for adverb,	**DO** for direct object,
S for subject,	**OP** for object of a preposition.

	TYPE	USE
EXAMPLE: The facts are not difficult <u>to see</u>.	*Inf*	*Adv*
1. Our club needs a place to build its float.	_____	_____
2. The astounding explosion of scientific knowledge has transformed our attitude toward life.	_____	_____
3. I enjoyed teaching at Baylor University.	_____	_____
4. The increased interest in the sciences has generally diverted our attention from the humanities.	_____	_____
5. The Okefenokee Swamp offers all lovers of nature a rewarding experience.	_____	_____
6. I am happy about your opportunity to tour Europe this summer.	_____	_____
7. Dr. Seigel's speech made a lasting impression on Jessie.	_____	_____
8. Apartment hunting can be fun.	_____	_____
9. Erik hesitated to answer the question.	_____	_____
10. After graduating from college, Sue worked for the American Telephone and Telegraph company.	_____	_____
11. To go to New York on such short notice is foolish.	_____	_____

	TYPE	USE

12. I am enjoying reading the six-volume biography of Benjamin Franklin.   _____ _____

13. Is the committee ready to vote on the question?   _____ _____

14. The chief inspector could do nothing except investigate the allegation.   _____ _____

15. William Faulkner's fame brought to Oxford, Mississippi, many well-
known scholars.   _____ _____

16. Watching the sun rise at sea is a memorable experience.   _____ _____

17. To gossip is a great temptation under the circumstances.   _____ _____

18. After six weeks of starving himself, he lost only six pounds.   _____ _____

19. The money kept in the cookie jar was quickly found by the thief.   _____ _____

20. Are you prepared to make financial sacrifices for your college education?   _____ _____

21. Everyone was in a hurry to catch the evening train.   _____ _____

22. Establishing her life's goals caused Jenny many sleepless nights.   _____ _____

23. Jeffrey always raises interesting questions in class.   _____ _____

24. Carl's latest interest has been scuba diving.   _____ _____

25. Because we arrived late, we did not have time to eat.   _____ _____

5
Recognizing Phrases

A **phrase** is a group of related words, generally having neither subject nor predicate and used as though it were a single word. It cannot make a statement and is therefore not a clause.

A knowledge of the phrase and how it is used will suggest to you ways of diversifying and enlivening your sentences. Variety in using sentences will remedy the monotonous "subject first" habit. For instance, the use of the participial phrase will add life and movement to your style, because the participle is an action word, having the strength of its verbal nature in addition to its function as a modifier.

We classify phrases as **gerund, participial, infinitive, absolute, prepositional,** and **appositive.** The following sentences will show how the same idea may be expressed differently by the use of different kinds of phrases:

> Sue swam daily. She hoped to improve her backstroke. ["Subject first" sentences.]
>
> By *swimming daily,* Sue hoped to improve her backstroke. [Gerund phrase.]
>
> *Swimming daily,* Sue hoped to improve her backstroke. [Participial phrase.]
>
> Sue's only hope of improving her backstroke was *to swim daily.* [Infinitive phrase.]
>
> *With a daily swim* Sue hoped to improve her backstroke. [Prepositional phrase.]

5a   The Gerund Phrase

A **gerund phrase** consists of a gerund and any complement or modifiers it may have. The function of the gerund phrase is always that of a noun:

> *Being late for breakfast* is Joe's worst fault. [The gerund phrase is used as the subject of the verb *is.*]
>
> She finally succeeded in *opening the camera.* [The gerund phrase is the object of the preposition *in.*]

Bill hated *driving his golf balls into the lake.* [The gerund phrase is the object of the verb *hated.*]

His hobby, *making furniture,* is enjoyable and useful. [The gerund phrase is an appositive.]

5b   The Participial Phrase

A **participial phrase** consists of a participle and any complement or modifiers it may have. It functions as an adjective:

Disappointed by his best friend, Roger refused to speak to him. [The participial phrase modifies the proper noun *Roger.*]

Having written the letter, Julie set out for the Post Office. [The participial phrase modifies the proper noun *Julie.*]

The boy *standing in the doorway* is the one who asked to borrow our rake. [The participial phrase modifies the noun *boy.*]

PUNCTUATION: *Introductory participial phrases are set off by commas. Other participial phrases are also set off by commas unless they are essential to the meaning of the sentence.* (See Chapter 19, Section b.)

5c   The Infinitive Phrase

An **infinitive phrase** consists of an infinitive and any complement or modifiers it may have. Infinitives function as adjectives, adverbs, or nouns:

She had a plane *to catch at eight o'clock.* [The infinitive phrase modifies the noun *plane.*]

To be in Mr. Foster's class was *to learn the meaning of discipline.* [The first infinitive phrase is the subject of the verb *was.* The second infinitive phrase is the predicate nominative after the verb *was.*]

Millie left early *to avoid the heavy traffic.* [The infinitive phrase modifies the verb *left.*]

After the night outdoors we were happy *to be warm and dry again.* [The infinitive phrase modifies the adjective *happy.*]

Ted has no plans except *to watch television.* [The infinitive phrase is the object of the preposition *except.*]

We decided *to go for a long walk.* [The infinitive phrase is the direct object of the verb *decided.*]

Her fiancé seems *to be very pleasant.* [The infinitive phrase is the predicate adjective after the verb *seems.*]

PUNCTUATION: *Introductory infinitive phrases used as modifiers are set off by commas.* (See Chapter 19, Section b.)

5d   The Absolute Phrase

A noun followed by a participle may form a construction grammatically independent of the rest of the sentence. This construction is called an **absolute phrase**. It is never a subject, nor does it modify any word in the sentence, but it is used *absolutely* or independently:

> *The bus having stopped,* the tourists filed out.
>
> *The theater being nearby,* I decided to walk.
>
> I shall do as I please, *all things considered.*

PUNCTUATION: An absolute phrase is always separated from the rest of the sentence by a comma. (See Chapter 19, Section b.)

5e The Prepositional Phrase

A **prepositional phrase** consists of a preposition followed by a noun or pronoun used as its object, together with any modifiers the noun or pronoun may have. The prepositional phrase functions usually as an adjective or an adverb:

> The plan *of the house* is very simple. [The prepositional phrase modifies the noun *plan.*]
>
> The river runs *through rich farmland.* [The prepositional phrase modifies the verb *runs.*]

PUNCTUATION: An introductory prepositional phrase, unless unusually long, is not set off by a comma. (See Chapter 19, Section b.)

5f The Appositive Phrase

An **appositive** is a word or phrase which explains, identifies, or renames the word it follows. An appositive may be a noun phrase (that is, a noun and its modifiers), a gerund phrase, an infinitive phrase, or a prepositional phrase:

> This book, *a long novel about politics,* will never be a best seller. [Noun phrase used as an appositive.]
>
> Jean knew a way out of her difficulty: *telling the truth.* [Gerund phrase used as an appositive.]
>
> His greatest ambition, *to make a million dollars,* was doomed from the start. [Infinitive phrase used as an appositive.]
>
> The rustler's hideout, *in the old cave by the river,* was discovered by the posse. [Prepositional phrase used as an appositive.]

An appositive may be **essential** (sometimes called **fused**) or **nonessential**; it is essential if it positively identifies that which it renames, frequently by use of a proper noun. Examples of both essential and nonessential appositives occur in the sentences below:

> The Victorian poets *Tennyson and Browning* were outstanding literary spokesmen of their day. [The appositive, *Tennyson and Browning,* identifies *poets* and thus is essential.]
>
> Tennyson and Browning, *two Victorian poets,* were outstanding literary spokesmen of their day. [The appositive, *two Victorian poets,* is nonessential because the poets are already identified by their names.]

PUNCTUATION: An appositive phrase is enclosed with commas unless it is essential. (See Chapter 19, Section b.)

Exercise 22 | **PHRASES**

In each of the following sentences identify the *italicized* phrase by writing in the space at the right

Prep if it is a prepositional phrase,   **Inf** if it is an infinitive phrase,
Part if it is a participial phrase,   **App** if it is an appositive phrase,
Ger if it is a gerund phrase,   **Abs** if it is an absolute phrase.

EXAMPLE: Betsy has a habit of *misplacing her car keys.*   *Ger*

1. *Introducing Dr. Sauls* is quite an honor.   _____

2. *Taking her doctor's advice,* she quit smoking.   _____

3. Dora made a kite *for her little brother.*   _____

4. *Born on a farm during the depression,* Barbara grew up knowing the value of hard work.   _____

5. The feeling of accomplishment *from a job well done* is wonderful.   _____

6. James Dickey, *a twentieth-century poet,* often writes about his own experiences.   _____

7. *All things considered,* Allen decided not to sell his car.   _____

8. We enjoyed *watching her dance.*   _____

9. The letters *addressed to Santa Claus* are always delivered on time.   _____

10. Julia and Charles, *members of the chess team,* are also twins.   _____

11. *The bell having rung,* we rushed to the door.   _____

12. Her secret dream is *to win the National Sportscar Race.*   _____

13. We all stood in front of the fire *warming our hands.*   _____

14. The theater was dark, *the play being over.*   _____

15. *After torrential rains,* the farmer must restore fertility to his land.   _____

16. *Being an authority* is sometimes an irksome responsibility.   _____

17. *Around the corner* is the house where Toni lives.   _____

18. If you have never skied before, you should start *practicing before the trip to Colorado.*   _____

19. Whom are you bringing *to the party?*   _____

20. We all went to New Orleans together *except Laura and Carol.*   _____

| Exercise 23 | PHRASES |

The sentences in the following exercise contain prepositional, verbal, and appositive phrases. Underline each phrase, and in the space at the right of each sentence show how each phrase is used by writing **Adj** for adjective, **Adv** for adverb, and **N** for noun.

EXAMPLE: <u>Growing roses</u> requires time and knowledge.   _N_

1. We are leaving for Fairbanks, Alaska, tomorrow morning.   _____

2. The speaker attended Bates College in Maine.   _____

3. Playing bridge well demands concentration.   _____

4. We found Aunt Lena reading some old letters.   _____

5. Have you telephoned the restaurant about reservations?   _____

6. To find the right size wrench is not always easy.   _____

7. Kevin, my first cousin, visited us last week.   _____

8. The farmer was careful to plow straight furrows.   _____

9. Scarborough's has a rugby sweater for sale.   _____

10. Uncle Fred assured us that the cows would return to the barn.   _____

11. Constantly nagging his children, Murray kept them upset.   _____

12. Our plane was delayed several hours in Los Angeles.   _____

13. Studying the humanities broadens one's outlook.   _____

14. The family plans to buy a new van this year.   _____

15. Andy will follow us on his bicycle.   _____

16. John Updike, the highly regarded novelist, was our guest lecturer this term.   _____

17. Little children are usually eager to please.   _____

18. Have you mastered the principles of Latin grammar?   ———

19. Bondurant, Minnesota's star quarterback, hopes that a professional team will
    draft him.   ———

20. Dinosaurs, enormous reptiles, roamed the earth centuries ago.   ———

21. Everyone wanted to postpone the examination.   ———

22. Having finished his class assignments, Larry took a brief nap.   ———

23. The Board approved the report outlining personnel procedures.   ———

24. Keeping her retirement a secret was impossible.   ———

25. I am trying to maintain an open mind.   ———

Exercise 24	PHRASES

In each of the following sentences underline the phrase. In the first space at the right identify the *type* of phrase by writing

        Prep for prepositional phrase,   **Inf** for infinitive phrase,
        Part for participial phrase,   **App** for appositive phrase.
        Ger for gerund phrase,

Then indicate in the second space its *use* by writing **Adj, Adv,** or **N.**

                                                                           TYPE   **USE**

EXAMPLE: Kate Peterson, philosopher and historian, was my major

          professor.   *App*   *N*

1. When I was a teen-ager, Andy Warhol, the pop artist, interested me.   _____ _____

2. Harris promised to support us.   _____ _____

3. We were too tired to play tennis.   _____ _____

4. Mac decorated his Christmas tree with candy canes and popcorn balls.   _____ _____

5. Jake was eager to receive his chemistry grades.   _____ _____

6. Eating a late supper caused Haskins a sleepless night.   _____ _____

7. During the winter many warm-blooded animals hibernate.   _____ _____

8. Carrying his pack, the tramp walked thirty miles.   _____ _____

9. Answering questionnaires and the telephone takes time.   _____ _____

10. Professor Quinlan did not enjoy directing graduate theses.   _____ _____

11. Diogenes searched the world to find an honest man.   _____ _____

12. Philip is able but is not willing to write the article.   _____ _____

13. Ernest's uncle, a carpenter, builds beautiful cabinets.   _____ _____

	TYPE	USE

14. We looked everywhere for a china soup tureen.   _____ _____

15. Marvin's job is to keep the yard clean.   _____ _____

16. Can you avoid apologizing to Madge?   _____ _____

17. Science and technology are an integral part of international affairs.   _____ _____

18. Martin wanted to drive Sally's new sports car.   _____ _____

19. Sara, May's younger sister, is attending veterinary school.   _____ _____

20. Priscilla is one of our best swimmers.   _____ _____

| Exercise 25 | **PHRASES** |

A.   Combine the following pairs of sentences, making one sentence a *participial* phrase. Punctuate each sentence correctly.

EXAMPLE: The Okefenokee Swamp is located in southeast Georgia and northeast Florida. It covers almost seven hundred square miles.

The Okefenokee Swamp, located in southeast Georgia and northeast Florida, covers almost seven hundred square miles.

1. The ringing telephone pierced the silence of the night. It sent a cold chill up Alice's spine.

2. Smoke drifted upward from the chimney. Emmett knew there would be a fire to warm him when he reached home.

3. The sun formed intricate designs on the floor. The sun was shining through the lace curtains.

4. Lester and I finished our shopping. We enjoyed dinner at Claudette's.

5. We had packed our camping gear. We headed for the desert.

6. Wade tried to get to sleep. He tossed and turned for hours.

7. I sharpened my pencils before class. I was ready to take the test.

8. Bryant looked at the wall clock. He realized that he was late for his date.

9. That is a handsome young man. He is standing by the fireplace.

10. Each of us wants to attend the college of his choice. Each must spend time preparing himself academically.

B.   Combine the following pairs of sentences, making one of the sentences an *appositive* phrase.

EXAMPLE: William Faulkner was an American novelist. He believed that "man will not merely endure: he will prevail."

William Faulkner, an American novelist, believed that "man will not merely endure: he will prevail."

1. Joseph is a gracious and reserved man. He is a biologist.

2. The California condor has been an endangered species since 1949. It is the largest bird in North America.

3. James Michener won the Pulitzer Prize in 1947 for *Tales of the South Pacific*. It was his first novel.

4. Many lines were knocked down by the ice storm. Some were telephone lines, and others were electric.

5. Vicky had eight puppies. Vicky is Charlie's collie.

6. *At Odds* by Carl N. Degler is a provocative study. It is an analysis of women and the family in America from the Revolution to the present.

7. Harry S. Truman was the thirty-third president of the United States. He was a man of great courage.

8. The Siberian tiger is capable of covering long distances in a single day. It is a cold-weather animal.

9. Fyodor Dostoevski was a Russian novelist. He was a master of the psychological novel.

10. Dr. Gray is the university president. He spoke to the alumni to express his appreciation to the group for its efforts.

Exercise 26 | PUNCTUATION OF PHRASES

In the following sentences insert all commas required by the rules stated in Chapter 5. In the blanks write the commas with the words that precede them. When the sentence requires no comma, write **C** in the space.

EXAMPLE: Carrying a small box, Dorothy ran over and
handed it to Grandmother.   _____ *box,* _____

1. William Butler Yeats an Irish poet and playwright was   _____
   awarded the Nobel Prize for literature in 1923.   _____

2. To meet the train on time I must leave immediately.   _____

3. Driving defensively Harry avoided a serious accident.   _____

4. My brother wearing his Miss Piggy shirt is campaigning   _____
   for president of student government.   _____

5. The class having ended I breathed a sigh of relief
   because I had not read the assignment.   _____

6. Wes handicapped by his inability to speak before a   _____
   group signed up for a speech course.   _____

7. The rain had washed mud into the lake making it
   murky.   _____

8. Dr. Loftis a heart specialist teaches at Emory University   _____
   Medical School.   _____

9. The date having been set for the trial the defense
   attorney notified his witnesses.   _____

10. To convince the jury of his client's innocence would
    be difficult.   _____

11. To tell the truth I am really quite bored by modern
    art.   _____

12. Gathering material for his novels takes Laurence Jamison
    to many interesting places.   _____

13. Having worked in the yard all day I was exhausted.   _____

14. The Oconee River swollen by recent rains, overflowed
    its banks.

    _____
    _____

15. Mary Gordon a contemporary writer is the author of
    Final Payments.

    _____
    _____

16. Irene's hobby collecting old coins, is expensive.

    _____
    _____

17. To prepare for my final examination in Russian I
    studied four hours a day.

    _____

18. The young man entering the library is our English
    professor.

    _____

19. Having recently returned from touring China Dr. Sanford
    will be an interesting speaker.

    _____

20. Watching television several hours a day Ben lost touch
    with the real world.

    _____

6

Independent Clauses

6a Independent Clauses

A group of words containing a subject and a verb and expressing a complete thought is called a sentence or an **independent clause**. Some groups of words which contain a subject and a verb, however, do not express a complete thought and therefore cannot stand alone as a sentence. Such word groups are dependent on other sentence elements and are called **dependent clauses**.

Sometimes an independent clause stands alone as a sentence. Sometimes two or more independent clauses are combined into one sentence without a connecting word. Then a semicolon is used to connect the independent clauses:

> The day is cold.
> The day is cold; the wind is howling.

Sometimes independent clauses are connected by one of the coordinating conjunctions, *and, but, for, or, nor, so,* and *yet.* As these conjunctions do not subordinate, an independent clause beginning with one of them may stand as a complete sentence. Independent clauses joined by a coordinating conjunction are separated by commas. Therefore, to punctuate correctly, you must distinguish between independent clauses and other kinds of sentence elements joined by coordinating conjunctions. In the following examples note that only independent clauses joined by coordinating conjunctions are separated by commas:

> The day was *dark* and *dreary*. [The conjunction *and* joins two adjectives, *dark* and *dreary*. No comma permitted.]
>
> The fallen tree *blocked* the highway and *delayed* travel. [The conjunction *and* joins the two verbs. No comma permitted.]
>
> She ran *up the steps* and *into the house*. [The conjunction *and* joints two phrases. No comma permitted.]

Mrs. Brown caught the fish, and *her husband cooked them.* [The conjunction *and* connects two independent clauses, and these are separted by a comma.]

Sometimes two independent clauses are connected by a **conjunctive**, or **transitional, adverb** such as one of the following:

however	moreover	nevertheless	therefore
then	accordingly	otherwise	thus
hence	besides	consequently	

A semicolon is necessary before any of these words beginning a second clause. After the longer *conjunctive adverbs* a comma is generally used:

We drove all day; *then* at sundown we began to look for a place to camp.

It rained during the afternoon; *consequently,* our trip to the mountains had to be postponed.

NOTE: Conjunctive adverbs can be distinguished from subordinating conjunctions by the fact that the *adverbs* can be shifted to a later position in the sentence, whereas the *conjunctions* cannot:

It rained during the afternoon; our trip to the mountains, *consequently,* had to be postponed.

SUMMARY OF PUNCTUATION: From the foregoing discussion and examples we can establish the following rules for the punctuation of independent clauses:

1. *Two independent clauses connected by a coordinating conjunction are separated by a comma:*

   Our goat chewed up the morning paper, *and* Father is angry.

   You should call Hank tonight, *for* he is all alone.

2. *Two independent clauses which are not connected by a coordinating conjunction are separated by a semicolon.* Remember that this rule also holds true when the second clause begins with a conjunctive adverb:

   Philip is quite strong; he is much stronger than I.

   We both wanted to go to the toboggan race; *however,* Mother had asked us to be home by six.

3. *A semicolon is used to separate independent clauses which are joined by a coordinating conjunction but which are heavily punctuated with commas internally:*

   Harry, George, and Kitty went to Sky Valley for skiing; but Tony and I were too tired to go.

4. *Short independent clauses, when used in a series with a coordinating conjunction preceding the final clause, may be separted by commas:*

   The audience was seated, the lights were dimmed, and the curtain was raised.

   NOTE: A series consists of at least three elements.

6b The Comma Splice

Use of a comma between two independent clauses not joined by a coordinating conjunction (Rule 2), is a major error called the **comma splice** (This term comes from the idea of splicing or "patching" together two clauses which should be more strongly separated.):

COMMA SPLICE: I enjoyed his company, I do not know that he enjoyed mine.

CORRECTION: I enjoyed his company, but I do not know that he enjoyed mine. (Using Rule 1)

I enjoyed his company; I do not know that he enjoyed mine. (Using Rule 2)

OR

I enjoyed his company; however, I do not know that he enjoyed mine. (Using Rule 2)

6c The Run-together Sentence

The **run-together sentence** results from omitting punctuation between two independent clauses not joined by a conjunction. Basically the error is the same as that of the comma splice: it shows ignorance of sentence structure:

Twilight had fallen it was dark under the old oak tree near the house.

When you read the sentence just given, you have difficulty in getting the meaning at first because the ideas are run together. Now consider the following sentence:

Twilight had fallen, it was dark under the old oak tree near the house.

The insertion of the comma is not a satisfactory remedy, for the sentence now contains a comma splice. There are, however, four approved devices for correcting the run-together sentence and the comma splice:

1. Connect two independent clauses by a comma and a coordinating conjunction if the two clauses are logically of equal importance:

   Twilight had fallen, and it was dark under the old oak tree near the house.

2. Connect two independent clauses by a semicolon if they are close enough in thought to make one sentence and you want to omit the conjunction:

   Twilight had fallen; it was dark under the old oak tree near the house.

3. Write the two independent clauses as separate sentences if you wish to give them separate emphasis:

   Twilight had fallen. It was dark under the old oak tree near the house.

4. Subordinate one of the independent clauses:

   When twilight had fallen, it was dark under the old oak tree near the house.

| Exercise 27 | THE COMMA SPLICE AND THE RUN-TOGETHER SENTENCE |

Mark correct sentences **C**, run-together sentences **R**, and sentences containing a comma splice **CS**.

EXAMPLE: The sun was obscured by the clouds, it was oppressively humid. _*CS*_

1. A few days later they boarded the cruise ship they had a tiny cabin. _____

2. A broad-shouldered, heavy-set soldier entered the room at first no one recognized him. _____

3. A report predicts that if current trends continue, the world in the year 2000 will be more polluted than it is today. _____

4. The attorney studied the jury a moment without speaking, then he addressed the court. _____

5. College students are often criticized for their crude pranks their good deeds too often go unnoticed. _____

6. The world's population is estimated to be around 4.5 billion people, it increased seventy-five percent during the last thirty years. _____

7. Their telephone has been disconnected I cannot get in touch with them. _____

8. The student nurse is very enthusiastic about the work she is doing at the hospital. _____

9. Grandmother has had her sewing machine for forty years, it continues to work perfectly. _____

10. Young children are curious and tend to get into everything, therefore, dangerous articles must be kept out of their reach. _____

11. Your imagination is running away with you, there are no squirrels in the attic. _____

12. Come out from behind the bushes, Bobby, I know you are there. _____

13. The reading lamp in the library is too dim I wish that someone would get a new bulb. _____

14. The colors in that painting are so lifelike that one can almost smell the flowers. _____

15. Edward announced that members of the men's garden club would meet again next Tuesday he will be unable to attend. _____

16. *The Shang Civilization* was written by Kwang-Chih Chang, it is a comprehensive history of one of China's earliest civilizations. _____

17. The drill team sponsored a garage sale to make money for their uniforms they raised over a thousand dollars. _____

18. The car was traveling entirely too fast on the wet highway the driver lost control. _____

19. The boy's parents are encouraging him to continue his education, he wants to join the Navy. _____

20. The new apartment complex will be completed in ninety days Vernon and Josephine hope to move in in March. _____

| Exercise 28 | THE COMMA SPLICE AND THE RUN-TOGETHER SENTENCE |

Mark correct sentences **C,** run-together sentences **R,** and sentences containing a comma splice **CS.**

EXAMPLE: The steps are slippery, therefore, please watch your step when you
leave.   *CS*

1. The boys' tennis team is going to camp next month, the camp is in Dallas.   _____

2. Smith's Hardware Store has donated five gallons of paint to our club now we
   need volunteers to paint the clubhouse.   _____

3. The man in the green sweater is Jack Barron, he is our new swimming coach.   _____

4. He did not study the assignment, therefore, he failed the test.   _____

5. As you know, I am not in favor of this project.   _____

6. Pam has not read *Macbeth* moreover, she has never seen the play.   _____

7. I tried several times to reach you on the telephone each time your line was busy. _____

8. As soon as he reached the campus, he tried to find some of his old friends.   _____

9. The landscape architect spent several hours sketching a new plan for the yard,
   he made numerous suggestions.   _____

10. The old home place was torn down last year a supermarket was built there.   _____

11. Change is inevitable, therefore, we must prepare ourselves for it.   _____

12. The policeman gave me a ticket for parking on the wrong side of the street, the
    fine was fifteen dollars.   _____

13. During the storm his yacht crashed upon a coral reef he was lucky to escape
    with his life.   _____

14. Jake has always been a great golfer, he plays golf every Saturday morning.   _____

15. I want to attend the club's next luncheon, however, I may be in Houston
    that day.   _____

16. Vacation provides me with time to catch up on my reading, but I never seem to
    get around to it.   _____

17. The computer made a mistake Dolly was assigned to a men's dormitory.   _____

18. Bertha wants to work for a legal firm this summer, I hope that she can.   _____

19. My mobile home is small and compact it is also quite comfortable.   _____

20. After jogging regularly for six months, I lost ten pounds I want to lose ten more by the end of the year.   _____

| Exercise 29 | PUNCTUATION OF INDEPENDENT CLAUSES |

In the following sentences insert all necessary commas and semicolons. Then in the space at the right write the correct punctuation mark with the word that precedes it. Write **C** if the sentence is correct.

EXAMPLE: Bobby and Hal are musicians in a rock band͵ but they play only for pleasure.   _____*band,*_____

1. The lane was poorly lighted therefore, I was unable to see the box in 'the middle of the path.   _____

2. Jessie could not find her billfold when she started to pay for the groceries.   _____

3. I recently read Paul Simon's *The Tongue-tied American* and I recommend it to both faculty and students.   _____

4. Lillian has a most incredibly beautiful voice but she doesn't plan to sing professionally.   _____

5. The greatest miracle of life is love it is a pity that John has turned his back on it.   _____

6. Drive slow and live long.   _____

7. His motorcycle is in the shop consequently, he borrowed my truck.   _____

8. Gainsborough's *Blue Boy* hangs in the Huntington main gallery directly across from Lawrence's *Pinkie* they are two frequently reproduced paintings.   _____

9. I am going to spend the next two hours on the beach although I really should be working.   _____

10. Gene's earnings as a freelance writer are adequate but he is excited about the prospect of a full-time position with *Saturday Review.*   _____

11. Give me your new address and I will send you the recipe for Russian tea.   _____

12. Learn from your mistakes don't brood over them.   _____

13. I lent her my copy of *Don Quixote* however, she hasn't returned it.   _____

14. Paula's plane will arrive at midnight I hope you can go with me to the airport.   _____

15. We will meet you at the theater and after the play we will have dinner at the Empress of China.   _____

16. Mark is a delightful person to be with although he is a little shy.   _____

17. Elsie spent the summer traveling now she is eager to begin school.   _____

18. Carolyn, one of my best friends, attended the University of Texas last year she wants to be a dietician.   _____

19. The ice storms this year have already cost our state millions in road repairs and winter is only half over.   _____

20. I cannot go to the store now I can, however, go after lunch.   _____

7

Dependent Clauses

Any clause beginning with a subordinating word like *what, that, who, which, when, since, before, after,* or *if* is a **dependent clause**. Dependent clauses, like phrases, function as grammatical units in a sentence—that is, as nouns, adjectives, and adverbs:

> I went to school. ⎱
> Too much time had elapsed. ⎰ [Both clauses are independent.]
>
> *When I went to school,* I studied my lessons. [The first clause is subordinate.]
>
> *Since too much time had elapsed,* she remained at home. [The first clause is subordinate.]

In the last two sentences *I studied my lessons* and *she remained at home* are complete statements. But the clauses *When I went to school* and *Since too much time had elapsed* do not express complete thoughts. They depend upon the independent statements to complete their meanings. Both of these dependent clauses function as adverbs.

7a   Noun Clauses

A **noun clause** is a dependent clause used as a noun, that is, as a subject, complement, object of a preposition, or appositive. Noun clauses are usually introduced by *that, what, why, whether, who, which,* or *how.* Some of these introductory words can introduce both noun and adjective clauses, since the function of the whole clause in the sentence, and not its introductory word, determines its classification. Most sentences containing noun clauses differ from those containing adjective and adverbial clauses in that with the clause removed they are no longer complete sentences.

> Your *plan* is interesting. [This is a simple sentence, containing no dependent clause. The subject is the noun *plan*. The following example sentences show that dependent noun clauses may be substituted for the word *plan*, and vice versa.]

93

What you intend to do [your plan] is interesting. [The italicized noun clause is the subject of the verb *is*. Notice that the noun *plan* can be substituted for the clause.]

Tell me *what you intend to do* [your plan]. [The italicized noun clause is the direct object of the verb *tell.*]

That is *what you intend to do* [your plan]. [The italicized noun clause is a predicate nominative.]

I am interested in *what you intend to do* [your plan]. [The italicized noun clause is the object of the preposition *in.*]

The fact *that he had not told the truth* soon became apparent. [The italicized noun clause is in apposition with the noun *fact.*]

PUNCTUATION: Noun clauses used as non-essential appositives are set off by commas.

7b Adjective Clauses

An **adjective clause** is a dependent clause which modifies a noun or pronoun. The common connective words used to introduce adjective clauses are the relative pronouns *who* (and its inflected forms *whom* and *whose*), *which, that*, and relative adverbs like *where, when*, and *why*. (*Where* and *when* can introduce all three kinds of clauses.)

The italicized clauses in the following sentences are all adjective clauses:

She is a woman *who is respected by everyone.*

Mr. Johnson, *whose son attends the University,* is our friend.

He saw the place *where he was born.*

It was a time *when money did not count.*

I know the reason *why I failed the course.*

Adjective clauses are classified as **essential** (restrictive) and **nonessential** (non-restrictive).

An *essential* clause, as its name indicates, is necessary in a sentence, for it identifies or points out a certain person or thing; a *nonessential* clause adds information about the word it modifies, but it is not essential in pointing out or identifying a certain person or thing:

Thomas Jefferson, *who was born on the frontier,* became President. [The name *Thomas Jefferson* has identified the person, and the italicized clause is not essential.]

A person *who loves to read* will never be lonely. [The italicized adjective clause is essential in identifying a particular kind of person.]

My father, *who was a country boy,* has lived in the city for years. [Since a person has only one father, an identifying clause is not essential.]

The girl *by whom I sat in class* is an honor student. [The italicized adjective clause is essential to the identification of *girl.*]

To determine whether an adjective clause is essential, you may apply this test: read the sentence leaving out the adjective clause and see whether the removal omits necessary identification. Try this test on the following sentence:

Jet pilots, *who work under a great deal of stress,* must stay in excellent physical condition.

You will see that the removal of the adjective clause does not change the basic meaning of the sentence. The italicized adjective clause is, therefore, nonessential.

Now read the following sentence, leaving out the italicized adjective clause:

Jet pilots *who are not in excellent physical condition* should not be allowed to fly.

If the adjective clause of this sentence is removed, the statement is not at all what the writer meant to say. The adjective clause is, therefore, essential.

PUNCTUATION: Nonessential adjective clauses are set off from the rest of the sentence by commas. (See Chapter 19, Section b.)

7c Adverbial Clauses

An **adverbial clause** is a dependent clause that functions exactly as if it were an adverb. Like an adverb it modifies a verb, an adjective, an adverb, or the whole idea expressed in the sentence's independent clause: e.g., *As luck would have it*, we missed his telephone call.

An adverbial clause is used to show *time, place, cause, purpose, result, condition, concession, manner,* or *comparison*. Its first word is a subordinating conjunction. Common subordinating conjunctions and their uses are listed below:

1. Time (*when, before, since, as, while, until, after, whenever*)

   I will stay *until you come.*
   When the whistle blew, the laborer stopped.

2. Place (*where, wherever, whence, whither*)

   He went *where no one had ever set foot before.*
   Wherever you go, I will go too.

3. Cause (*because, since, as*)

   Since I had no classes on Saturday, I went home.
   Because he was afraid of being late, Bob ran all the way.

4. Purpose (*in order that, so that, that*)

   My family made many sacrifices *so that I could have an education.*
   Men work *that they may eat.*

5. Result (*so . . . that, such . . . that*)

   The weather was *so* cold *that I decided not to walk to school.*

6. Condition (*if, unless*)

   You will hurt your hand *if you are not careful.*
   Unless you apply at once, your name will not be considered.

7. Concession (*though, although*)

   Although she had no money, she was determined to go to college.

8. Manner (*as, as if, as though*)

   She looked *as though she wanted to laugh.*
   Do *as you like,* but take the consequences.

9. Comparison (*as, than*)

> He is older *than his brother.*
>
> He is as tall *as his brother.*

PUNCTUATION: Introductory adverbial clauses are always set off by commas:

> *Although he had tests to take and a term paper to write,* he went home for the weekend.
>
> *While I was eating lunch,* I had a phone call from my brother.

7d Kinds of Sentences

For the purpose of varying style and avoiding monotony, you may need to be able to distinguish the four basic types of sentences. According to the number and kind of clauses (phrases do not affect sentence type), sentences may be grouped into four types: **simple, compound, complex,** and **compound-complex.**

1. A **simple** sentence is a single independent clause; it has one subject and one predicate. But it may have as a subject more than one noun or pronoun and as a predicate more than one verb:

> Robert has a new car. [Single subject and single predicate.]
>
> *Robert* and his *brother* have a new car. [There is one verb, *have*, but the subject consists of two nouns.]
>
> Robert *washed* and *polished* his new car on Sunday. [There is one subject, *Robert*, but two verbs.]
>
> *Robert* and his *brother washed* and *polished* their new car. [The subject consists of two nouns, *Robert* and *brother*; and the predicate consists of two verbs, *washed* and *polished.*]

2. A **compound** sentence contains at least two independent clauses and no dependent clause:

> Mary likes the mountains, but Jackie prefers the seashore.
>
> A lamp was lighted in the house, the happy family was talking together, and supper was waiting.

3. A **complex** sentence contains only one independent clause and one or more dependent clauses (the dependent clauses are in italics):

> The toy truck *that you gave Molly for her birthday* is broken.
>
> *Why he refused to contribute to the fund* we do not know.

4. A **compound-complex** sentence has at least two independent clauses and one or more dependent clauses (the independent clauses are in italics):

> *My friend was offended by my attitude,* and *I was sorry* that she was hurt.
>
> *We spent the morning looking for the home of the woman* who paints landscapes, but *we were unable to find it.*

Exercise 30	CLAUSES

In the following sentences underline each dependent clause. In the space at the right, write **Adj** if the clause is an adjective clause, **Adv** if it is an adverbial clause, and **N** if it is a noun clause. If the sentence contains no dependent clause, leave the space blank.

EXAMPLE: <u>After he took French 101 three times,</u> Carl finally passed the course.   *Adv*

1. For those who travel a great deal, all motels begin to look alike.   _____

2. I can tell by the sound of those footsteps that Joan is coming.   _____

3. After the dog was clipped for the summer, she looked much cooler.   _____

4. The coach told her team members that she was proud of them.   _____

5. Kurt Herbert Adler, general director of the San Francisco Opera, was educated in Vienna.   _____

6. Eva, who has a friendly, easy-going manner, is our new business manager.   _____

7. The class thought that Professor Humphries was dictatorial and irascible.   _____

8. Emmett found it necessary to explain to his son why no one should go swimming alone.   _____

9. Because the cost of gas has increased, riding the bus to work is the most economical way to go.   _____

10. Did you know that computers can communicate with each other?   _____

11. A good secretary can run the office when the boss is out of town.   _____

12. David told his mother that he didn't want to go to a barber but to a hair stylist.   _____

13. Bob went to his car only to find that he had a flat tire.   _____

14. Martha asked how to find the difficult word in the dictionary.   _____

15. If you need a copy of my itinerary, my assistant has it.   _____

16. Mark loves paddling his canoe on the lake which is behind his house.   _____

17. Eating was Roger's chief activity, and his waistline attested to that fact.   _____

18. Esther could not find the dress pattern that she was looking for.   _____

19. Although you do not like spinach, you know that it is good for you.   _____

20. Because of a decrease in business, railroad service was discontinued between the two cities.   _____

21. Charlotte did not understand why the elevators were slow whenever she was in a hurry.   _____

22. Even though the mornings were cool and pleasant, the afternoons were hot and sultry.   _____

23. Our house was unnaturally quiet when the children were away.   _____

24. Because there was nothing to watch on television, Ward decided to clean his apartment.   _____

25. Please water my plants while I am on vacation.   _____

| Exercise 31 | CLAUSES |

Give the function of each of the *italicized* clauses by writing the proper abbreviation in the space at the right:

S for subject,	**OP** for object of a preposition,
DO for direct object,	**Adj** for adjective modifier,
PN for predicate nominative,	**Adv** for adverbial modifier.

EXAMPLE: Nearly everyone agrees *that salt causes hypertension.* <u>DO</u>

1. Have you read Rebecca Harding Davis's obscure novel *which was published in an 1861 issue of a popular magazine?* _____

2. Stanley is the only one *who can predict the outcome.* _____

3. My sister says *that boots are a backpacker's best friend.* _____

4. The couple *with whom I chatted* have recently returned from Spain. _____

5. *After Denise finishes college,* she will spend a year in Europe. _____

6. The problem is *that we lack money for your project.* _____

7. Venice is a city *that always appears to be moving.* _____

8. His wife, *who is Canadian,* gets the urge to replace the slipcovers every two or three years. _____

9. Everyone was up early the day after Thanksgiving *because all the stores were having sales.* _____

10. Since its beginning the space program, *which is highly publicized,* has been a dramatic testimony to our technological achievements. _____

11. After many years she returned to the neighborhood *where she had spent her childhood.* _____

12. *Although he owns a mountain home in North Carolina,* Tom and his family spend very little time there. _____

13. *If you have never hung wallpaper,* you should practice *before you begin.* _____
_____

14. Do you believe *that history repeats itself?* _____

15. One thing *that we have learned in space science* is *how little we know.*   _____

_____

16. *That we could get tickets this late to see the play* surprised me.   _____

17. Do you have any suggestions on *how we can improve the quality of our product?*   _____

18. *When Dr. Butler first came to Kansas State,* he agreed to give a series of lectures on differential geometry.   _____

19. *As far as I know,* neither Ralph nor Paul is attending the concert.   _____

20. *How many library books are not being returned* is quite important to the library committee.   _____

21. The fact is *that we appreciate Jane's abilities more every day.*   _____

22. Did you keep a count of *how many students registered today?*   _____

23. The plot was *so* intriguing *that I could not put the book down.*   _____

24. *When we visited Monticello,* we saw many devices invented by Jefferson for his home.   _____

25. Do you know *when she arrived in town?*   _____

Exercise 32	REVIEW OF CLAUSES

In the following sentences enclose the dependent clauses in parentheses. In the spaces at the right indicate the number of independent and dependent clauses in each sentence. Be able to tell the function of each of the dependent clauses. (Note that some sentences may not contain a dependent clause.)

	IND.	DEP.
EXAMPLE: Houston, Texas, is a city (which is attracting many young people.)	1	1
1. If I had known that you were coming, I would have invited several of your classmates for dinner.	___	___
2. When Pythagoras discovered something new in geometry, legend says that he sacrificed an ox to the Muses.	___	___
3. Did you know that the Milners have a new baby?	___	___
4. That Laura is a bright child is shown by her ability to make puns.	___	___
5. When one buys antiques, he sometimes finds that not all dealers are honest.	___	___
6. After Chuck had visited the University of Virginia, he knew that he wanted to go there.	___	___
7. Even though Milton is an avid outdoorsman, his wife, Janet, is not.	___	___
8. The McDonalds live on a twenty-five acre farm near Enid, Oklahoma.	___	___
9. What Rick does with his money is a mystery to his parents.	___	___
10. Phyllis said that she is going to learn to paint when she finishes her degree in chemistry.	___	___
11. Wealth, which is highly valued in our society, does not always guarantee happiness.	___	___
12. My aunt, who is allergic to milk, must watch her diet; therefore, cooking for her is somewhat difficult.	___	___

101

IND.   DEP.

13. I have recently read several spy novels which were written by Helen MacInnes.   ____ ____

14. Children who spend several hours a day watching television often have difficulty with their school work.   ____ ____

15. Although the ambassador had spent ten years in Sweden, he could not carry on a conversation in Swedish.   ____ ____

16. That old house was ready for a wrecking crew before we renovated it.   ____ ____

17. If you can't find anyone else to go with you to the movie, Henry says that he will go, but I warn you that he'll talk the entire time.   ____ ____

18. Martha did not understand that problem at all.   ____ ____

19. Because of a stalled car on the freeway, we did not arrive until after the first act of the play was over.   ____ ____

20. When Somerset Maugham's *Cakes and Ale* appeared in 1930, it achieved overnight notoriety.   ____ ____

21. How many articles did you read before you completed your research?   ____ ____

22. After reading the reviews, we wanted to buy tickets for the Saturday night performance.   ____ ____

23. The only person who showed curiosity was a small boy who had not learned that he shouldn't say that the emperor had no clothes.   ____ ____

24. As we sat on the grass, a gentle rain started falling.   ____ ____

25. Hoping to change Father's mind, I tried to argue my point.   ____ ____

Exercise 33	CLAUSES

Complete each of the sentences below by writing in the spaces an *adjective clause*, an *adverbial clause*, or a *noun clause* as indicated above each space.

(adverbial clause)

EXAMPLE: <u>After we had finished work,</u>_____we went to Herren's
for dinner.

(noun clause)
1. Circumstances often dictate _____

(adverbial clause)
2. Larry and Helen stood on the porch and watched the birds _____

___ _____

(adjective clause)
3. Henrietta's wedding dress, _____
was delivered today.

(noun clause)
4. Tell Louise _____

(adjective clause)
5. I do not like recorded telephone messages _____

___ _____

(noun clause)
6. _____is extremely doubtful.

(adjective clause)
7. Employees _____must have security
clearance.

(adverbial clause)

8. _____ he never finished it.

(adjective clause)

9. The changes in class scheduling _____
were adopted by the faculty.

(adverbial clause)

10. _____ we will be ready.

| Exercise 34 | PUNCTUATION OF CLAUSES |

In the following sentences supply commas and semicolons where they are needed. In the spaces at the right, write the marks of punctuation with the words that precede them. Write **C** if the sentence is correct.

EXAMPLE: When I came into the house⌃ the telephone was ringing. _____*house,*_____

1. Once we had climbed on the bus and scrambled for our seats Mr. Waterford began counting heads. _____ _____

2. Irene who is interested in opening a decorating shop needs advice from an experienced business woman. _____ _____

3. That the First National Bank owns this property is not generally known. _____ _____

4. Summer was surely over Mrs. Brown's maple trees were tinged with gold. _____ _____

5. When Louis finally reached Marcus Place he saw the sign pointing to the interstate highway. _____ _____

6. We went to Everybody's for pizza then we dropped by Doug's apartment for coffee. _____ _____

7. Jerry left the car parked at the curb and went into the grocery store. _____ _____

8. There is no need to debate the issue the sponsors of the arms bill have the votes they need for its passage. _____ _____

9. The country singer who is to appear here Saturday night has agreed to give Mark an interview. _____ _____

10. They hiked at least another mile upstream and at last they saw the falls. _____ _____

11. The appeals court upheld the ruling by Judge Balfour who has been on the bench for more than a decade. _____ _____

12. I read the construction company's ad in the morning paper and applied for the job the same day. _____ _____

13. The radio blared forth the smell of coffee filled the apartment yet Watson slept on.

_____
_____

14. Did you buy your table at the flea market or is that the one you found in your mother's attic?

_____
_____

15. Mr. Hooper paced up and down his office the florist had not delivered the roses he had ordered for Ms. Rigby.

_____
_____

16. My opinion has changed since I read the editorial in the New York *Times.*

_____
_____

17. Mother could not decide where she wanted the piano consequently the movers placed it squarely in the middle of the living room.

_____
_____

18. The photographs that have been hung in the north gallery are the work of my friend Simon Jones.

_____
_____

19. Interpol which is the international crime information center has its headquarters in France.

_____
_____

20. After Melvin had attended the Southeast Computer Show he decided to invest in a home computer.

_____
_____

21. Time is always a problem for Morris as I'm sure everyone knows.

_____
_____

22. The Woodwards having been to Williamsburg want to spend Christmas there.

_____
_____

23. Frances, call me when you hear from the travel agent.

_____
_____

24. When you hear from him then we can begin planning our trip.

_____
_____

25. In last night's game Finley hit a homer popped up and struck out twice.

_____
_____

| Exercise 35 | KINDS OF SENTENCES |

Identify the type of sentence by writing one of the following abbreviations in the space at right:

S   if the sentence is simple,   **Cx**   if the sentence is complex,
Cp   if the sentence is compound,   **Cp-Cx**   if the sentence is compound-complex.

EXAMPLE: Maria has asked that we come to her house at eight.   *Cx*

1. Several accountants attended the seminar to increase their understanding of the small-business computer.   _____

2. Ernest, who is a biology major, attends labs three afternoons a week.   _____

3. The waitress at the diner served advice and encouragement along with ham and eggs.   _____

4. The bare light bulb swung from the middle of the kitchen ceiling, and the shadows moved up and down the walls.   _____

5. We met to discuss plans for the dance but spent most of the time discussing Jo.   _____

6. Maybe Huck Finn was right after all, for modern science recognizes non-medical means of curing warts.   _____

7. The recession was milder than the economists had predicted; consequently, a new optimism spread through the business community.   _____

8. Although I was famished, I did not have time to go to the cafeteria, which is on the sixth floor of the building across the street.   _____

9. Eurail passes are still considered a good bargain for tourists wishing to see Europe.   _____

10. The Gerald R. Ford Library, which contains Ford's presidential papers, is at the University of Michigan in Ann Arbor.   _____

11. We put everything we could find in the soup: carrots, potatoes, tomatoes, and of course onions.   _____

12. Stop with me at Harvey's; we can solve all our problems with a hamburger and a chocolate milk shake.   _____

13. Sidney and Joe climbed row after row before they found their seats; nevertheless, they were pleased to be in the coliseum at all.   _____

14. That the wind had shifted was soon evident to the crew of the fishing boat.   _____

15. The annual inflation rate had risen to ten percent despite the government's tight money policy.   _____

16. We needed the rain badly, but none of us welcomed the cold, gray Sunday.   _____

17. The baskets of peaches lined up on the roadside stand frequently caught the attention of passing motorists.   _____

18. To get to Harborside Inn, you will have to turn left at the bottom of this hill; then go straight until you come to the sound.   _____

19. The appearance of the Rolling Stones was described by the reporter as "the musical happening of the year," and the audience could not have agreed more.   _____

20. The book shop, which occupies a small Victorian house near the center of town, has not been open more than a week or two.   _____

21. Humphrey, my friend who rides to work with me, has recently been promoted; furthermore, he is being transferred to Dallas.   _____

22. A crowd gathered in front of the auditorium, waiting for the appearance of Sylvester.   _____

23. The stock market rose sharply after the President announced his new economic policy, and the Dow Jones average reflected this significant gain.   _____

24. The classified section of today's paper is filled with help-wanted ads, so I believe that I can find a job.   _____

25. *Billboard,* a magazine addressed to the entertainment world, is published in New York.   _____

8

Agreement of Subject and Verb

The verb in every independent or dependent clause must agree with its subject in person and number. (There are **three persons**: the **first person** is the speaker, the **second person** is the person spoken to, and the **third person** is the person or thing spoken about. There are **two numbers**: the **singular**, denoting one person or thing, and the **plural**, denoting more than one person or thing.) A careful study of the conjugation of the verb in Chapter 1 will show you that a verb can change form not only in *tense* but also in *person* and *number*. If you can recognize the subject and the verb, you should have no trouble making the two agree. Although there is ordinarily no problem in doing so, certain difficulties need special attention.

8a Intervening Expressions

The number of the verb in a sentence is not affected by any modifying phrases or clauses standing between the subject and the verb but is determined entirely by the number of the subject:

> The *evidence* which they submitted to the judges *was* [not *were*] convincing. [*Evidence* is the subject of the verb *was*.]

> The new *library* with its many books and its quiet reading rooms *fills* [not *fill*] a long-felt need. [*Library* is the subject of the verb *fills;* the phrase *with its many books...* has nothing to do with the verb.]

> A list of eligible candidates *was* [not *were*] posted on the bulletin board. [*List* is the subject of the verb *was posted.*]

> Our big pine tree as well as a small oak *was* [not *were*] damaged by the high winds. [*Tree* is the subject of the verb *was damaged;* the intervening phrase *as well as a small oak* is not a part of the subject.]

> The famous golfer along with his many fans *was* [not *were*] heading toward the ninth

green. [*Golfer* is the subject of the verb *was heading; along with his many* fans is not a part of the subject.]

My father, together with my two brothers, *is* [not *are*] planning to build a cabin at the lake. [*Father* is the subject of the verb *is planning*. The phrase that comes between the subject and the verb is not a part of the subject.]

8b   Verb Preceding the Subject

In some sentences the verb precedes the subject. This reversal of common order frequently leads to error in agreement:

There *is* [not *are*] in many countries much *unrest* today. [*Unrest* is the subject of the verb *is.*]

There *are* [not *is*] a *table*, two *couches*, four *chairs*, and a *desk* in the living room. [*Table, couches, chairs,* and *desk* are the subjects of the verb *are.*]

Where *are* [not *is*] *Bob* and his *friends going*? [*Bob* and *friends* are subjects of the verb *are going.*]

8c   Indefinite Pronouns

The indefinite pronouns or adjectives *either, neither,* and *each,* as well as such compounds as *everybody, anybody, everyone, anyone,* are always singular. *None* may be singular or plural. The plural usage is commoner:

Each of the plans *has* [not *have*] its advantages.

Everyone who heard the speech *was* [not *were*] impressed by it.

Every bud, stalk, flower, and seed *reveals* [not *reveal*] a workmanship beyond the power of man.

Is [not *Are*] *either* of you ready for a walk?

None of the men *have* brought their wives.

None of the three *is* [*are*] interested.

None—no, not one—*is* prepared.

8d   Compound Subjects

Compound subjects joined by *and* normally require a plural verb:

Correctness and *precision are* required in all good writing.

Where *are* the *bracelets* and *beads*?

NOTE: When nouns joined by *and* are thought of as a unit, the verb is normally singular:

The *sum* and *substance* of the matter *is* [not *are*] hardly worth considering.

My *friend* and *coworker* Mr. Jones *has* [not *have*] gone abroad.

8e   Subjects Joined by *Or* and *Nor*

Singular subjects joined by *or* or *nor* take a singular verb. If one subject, however, is singular and one plural, the verb agrees in number and person with the nearer one:

Either the *coach* or the *player was* [not *were*] at fault.

Neither the *cat* nor the *kittens have* been fed. [The plural word *kittens* in the compound subject stands next to the verb *have been fed.*]

Neither the *kittens* nor the *cat has* been fed. [The singular subject *cat* stands next to the verb, which is therefore singular.]

Neither my *brothers* nor *I am* going. [Note that the verb agrees with the nearer subject in person as well as in number.]

8f   Nouns Plural in Form

As a general rule use a singular verb with nouns that are plural in form but singular in meaning. The following nouns are usually singular in meaning: *news, economics, ethics, physics, mathematics, gallows, mumps, measles, shambles, whereabouts:*

The *news is* reported at eleven o'clock.

Measles is a contagious disease.

The following nouns are usually plural: *gymnastics, tactics, trousers, scissors, athletics, tidings, acoustics, riches, barracks:*

Athletics attract him.

The *scissors are* sharp.

Riches often *take* wing and *fly* away.

Plural nouns denoting a mass, a quantity, or a number require a singular verb when the subject is regarded as a unit.

Five *dollars is* too much for her to pay.

Fifty *bushels was* all the bin would hold.

Though usage is mixed, phrases involving addition, multiplication, subtraction, and division of numbers preferably take the singular:

Two and two is [are] four.

Two times three is six.

Twelve divided by six is two.

In expressions like *some of the pie(s), all of the money, all of the children,* the number of *some* and *all* is determined by the number of the noun in the prepositional phrase:

Some of the pie *is* missing.

Some of the pies *are* missing.

8g   The Subject of Some Form of *To Be*

When one noun precedes and another follows some form of the verb *to be,* the first noun is the subject, and the verb agrees with it and not with the complement even if the complement is different in number:

The only *fruit* on the market now *is* peaches.

Peaches are the only fruit on the market now. [In the first sentence *fruit* is the subject; in the second, *peaches.*]

8h   Relative Pronoun as Subject

When a relative pronoun (*who, which,* or *that*) is used as the subject of a clause, the number and person of the verb are determined by the antecedent of the pronoun, the word to which the pronoun refers:

> This is the student *who is* to be promoted. [The antecedent of *who* is the singular noun *student;* therefore, *who* is singular.]
>
> These are the students *who are* to be promoted. [The antecedent of *who* is the plural noun *students.*]
>
> Should I, *who am* a stranger, be allowed to enter the contest? [*Who* refers to *I; I* is first person, singular number.]
>
> She is one of those irresponsible persons *who are* always late. [The antecedent of *who* is *persons.*]

If sentences such as the last one give you trouble, try beginning the sentence with the "of" phrase, and you will readily see that the antecedent of *who* is *persons* and not *one*:

> Of those irresponsible *persons who are* always late she is one.

8i   Collective Nouns

Some nouns are singular in form but plural in meaning. They are called **collective nouns** and include such words as *team, class, committee, crowd,* and *crew.* These nouns may take either a singular or a plural verb: if you are thinking of the group as a unit, use a singular verb; if you are thinking of the individual members of the group, use a plural verb:

> The *crew is* striking for higher pay. [The crew is acting as a unit.]
>
> The *crew are* writing reports of the wreck. [The members of the crew are acting as individuals.]

8j   Nouns with Foreign Plurals

Some nouns retain the plural forms peculiar to the languages from which they have been borrowed: *alumni, media, crises.* Still other nouns occur with either their original plural forms or plural forms typical of English: *aquaria* or *aquariums, criteria* or *criterions.* If you are in doubt as to the correct or preferred plural form of a noun, consult a good dictionary.

NOTE: Be careful not to use a plural form when you refer to a singular idea. For instance, write *He is an alumnus of Harvard,* not *He is an alumni of Harvard.*

Exercise 36	SUBJECT-VERB AGREEMENT

Write the correct form of the *italicized* verb in the space at the right.

EXAMPLE: In the window of the toy store (*were, was*) a fire engine
and a dozen dolls.   _____*were*_____

1. Over there on the table (*are, is*) a registration form and name tag.   _____

2. The macaroni and cheese that Jack brought (*need, needs*) to go
into the oven.   _____

3. The plaid pants (*are, is*) the very thing to wear with a red shirt.   _____

4. The organ as well as the piano often (*accompany, accompanies*)
the choir on Sunday mornings.   _____

5. Neither of the nurses you met (*are, is*) Griffin's cousin.   _____

6. The ad states that ten thousand Americans (*work, works*) for
Volkswagen.   _____

7. Each of the offices in the new bank building (*overlook, overlooks*)
the courtyard.   _____

8. The pair of boots that I bought at Rimple's (*are, is*) similar to a
pair that you have.   _____

9. The Public Service Commission (*have, has*) not agreed among
themselves concerning the rate hike requested by the power
company.   _____

10. Even though some of the beads (*are, is*) lost, Carol wants to re-
string the ones that she has.   _____

11. The committee (*have, has*) struggled with the question of how to
distribute the food and clothing.   _____

12. My old friend and former roommate (*are, is*) going hunting with
me one day next week.   _____

13. Shortcake topped with strawberries (*are, is*) still my favorite
dessert.   _____

14. According to Irving, ethics (*are, is*) frequently discussed in Dr.
    Jensen's philosophy class.   _____

15. Baltimore is one of those cities which (*have, has*) renewed their
    waterfronts.   _____

16. (*Are, Is*) either of the employment agencies aware that you are
    an experienced accountant?   _____

17. I do believe that every one of the catalogues (*feature, features*) an
    attractive calendar.   _____

18. Alice had to tell the officer that the whereabouts of her driver's
    license (*were, was*) unknown.   _____

19. Did you hear that ten degrees Fahrenheit (*are, is*) to be the high
    tomorrow?   _____

20. Only part of the wheat (*are, is*) being stored in the silos. _____

Exercise 37 | SUBJECT-VERB AGREEMENT

Write the correct form of the *italicized* verb in the space at the right.

EXAMPLE: The Board of Trustees (*are, is*) meeting at noon to consider the
budget.   *is*

1. Everybody living on our street (*were, was*) able to hear the bluegrass band
holding forth in the park last night.   _____

2. Scissors (*seem, seems*) to be an essential possession of men with beards.   _____

3. Neither the reporters nor the governor's aide (*have, has*) suggested that the
bill will be vetoed.   _____

4. Some of the parcels of land along the freeway (*are, is*) selling for exorbitant
prices.   _____

5. Two gallons of gasoline (*are, is*) all that Harry's Chevette uses to go to
Lexington and back.   _____

6. Where (*are, is*) Elvira's necklace and bracelet?   _____

7. Every record and tape in MacTaggart's collection (*were, was*) chosen with
great care.   _____

8. The phenomena associated with a solar eclipse (*were, was*) the subject of
the television program.   _____

9. Fifty-one percent of our stockholders (*are, is*) willing to accept your plan
for the merger.   _____

10. Sometimes the same statistics (*are, is*) used to support opposing points
of view.   _____

11. According to the dictionary, statistics (*are, is*) a branch of mathematics. _____

12. Mathematics (*have, has*) been taught by Dr. Steiner since 1969.   _____

13. The lobby of the hotel with all its sofas and plants and people (*are, is*)
terribly crowded.   _____

14. There (*are, is*) in most small towns somebody who can identify the
skeletons in every closet.   _____

15. Everybody whom Rufus has heard from (*are, is*) willing to help with the party after the basketball game.   _____

16. Either of the houses of the General Assembly (*are, is*) able to initiate consideration of the constitutional amendment.   _____

17. The fruit that this section of the state is noted for (*are, is*) grapes.   _____

18. Neither my friends nor I (*are, am*) interested in a canoe trip this weekend.   _____

19. Some of the money in my savings account (*were, was*) given me by my grandmother.   _____

20. Some of this year's taxes (*were, was*) used to finance the municipal center.   _____

| Exercise 38 | **SUBJECT-VERB AGREEMENT** |

Write the correct form of the *italicized* verb in the space at the right.

EXAMPLE: (*Are, Is*) neither of the sweaters large enough for Max?   _____*Is*_____

1. The magazine filled with recipes and ideas for decorating (*make, makes*) a good gift.   _____

2. Dimming the headlights (*are, is*) the only decent thing to do when one is driving on a freeway at night.   _____

3. Some of the apples that Sheila brought from the mountains (*are, is*) still in the truck.   _____

4. There at the foot of the escalator (*were, was*) the counters piled with Christmas ornaments.   _____

5. Henry VI is credited with the observation that "Riches (*are, is*) ready snares."   _____

6. No one of us (*have, has*) the right to decide upon a name for the literary magazine.   _____

7. I can hardly believe that the whereabouts of Rupert and his St. Bernard (*are, is*) not known.   _____

8. Over half of the daily papers in the state (*are, is*) supporting Kohn for governor.   _____

9. Four ounces of yogurt (*are, is*) in this carton but only three in that one.   _____

10. *One Hundred Favorite Folktales,* a collection made by Stith Thompson, (*were, was*) published in 1968.   _____

11. Either of the sports magazines probably (*contain, contains*) an account of the rhubarb you're talking about.   _____

12. The criteria that the zoological society uses for selecting animals (*have, has*) been announced.   _____

13. When (*are, is*) Jose and the stage crew to complete the sets for *A Delicate Balance?*   _____

14. A group of delegates to the hairdressers' convention (*want, wants*) to make reservations for dinner tonight. _____

15. Stacked on the corner of the secretary's desk (*were, was*) a dictionary, a thesaurus, and the latest issue of *Vogue.* _____

16. Every member of the tennis team (*were, was*) extremely pleased with the new courts. _____

17. Neither Zimmerman nor his law partners (*are, is*) interested in opening another office in Middletown. _____

18. The data that Harriet included in her article (*were, was*) gathered while we were in college. _____

19. At cookouts pork and beans (*are, is*) a favorite of my neighbors. _____

20. Each key on this ring (*fit, fits*) one of the doors in the dormitory. _____

Exercise 39	SUBJECT-VERB AGREEMENT

Write the correct form of the *italicized* verb in the space at the right.

EXAMPLE: Where (*are, is*) the needle and thread I left on the table?   *are*

1. The sheriff along with two of her deputies (*were, was*) checking licenses at the North Road exit.   _____

2. Shortly before noon a fleet of Cadillacs (*were, was*) seen arriving at the embassy.   _____

3. The glad tidings (*are, is*) that I can still get into my red velvet skirt.   _____

4. At the back of each issue of the literary journal (*are, is*) a list of the contributors' names.   _____

5. The golf team (*are, is*) leaving this afternoon for a match at the University of Florida.   _____

6. What (*are, is*) the criteria for the job of diplomatic courier?   _____

7. The director with the help of her staff (*have, has*) planned a series of films on African arts.   _____

8. Today was one of those perfect October days which (*serve, serves*) to measure all other days.   _____

9. (*Are, Is*) the World Series to be played in September or October?   _____

10. Eight times $3.35 (*are, is*) $26.80.   _____

11. The alumnae (*have, has*) been asked to participate in a recruitment workshop this summer.   _____

12. Montgomery said that the ethics of John's decision (*was, were*) questionable.   _____

13. According to my bank statement, $12.55 (*are, is*) all I have left in my checking account.   _____

14. Neither the manager nor the players (*were, was*) available for comment.   _____

15. Maxwell's is one of those hardware stores that (*offer, offers*) everything from thumb tacks to brass andirons.   _____

16. Every rose, snapdragon, and daisy (*have, has*) been placed perfectly in the bride's bouquet.

_____

17. Much to his dismay neither of the microfilm readers (*were, was*) working.

_____

18. Seemingly, none of the shoppers in the mall (*have, has*) become aware of the freezing rain that is coating the streets.

_____

19. The accoustics in the old music hall (*are, is*) as good as any the director remembers.

_____

20. My father and my best friend (*have, has*) promised to go backpacking with me.

_____

| Exercise 40 | SUBJECT-VERB AGREEMENT |

In each of the following sentences fill in the blank with the correct form of the verb **to be** in the present tense. Then write the correct form again in the space at the right.

EXAMPLE: On the top shelf ____*is*____ the box of manila envelopes.   ____*is*____

1. Most of the contemporary paintings in the collection _____ to be hung
   in this gallery.   _____

2. _____ Mr. Franck and his client aware that the courthouse is closed on
   Saturdays?   _____

3. There _____ no two ways about it: Alfred intends to marry Fritzie.   _____

4. Fifty cents _____ all that I have in my change purse.   _____

5. Around the corner and halfway down the block _____ a drug store and a
   delicatessen.   _____

6. Every last one of my brothers and sisters _____ looking forward to the
   World Series.   _____

7. The spaghetti as well as the ravioli _____ particularly good at Luci's.   _____

8. Every morning two quarts of milk _____ delivered to our house.   _____

9. Forgotten by all but the oldest citizens in Louisburg _____ Sam Cooley
   and his hound dog.   _____

10. The media _____ sending representatives to the opening of Ann Levant's
    campaign headquarters.   _____

11. My favorite Sunday night supper _____ a bowl of oyster stew or clam
    chowder.   _____

12. The flock of geese _____ headed south toward the Outer Banks.   _____

13. Measles _____ rampant among the children in our apartment complex.   _____

14. A truck piled high with odds and ends of furniture _____ parked by the
    side of the road.   _____

15. The tactics that the students use to manage Miss Rosewater _____ one
    part deception and nine parts flattery.   _____

16. Neither of the maps of Canada _____ detailed enough to include the town
    of Wabush.   _____

17. Have you noticed that every one of the young women selling cosmetics at
    Wolfe's _____ carefully trained?   _____

18. The crises occurring in the Middle East _____ so frequent that I have
    difficulty keeping up with them.   _____

19. The long and short of your argument _____ that no one should have to go
    hungry.   _____

20. The Dean said that about one-half of our students _____ accustomed to
    riding the subway to classes.   _____

9

Agreement of Pronoun and Antecedent

Pronouns, as we saw in Chapter 1, are words that are used in the place of nouns when repetition of a noun would be awkward. *The dog hurt the dog's foot* is clearly an unnatural expression. Usually a pronoun has a definite, easily recognized *antecedent* (the noun or pronoun to which it refers), with which it agrees in *person, number,* and *gender.* The *case* of a pronoun, however, is not dependent on the case of its antecedent.

9a Certain Singular Antecedents

Use singular pronouns to refer to singular antecedents. *Each, either, neither, anyone, anybody, everyone, everybody, someone, somebody, no one, nobody* are singular, and pronouns referring to them should be singular:

> *Each* of the girls has *her* own car.
>
> *Neither* of the boys remembered *his* poncho.
>
> Does *everyone* have *his* ticket?

NOTE: In the last of the preceding examples *his* is used even though its antecedent may be either male or female. You should be aware of and sensitive to objections to this traditional practice, but you should also recognize that no completely satisfactory solution exists, inasmuch as our language has no singular form that refers to persons of either sex. Because the expressions *he or she, his or her,* and *him or her* are awkward, you are justified in using the masculine pronouns (or possessive adjectives) in a universal sense. It is often possible, however, to avoid the problem by rephrasing the sentence:

> Does *everyone* have *a* ticket?
>
> Do *we* all have *our* tickets?
>
> *Who* doesn't have *a* ticket? etc.

9b Collective Nouns as Antecedents

With *collective nouns* use either a singular or a plural pronoun according to the meaning of the sentence. Since collective nouns may be either singular or plural, their correct usage depends upon (1) a decision as to meaning (See Chapter 8, Section 8i) and (2) consistency:

> The *team* has elected Jan as *its* captain. [The team is acting as a unit and therefore requires the singular pronoun *its*.]

> The *team* quickly took *their* positions on the field. [Here each member of the team is acting individually.]

Exercise 41 | AGREEMENT OF PRONOUN AND ANTECEDENT

From the *italicized* forms in parentheses choose the correct pronoun for each sentence and write it in the space at the right.

EXAMPLE: Our soccer team won the championship in (*their, its*) league.   _____*its*_____

1. Each of the joggers soon set (*their, his*) own pace.   _____

2. On our tour of New England no one was allowed to leave (*their, her*) luggage on the bus overnight.   _____

3. Although Dan participated in athletics only as an observer, he still considered (*them, it*) an important part of his life.   _____

4. The Federal Communications Commission published (*their, its*) study concerning ownership of television cable systems.   _____

5. The international crisis resolved (*themselves, itself*) as quickly as (*they, it*) had arisen.   _____

6. Either Martha or Joan left (*their, her*) briefcase by a chair in the conference room.   _____

7. The data generated by the computer proved (*their, its*) worth when George compiled his annual report.   _____

8. Every collie in the kennel had (*their, its*) registration papers.   _____

9. Every representative attending the Garden Club Council will announce the date of the flower show to (*their, her*) own club.   _____

10. Gymnastics had not been an interest of mine until I watched (*them, it*) on television.   _____

11. That Wilson College faithfully observes (*their, its*) traditions is evident to all of us.   _____

12. As Steve's fascination with politics increased, (*they, it*) consumed more and more of his time.   _____

13. Everybody grabbed up (*their, his*) books and papers when the fire alarm sounded.   _____

14. The news from Central America is often so complex that I have difficulty following (*them, it*).   _____

15. Anybody who has lost (*their, her*) glasses knows something of my present frustration.   _____

16. Economics may be a "dismal science," but (*they, it*) can challenge the best of minds.   _____

17. Do you remember whether General Motors offered (*their, its*) customers rebates on smaller models?   _____

18. Every entrant in the bass tournament must fill out (*their, his*) registration form at the marina.   _____

19. On Tuesday the alumnae had (*their, her*) first opportunity to meet President Simmons.   _____

20. If I ever find my scissors, I want to have (*them, it*) sharpened.   _____

Exercise 42 | AGREEMENT OF PRONOUN AND ANTECEDENT

In the following sentences underline each pronoun or pronominal adjective incorrectly used; then write the correct form and, if necessary, the correct form of the verb in the space at the right. Write **C** if the sentence is correct.

EXAMPLE: Neither of the drivers has <u>their</u> own truck. _____*his/her*_____

1. This article reports that the U.S.S.R. has their own domestic problems. _____ _____

2. Have either of these cats had their rabies shot? _____ _____

3. No one has yet offered to drive their car to the meeting in Wilmington. _____ _____

4. Each of the cabinet makers were widely recognized for their crafts- manship. _____ _____

5. Every summer both of the pools in the community offers its swimmers courses in lifesaving. _____ _____

6. Most of the houses in this block were restored by their owners. _____ _____

7. Every president of the corporation have had their portrait painted. _____ _____

8. Neither Helen nor Anne have offered their opinion concerning this section of the copyright law. _____ _____

9. Although the pear trees have their new leaves, the pecan trees are as bare as they have been all winter. _____ _____

10. If we are to have enough food to go around, everybody must bring a lunch for themselves and their date. _____ _____

11. Mumps are an unpredictable disease: some of the family contracted them and others did not. _____ _____

12. At the beginning of the third quarter Kentucky was deep in their own
territory.

13. Mathematics have their roots in the history of the Middle East.

14. One of those hardware sales representatives left their case of samples at
the reception desk.

15. Has anybody listened to enough of their French tapes to pronounce
cherchez la femme?

16. Because it is not getting enough power, one of the computers is down
this morning.

17. This criteria should be included in the classified ad.

18. Do either of the applicants for the job have their degree in marketing?

19. The barracks located across from the post exchange need their roofs
repaired.

20. The data in this chart has lost its usefulness since the publication of the
latest census figures.

10
Reference of Pronouns

The word to which a pronoun refers should always be clear to the reader; that is, a **pronoun** and the **antecedent** to which it refers must be instantly identified as belonging together. Even when a pronoun agrees properly with its antecedent in person and number, it may still be confusing or misleading if there is more than one possible antecedent. Therefore, it is sometimes necessary to repeat the antecedent or to reword the whole sentence for the sake of clarity.

10a Ambiguous Reference

Sometimes a sentence contains more than one word to which a pronoun may grammatically refer (the term *ambiguous* means "capable of more than one interpretation"). The sentence should be written in such a way that the reader has no doubt which word is the antecedent:

> Albert told his uncle that his money had been stolen. [The first *his* is clear, but the second *his* could refer to either *Albert* or *uncle*.]
>
> Albert told his uncle that Albert's money had been stolen. [The meaning is clear, but the sentence is unnatural and awkward.]

To avoid the ambiguous reference of the first sentence and the awkward repetition of the second, reword the sentence:

> Albert said to his uncle, "My money has been stolen."

Another kind of ambiguous reference (sometimes called *divided* or *remote* reference) occurs when a modifying clause is misplaced in a sentence:

> INCORRECT: The colt was almost hit by a car which jumped over the pasture fence.
>
> CORRECT: The colt which jumped over the pasture fence was almost hit by a car.

NOTE: A relative pronoun should always be placed as near as possible to its antecedent. (See Chapter 15.)

10b   Broad Reference

Usually a pronoun should not refer broadly to the whole idea of the preceding clause:

> She avoided using slang, which greatly improved her speech. [*Which* has no clearly apparent antecedent but refers broadly to the whole idea in the first clause.]

> She talked endlessly about her operation, and this was tiresome.

A method often used to improve such sentences is to supply a definite antecedent or to substitute a noun for the pronoun:

> She avoided using slang, a practice which greatly improved her speech.

> She talked endlessly about her operation, and this chatter was tiresome.

As you can see, these sentences are awkward, adding unnecessary words. A better method is to get rid of the pronoun and make a concise, informative sentence that says everything in one clause:

> By avoiding slang, she greatly improved her speech.

> Her endless talk about her operation was tiresome.

10c   Weak Reference

A pronoun should not refer to a word which is merely implied by the context. Nor, as a common practice, should the pronoun refer to a word used as a modifier:

> INCORRECT: My father is a chemist. *This* is a profession I intend to follow. [The antecedent of *This* should be *chemistry*, which is implied in *chemist* but is not actually stated.]

> CORRECT: My father is a chemist. Chemistry is the profession I intend to follow.

> ALSO CORRECT: My father's profession of chemistry is the one I intend to follow.

> INCORRECT: When she thrust a stick into the rat hole, it ran out and bit her. [*Rat* in this sentence is the modifier of *hole*.]

> CORRECT: When she thrust a stick into the rat hole, a rat ran out and bit her.

10d   Impersonal Use of the Personal Pronoun

Remember that pronouns are frequently used impersonally and when so used do not have antecedents. Notice the correct impersonal use of *it* in statements about *weather, time,* and *distance*:

> *It* looks like rain. [Reference to weather.]

> *It* is now twelve o'clock. [Reference to time.]

> How far is *it* to the nearest town? [Reference to distance.]

Avoid the use of *you* and *your* unless you are directing your statement specifically to the reader. Instead, use an impersonal word like *one* or *person.* Also note that the pronoun *you* can never refer to an antecedent in the third person:

> INCORRECT: If *you* want to excel in athletics, *you* should watch your diet. [Incorrect when referring to athletes in general.]

CORRECT: If *one* wants to excel in athletics, *he* should watch his diet.

INCORRECT: When a woman marries, *you* take on new responsibilities. [Here *you* refers incorrectly to *woman*, an antecedent in the third person.]

CORRECT: When a woman marries, *she* takes on new responsibilities.

INCORRECT: All those planning to attend the meeting should get *your* registration fees in on time. [Here *your* incorrectly refers to the third person plural antecedent *those*.]

CORRECT: All those planning to attend the meeting should get *their* registration fees in on time.

A rewording of the sentence often produces a clearer and more emphatic sentence while eliminating the problem of the correct pronoun to use:

CORRECT: Those who wish to excel in athletics should watch their diets.

CORRECT: To marry is to take on new responsibilities.

CORRECT: Registration fees must be in on time for those who plan to attend the meeting.

| Exercise 43 | REFERENCE OF PRONOUNS |

Write **R** after each sentence that contains an error in the reference of a pronoun. Then rewrite the sentence correctly. Write **C** if the sentence is correct.

EXAMPLE: The snow had covered the streets and sidewalks, which meant I would
have to wear my boots.   *R*

*Because the snow had covered the streets and sidewalks, I would have
to wear boots.*

1. The clock on the bank struck twelve, which meant I was late for my appointment
   with Theresa.   _____

2. The leaves are piled in great heaps along the curb; this makes parking difficult.   _____

3. If you major in teacher education, Carlos, one will spend some time as an
   apprentice in a classroom.   _____

4. The benches are made of redwood and wrought iron, which have been placed
   along the paths in the park.   _____

5. Sue told Louisa that she would enjoy majoring in interior design.   _____

6. Although several members of his family are musicians, Stedman has not the
   slightest interest in it.   _____

7. It was May before I finally decided to spend the summer working at Wolfe's.   _____

8. Every year the squirrels raid our pecan trees and succeed in stealing half of them.   _____

9. The books which I have decided to take with me to the beach include a collection of Caroline Gordon's short stories.   _____

10. Jacob's description of Alpine skiing has made me want to visit them next winter.   _____

11. The announcers discussed the pitcher's record in great detail, which caused my father to miss Mulligan's home run.   _____

12. The street was paved with cobblestones, which wound through the oldest section of the city.   _____

Exercise 44	REFERENCE OF PRONOUNS

Write **R** after each sentence that contains an error in the reference of a pronoun. Then rewrite the sentence correctly. Write **C** if the sentence is correct.

EXAMPLE: The antique dealer makes trips to Europe twice a year to buy them for
his shop.   *R*

*The dealer makes trips to Europe twice a year to buy antiques for
his shop.*

1. Meredith has always wanted to be a veterinarian, so I am not surprised that she is
preparing to study it.   _____

2. Mrs. Popper often forgets the key to her apartment, which tries the patience of
the manager.   _____

3. After one has camped out in freezing weather, you really appreciate a warm bed.   _____

4. How far is it to Babylon?   _____

5. I am afraid that Margie's recipe for lemon pie does not call for a real one.   _____

6. Carlos's interest in horseback riding stems from the fact that his grandparents
raise them.   _____

7. Philip was an excellent sky diver; he learned it while he was a paratrooper. _____

8. The economist forecast a rise in production; this was certainly encouraging to all of us looking for jobs. _____

9. If one knows what Mrs. Askew thinks, then you know what Mr. Askew thinks. _____

10. The carpets were loaded into the van, which Mr. Halifax had bought many years ago in Iran. _____

11. At Thanksgiving the kitchen, where Aunt Julia presides over the measuring and mixing, becomes the center of our house. _____

12. The brick wall had been handsome in its day, but now many of them were crumbling into dust. _____

| Exercise 45 | REFERENCE OF PRONOUNS |

Write **R** after each sentence that contains an error in the reference of a pronoun. Then rewrite the sentence correctly. Write **C** if the sentence is correct.

EXAMPLE: Reading a Canadian history should serve as a good introduction to it.   _R_

> *Reading a Canadian history should serve as a good introduction to the country.*

1. The broker advised her not to buy stock in the gold mine, which she ignored.   _____

2. If a person is interested in playing racquet ball, you should join the Knox Street Y.M.C.A.   _____

3. The newly elected mayor, who will take office in January, has begun making plans for his administration.   _____

4. She wore her hair piled high on her head, which was softly curled.   _____

5. Pirates still roam the high seas; this is recognized by the U.S. Maritime Association.   _____

6. Dan told his father that he would have to earn more money if he expected to make ends meet.   _____

7. At the height of the thunderstorm the lights went out, which brought our poker game to a quick end.   _____

8. It is entirely too cold to walk all the way to the Silver Screen.   _____

9. The truck is hauling produce from Florida, which is refrigerated.   _____

10. I must put the casserole in the oven, which Mother made this morning.   _____

11. Carl Sagan stated that there are "far more galaxies than people"; this amazes me.   _____

12. Remember to fill the bird feeder; they will have difficulty finding food in this kind of weather.   _____

11

Case of Pronouns

Nouns and pronouns have three case functions: the **nominative**, the **objective**, and the **possessive**. Except in the possessive, nouns do not show case by change of form and consequently do not present any problems of case. The chief difficulties are in the correct use of pronouns.

11a The Nominative Case

The **nominative case** is used (1) as the subject of a verb (*I* shall come); (2) as the complement after *is, are,* and the other forms of the verb *to be* (It is *I*); or (3) as an appositive of the subject or of the complement after forms of the verb *to be* (Two of us—*he* and *I*—called). Ordinarily the case of a pronoun which comes before a verb presents no difficulties, for we naturally write "I am going," not "Me am going." But all constructions requiring the nominative case are not so simple as this one. Study carefully the following more difficult constructions:

1. A clause of comparison introduced by *as* or *than* is often not written out in full. The verb is then understood. The subject of this understood verb is in the nominative case:

> No one can do the work as well as *he* (can).
>
> He knows more about the subject than *she* (does).

2. After forms of the linking verb *to be*, nouns and pronouns used to identify the subject agree in case with the subject. Nouns and pronouns used in this way are called **predicate nominatives** and are in the nominative case:

> It was *they* [not *them*].
>
> The persons referred to were her sister and *she* [not *her*].
>
> He answered, "It could not have been *I* [not *me*]."

3.   Pronouns are frequently combined with a noun or used in apposition with a noun. If they are thus used with the subject of the sentence or with a predicate nominative, they are in the nominative case:

> *We* boys will be responsible for the equipment.
>
> Two photographers—*you* and *he*—must attend the convention.

If you read these sentences omitting the nouns, the correct form of the pronoun will at once be clear.

4.   The position of the relative pronoun *who* often causes confusion, especially if it follows a verb or a preposition. The role of the relative pronoun within the dependent clause determines its case. Thus if *who* is the subject of the verb in the dependent clause, it is in the nominative case:

> You know *who* sent the money. [Since *who* is the subject of the verb *sent* and not the object of *know*, it must be in the nominative case. The whole clause *who sent the money* is the object of *know*.]
>
> Give the praise to *whoever* deserves it. [*Whoever* is the subject of *deserves*. The whole clause *whoever deserves it* is the object of the preposition *to*.]

5.   Parenthetical expressions such as *you think, I believe, I suppose,* and *he says* often stand between a verb and the pronoun which is the subject. The pronoun must still be in the nominative case:

> *Who* do you think called me last night? [The expression *do you think* has nothing to do with the case of *who*. Leave it out, or place it elsewhere in the sentence, and you will see that *who* is the subject of *called*.]
>
> The man *who Jim* says will be our next governor is in the room. [Leave out or place elsewhere *Jim says*, and you will see that *who* is the subject of *will be*.].

11b   The Objective Case

The **objective case** of a pronoun is used when the pronoun is the direct or indirect object of a verb, the object of a preposition, or an appositive of an object:

1.   Compound subjects present a special difficulty:

> He wrote a letter to Mary and *me*. [Both words *Mary* and *me* are objects of the preposition *to* and therefore in the objective case. Omit *Mary and* or shift *me* to the position of *Mary*, and the correct form is at once apparent.]
>
> She gave George and *him* the address. [*Him* is part of the compound indirect object.]
>
> They invited William and *me* to the barbecue. [*Me* is part of the compound direct object.]

2.   You will also have to watch the case of a pronoun combined with a noun in apposition with an object:

> She spoke cordially to *us* boys.
>
> They told three of us girls—Mary, Sue, and *me*—to go.

3. *Whom*, the objective case of *who*, deserves special consideration:

> *Whom* were you talking to? [To *whom* were you talking?]
>
> He is the boy *whom* we met on the plane. [*Whom* is the object of the verb *met*. The subject of *met* is *we*. Remember that the case of the relative pronoun is determined by its role within the dependent clause.]
>
> *Whom* do you think we saw last night? [The parenthetical expression does not change the fact that *whom* is the object of *saw*.]

11c   Case of Pronouns Used with Infinitives

An infinitive phrase, as you have learned already, can have both an object and adverbial modifiers. In addition, an **infinitive** may have a subject. There are rules governing the case of pronouns when they are subjects or complements of infinitives:

1. When a pronoun is the subject of an infinitive, it will be in the objective case:

> We want *him* to be elected.

2. If the infinitive is a form of the verb *to be* and if it has a subject, its complement will also be in the objective case:

> She took him to be *me*.

3. If the infinitive *to be* does not have a subject, its complement will be in the nominative case:

> The best player was thought to be *he*.

11d   The Possessive Case

Personal pronouns and the relative pronoun *who* have **possessive case** forms, which may be used with a noun or a gerund.

1. When the possessive forms *my, our, your, her, his, its,* and *their* modify nouns or gerunds, they are classified as **possessive adjectives**:

> *My* book is on the table. [*My* is a possessive adjective, modifying *book*.]
>
> We appreciate *your* giving to the Community Chest. [Not *you giving*. The object of the verb *appreciate* is the gerund *giving*; therefore, *your* is merely the possessive adjective modifying the gerund.]

2. Personal and relative pronouns form their possessives without the apostrophe:

> The boy *whose* car is in the driveway works here.
>
> The dog chewed *its* bone.

NOTE: Notice the difference between *its*, the possessive form, and *it's*, the contraction of *it is*:

> *It's* time for your car to have *its* oil changed.

Exercise 46	CASE OF PRONOUNS

In the following sentences underline each pronoun that is used incorrectly, and then write the correct form in the space at the right. Write **C** if the sentence is correct.

EXAMPLE: Did anyone tell Mary or he about the change of time?   _him_

1. Me and Hilda have already made plans to buy season tickets. _____

2. You wearing those satin sandals to a street dance is out of the question. _____

3. When Sandy gets to the travel agency, who should he ask for? _____

4. Because there were no more seats in the waiting room, the large woman squeezed between Henry and I. _____

5. Address the card to either of us, George or I. _____

6. Whom do you think will be Mr. Morganstern's choice for drum major? _____

7. Elmer considers her to be the most devastating girl he has ever seen. _____

8. The boy who was sitting across from you and I on the train is Tom's cousin. _____

9. No one can type the report as quickly as him. _____

10. Of we four, Henrietta is the best bridge player. _____

11. We golfers need to get an early start if we are going to play eighteen holes before lunch. _____

12. The fire must have started near midnight, because the sirens woke he and his dog soon after that time. _____

13. The grocer sold she and Jules the last gallon of cider he had. _____

14. Louisa and him often ride their bicycles out to Gaines Point for a picnic supper. _____

15. One of them Oriental rugs is just what you need for your dining room. _____

16. Marvin is concerned about you having to walk all the way to Fourth Street by yourself.   _____

17. Sophie often invites we two for supper on Sunday nights.   _____

18. Who did you see when you stopped by Rose's apartment?   _____

19. Although Marcia is tall, she is not as tall as him.   _____

20. We haven't the slightest notion who will be asked to head the Student Activities Committee.   _____

21. Three of us—Harold, John and me—plan to do some backpacking during the holidays.   _____

22. I heard that Watkins and her plan to be married in April.   _____

23. Your father seemed surprised to see he and Myrtle having lunch at Knickers.   _____

24. Who did you say was reading a novel by Anne Tyler?   _____

25. The editor thinks that it was her who phoned in the story about Harry's rescuing the child.   _____

| Exercise 47 | **CASE OF PRONOUNS** |

In the following sentences underline each pronoun that is used incorrectly, and then write the correct form in the space at the right. Write **C** if the sentence is correct.

EXAMPLE: Who is the telephone for?   *Whom*

1. I am certain that the woman wearing the red velvet jacket is her.   _____

2. This building belongs to Angus McDougal and he.   _____

3. Give the invoices to whomever is in charge of billing.   _____

4. The television series lost much of it's audience when the villain was dropped from the cast.   _____

5. Send for either Lilly or I if you have trouble moving the chest of drawers.   _____

6. The hospital corridor was poorly lighted, but I took the paramedic to be he.   _____

7. Between you and I Morris spends most of his afternoon in Blaze's Game Room.   _____

8. Does the World War I song begin with the line "Its a long way to Tipperary"?   _____

9. Us three can certainly assume the responsibility for setting up the tables for the meeting.   _____

10. Uncle Joseph has asked Jim and I to work at the bakery during the holidays.   _____

11. Could it have been her who brought us the fresh vegetables?   _____

12. No one enjoys a weekend in San Francisco more than them.   _____

13. Mr. Dronesberry has divided the chore of addressing the letters among we four.   _____

14. Us considering a trip to Labrador in the dead of winter seemed absurd.   _____

15. The debate between Andy and him became more and more heated as the
    evening wore on.   _____

16. The author of the ghost story is thought to be him.   _____

17. My brother Horace is smaller than me.   _____

18. Otherwise, he looks rather like me.   _____

19. Not many boys I know tinker with a car as endlessly as her.   _____

20. Everyone except she and Philip has been skiing at Sky Valley many times.   _____

Exercise 48 | CASE OF PRONOUNS

In the space at the right, write the correct form of the pronoun *who (whoever)*.

EXAMPLE: The manufacturer (*who, whom*) makes these tools has an office
    in Chicago.   *who*

1. I want you to meet my favorite uncle, (*who, whom*) everyone calls Charlie.   _____

2. One never knows (*who, whom*) will arrive at Alan's house for supper.   _____

3. Have the media been told (*who, whom*) will serve as grand marshal for
the Fourth of July parade?   _____

4. To (*who, whom*) do you wish to speak?   _____

5. (*Whoever, whomever*) takes the mail to the Post Office can also buy some
stamps.   _____

6. If I should decide to buy a hunting license, (*who, whom*) should I see?   _____

7. Angela has not found anyone (*who, whom*) is able to go with her on a dig
this summer.   _____

8. (*Who, Whom*) are these files intended for?   _____

9. Oliver cannot remember (*whose, who's*) turn it is to bring refreshments.   _____

10. (*Who, Whom*) did you say was negotiator for the United States?   _____

11. (*Whose, Who's*) interested in spending the day with Alex and me at the
Smithsonian?   _____

12. Ask (*whoever, whomever*) answers the telephone whether the concert
begins at eight or eight-thirty.   _____

13. Stuart Roth is the man (*who, whom*) I think serves as director of public
relations.   _____

14. (*Whose, Who's*) camera is that on my beach towel?   _____

15. Grandmother wants to know (*who, whom*) will volunteer to slice the
turkey.   _____

16. (*Whoever, Whomever*) recruited that tailback certainly did a good day's work.   _____

17. The old woman (*who, whom*) you saw at the bus stop lives in the apartment next to mine.   _____

18. Do you know (*who, whom*) can identify the people in this old photograph?   _____

19. We invited (*whoever, whomever*) seemed interested to the film being shown at the Goethe Institute.   _____

20. Raphael is a man (*who, whom*) you can depend upon.   _____

| Exercise 49 | REVIEW OF AGREEMENT AND CASE |

Underline each word that is incorrectly used. Then write the correct word in the space at the right. Write **C** if the sentence is correct.

EXAMPLE: The owner of the plane is either <u>her</u> or her brother.   *she*

1. Neither of us were ever able to decide whether the movie had been worth the price of the ticket.   _____

2. A singer and songwriter is to discuss the history of jazz in my music appreciation class.   _____

3. On the platform constructed for the occasion was seated the mayor, three of the commissioners, and Senator Bragg.   _____

4. Carolyn, Sarah, and me have bought the groceries that we will need to take with us to the lodge.   _____

5. The phenomenon of miniskirts is reappearing on the pages of the fashion magazines.   _____

6. Never count on him keeping a secret.   _____

7. Surely the media will send its most experienced people to the airport to interview the Secretary of State.   _____

8. The person whom I think addressed the convention on Thursday is the president of one of the unions.   _____

9. The chief along with a dozen firemen were on the scene minutes after the alarm had been turned in.   _____

10. No one else that I know can manage time as well as her.   _____

11. The company representative demonstrated the word processor for Kenneth and I.   _____

12. I agree with the idea of you job hunting during the spring break.   _____

13. Either radio or television are sure to carry the championship game.   _____

14. Buried in the last section of Thursday's paper was one story about the origin of yogurt and another about its present popularity.   _____

15. The golfer with the day's highest score was announced to be her.   _____

16. Frampton wants we three to drop by his house before we go to Margaret's.   _____

17. The article which states that law firms are discovering that computers can aid them in their research is in a recent law journal.   _____

18. Everybody has their own way of packing their luggage for a trip.   _____

19. Are either of these models the girl on the cover of this month's *Mademoiselle?*   _____

20. I believe that it was him who gave us directions to the Omni.   _____

21. Cooking a turkey with all the trimmings require more time than I have.   _____

22. The old man who I brought to the rally was interested in conservation before you and I were born.   _____

23. Maria's is one of those restaurants that serves authentic Mexican food.   _____

24. The sum and substance of the matter are that Delaney can outrun everyone else on the team.   _____

25. Khaki, our cocker spaniel, has three new puppies that look exactly like her.   _____

26. The differences between you and he are not as great as you might think.   _____

27. Neither my father nor I are skillful enough to install the kitchen cabinets.   _____

28. Me preparing a dinner for twenty-five people on such short notice is out of the question.   _____

29. About seven or eight dollars is the cost of a ticket to hear the symphony.   _____

30. Most of the vegetation along the river bank are broadleaved evergreens.   _____

31. Official data concerning the population of that small country is difficult
    to secure.   _____

32. Phil along with a partner named Henry Morse sell high fidelity equipment
    in a shop at the north end of the mall.   _____

33. Do either of the electricians know what is wrong with the computer in the
    registrar's office?   _____

34. Every one of the campaign workers in your group has already turned in
    their report.   _____

35. Neither Antonio nor his brothers was at Westside High School when I was.   _____

12

Adjectives and Adverbs

Adjectives and adverbs, as you saw in Chapter One, are words which modify, describe, or add to the meaning of other words in a sentence. It is important to remember the special and differing functions of these two kinds of modifier; *adjectives* modify only nouns and other substantives; *adverbs* modify verbs, adjectives, adverbs, and certain phrases and clauses.

12a Adjective and Adverb Forms

An adverb is frequently formed by adding *-ly* to the adjective form of a word: for example, the adjectives *rapid, sure,* and *considerate* are converted into the adverbs *rapidly, surely,* and *considerately* by this method. But there are numerous exceptions to this general rule. Many common adverbs, like *well, then,* and *quite,* do not end in *-ly*; moreover, there are many *adjectives* that do end in *-ly*, like *manly, stately, lonely,* or *unsightly.*

Sometimes the same form is used for both adjective and adverbial forms: *fast, long,* and *much,* for example. (There are no such words as *fastly, longly,* or *muchly*.) Certain adverbs have two forms, one being the same as the adjective and the other ending in *-ly: slow, slowly; quick, quickly; loud, loudly;* etc. The first form is often employed in short commands, as in the sentences *Drive slow* and *Speak loud.*

12b Predicate Adjectives

In any sentence which follows a "subject-verb-modifier" pattern, you must be especially careful to determine whether the modifier is describing the subject or the verb:

John talks *intelligently.*

John is *intelligent.*

In the first sentence the modifier clearly describes how John talks — that is, it modifies the verb *talks*; consequently, the adverb *intelligently* is needed. But in the second sentence the modifier describes the subject *John*; therefore, an adjective is used. In this construction the adjective following the linking verb *is* is called the **predicate adjective.**

The term **linking verb**, as you learned from Chapter One, refers to certain intransitive verbs which make a statement not by expressing action but by expressing a condition or state of being. These verbs "link" the subject of the sentence with some other substantive that re-names or identifies it or with an adjective that describes it. Any adjective that appears after a subject-linking verb construction is called the **predicate adjective.** The verbs most commonly used as linking verbs are the following:

appear	become	remain	stay
be	grow	seem	feel (as an emotion)

Along with these are the five "sense" verbs, which are usually linking verbs:

look	feel	smell	taste	sound

The following sentences illustrate the use of predicate adjectives:

The little dog was *glad* to be out of his pen. [*Glad*, a predicate adjective, follows the linking verb *was* and describes *dog*.]

Father appeared *eager* to drive his new car.

Laurie became *angry* at being put to bed.

Jackie seems *happy* in her new job.

Please remain *quiet*, and I will give you your seat assignments. [*Quiet*, the predicate adjective, describes the subject, *you*, understood.]

The day grew *dark* as the clouds gathered.

Peggy looks *sporty* in her new tennis outfit.

I feel *confident* that Ty will win his case.

That cinnamon bread smells *delicious.*

The rain sounds *dismal* beating on the roof.

Almond toffee ice cream tastes *marvelous.*

This warm robe feels *comfortable.*

A practical test to follow in determining whether to use an adjective or an adverb is to try to substitute some form of the verb *to be* for the verb in the sentence. If the substitution does not substantially change the meaning of the sentence, then the verb should be followed by an adjective. For instance, *She is smart in her new uniform* has essentially the same meaning as *She looks smart in her new uniform*; therefore, the adjective *smart* is the correct modifier.

Occasionally, one of the "sense" verbs is followed by an adverb because the verb is being used not as a *linking* verb but as an *action* verb: *He looked nervously for his keys. Nervously* describes the act of looking, so the adverb is used to express how the looking was done. The substitution test would show immediately that an adjective would be incorrect in the sentence.

12c Misuse of Adjectives

Using an adjective to modify a verb is a common error but a serious one. The sentence *The doctor spoke to the sick child very kind* illustrates this error. *Kind* is an adjective and cannot be used to modify the verb *spoke*; the adverb *kindly* must be used.

Four adjectives which are frequently misused as adverbs are *real, good, sure,* and *some.* When the adverbial form of these words is needed, the correct forms are *really, well, surely,* and *somewhat:*

> The mountain laurel is *really* (or *very,* not *real*) colorful.
> You did *well* (not *good*) to stop smoking so quickly.
> I *surely* (not *sure*) hope to see him before he leaves.
> I feel *somewhat* (not *some*) better today.

NOTE: Remember that *well* can also be an adjective, referring to a state of health, as in *I feel well now, after my long illness.*

12d Comparison of Adjectives and Adverbs

When you wish to indicate to what extent one noun has a certain quality in comparison with that of another noun, you change the form of the modifying adjective that describes the quality: My dog is *bigger* than your dog. My dog is the *biggest* dog in town.

Descriptive adverbs, like adjectives, may be compared in the same way:

> We awaited the holidays *more eagerly* than our parents did.
>
> The shrimp and the oysters were the foods *most rapidly* eaten at the party.

Adjectives and adverbs show or imply comparison by the use of three forms, called **degrees**: the **positive, comparative,** and **superlative degrees.**

POSITIVE DEGREE

The **positive degree** of an adjective or adverb is its regular form:

> He is a *fine* man.
> John took notes *carefully.*

COMPARATIVE DEGREE

The **comparative degree** of an adjective or adverb compares two things, persons, or actions:

> He is a *finer* man than his brother.
> John took notes *more carefully* than Bob did.

SUPERLATIVE DEGREE

The **superlative degree** compares three or more persons, things, or actions:

> He is the *finest* man I know.
> John took notes *most carefully* of all the boys in his class.

The comparative degree is regularly formed by adding *-er* to the positive form of an adjective or adverb or by using *more* or *less* before the positive form. The superlative degree is formed either by adding *-est* to the positive or by using *most* or *least* before the positive. The number of syllables in the word determines which of these forms must be used:

	Positive	Comparative	Superlative
Adj.	strong	stronger	strongest
	pretty	prettier	prettiest
	difficult	more difficult	most difficult
Adv.	quietly	more quietly	most quietly
	easily	more easily	most easily
	fast	faster	fastest

The comparison of some words is irregular, as of *good* (*good, better, best*) and *bad* (*bad, worse, worst*).

Be careful not to use the superlative form when only two persons, groups, objects, or ideas are involved:

Tom is the *healthier* (not *healthiest*) of the two brothers.

Certain adjectives and adverbs such as *perfect, unique, round, square, dead,* and *exact* cannot logically be used in the comparative or superlative degrees, and most should not be modified by words like *quite* or *very*. These words in their simplest forms represent the superlative, incapable of being added to or detracted from:

ILLOGICAL: Samuel is the *most unique* person I know.

LOGICAL: Samuel is a unique person.

ALSO LOGICAL: Samuel is an *almost unique* person.

ILLOGICAL: Beth's engagement diamond is the *most perfect* stone I've seen in years.

LOGICAL: Beth's engagement diamond is a *perfect* stone.

ALSO LOGICAL: Beth's engagement diamond is the *most nearly perfect* stone I've seen in years.

| Exercise 50 | ADJECTIVES AND ADVERBS |

Underline the word or words modified by the *italicized* adjective or adverb. Then in the space right, write **Adj** if the italicized word is an adjective, **Adv** if it is an adverb.

EXAMPLE: My wheels <u>spun</u> *uselessly* on the ice.   *Adv*

1. *Gradually* we gathered around Harry's television set to watch the last of the Rose Bowl game.   _____

2. Martin can *surely* create a marvelous stew.   _____

3. I do not believe that *six* people will fit into your Honda.   _____

4. She has used her microwave oven *more* frequently than she imagined she would.   _____

5. The society is extremely *happy* about the efforts to restore the buildings in this block.   _____

6. The spice cake tastes *heavenly*.   _____

7. I wonder why Grace has *not* called to tell me about her weekend.   _____

8. *Not* a copy of O'Hara's latest novel is left at the bookstore.   _____

9. The sky is *somewhat* clearer today.   _____

10. Rudolph has *some* hope of graduating this summer, according to his roommate.   _____

11. We walked *farther* up Fifth Avenue than we had intended.   _____

12. Matthew looks even *younger* than when I saw him last.   _____

13. We looked *carefully* for the diamond pin both in the grass and along the walkway.   _____

14. The audience grew *quiet* when the slight young woman stepped onto the stage.   _____

15. The covered bridge is *too* narrow for more than one car to cross at a time.   _____

16. Rosa's charm is *unique*.   _____

17. The boots I bought in Montana remain *supple* and soft. _____

18. As the rain came *down* in torrents, I struggled to open my umbrella. _____

19. Quinton paced up and down the concourse, wondering when *Melba's* flight would arrive. _____

20. While the creole sauce simmered *slowly,* we began peeling the shrimp. _____

21. The parking area at the mall seems *unusually* crowded for a Monday. _____

22. The speaker's voice became *strong* as he gained confidence. _____

23. When Winston begins an argument, he is always *sure* of his facts. _____

24. The conductor feels *good* about the band's performance at the festival. _____

25. Although the student had not felt *well* all week, his health improved rapidly as Friday approached. _____

26. Mortimer plays *well,* no matter what the game. _____

27. This knife is *too* dull to slice the ham. _____

28. Dad is *really* pleased that I am looking for a job. _____

29. Is that a *real* kilt, or something you created yourself? _____

30. *Never* have I seen a desk as cluttered as this one! _____

| Exercise 51 | ADJECTIVES AND ADVERBS |

Underline any adjective or adverb that is incorrectly used. Then write the correct form in the space at the right. Write **C** if the sentence is correct.

EXAMPLE: I <u>sure</u> wish we could find tickets to the concert. _____*surely*_____

1. Which of those two video games is best? _____

2. The wind blew so brisk that he wore his raccoon coat and carried a blanket as well. _____

3. The stock market dropped sharp, just at the end of the day. _____

4. Can you think of anything that tastes more deliciously than the morning's first cup of coffee? _____

5. The rose that won first prize is a most perfect specimen. _____

6. Despite the snowstorm the huge jet landed smooth and taxied slowly toward Gate 7. _____

7. To tell the truth, Hannah, your story sounds suspiciously. _____

8. The hikers climbed steady all morning, hoping to reach the campsite by noon. _____

9. Call Max for a real good price on a new battery. _____

10. Flo looked especially pretty in the grey silk dress. _____

11. I woke to the sound of the family cat, purring soft by my side. _____

12. The car stopped sudden when the outline of the stalled van loomed in the fog. _____

13. Lawrence says that his interview with the director went good. _____

14. A pound of ground beef is some cheaper here than at Hamby's. _____

15. Neal has won so many trophies that he has a special built case for them.   _____

16. I sure was hot by the time I had finished mowing the front lawn.   _____

17. Duke seemed sure that he would be able to take his opponent in the first round.   _____

18. Jo's heart beat rapid when she heard the key turn in the lock.   _____

19. Your help in finding information about John Heisman was muchly appreciated.   _____

20. I feel badly about forgetting to let you know that the committee is not meeting this afternoon.   _____

21. Jane works steadier than anyone else in our office.   _____

22. Reporters frequently reminded us that Luci was the youngest of the two Johnson girls.   _____

23. We meet regular at the Varsity to have lunch and watch the noon news.   _____

24. Mary Bell appeared eager to hear the least bit of news that I brought from home.   _____

25. I need to watch expenses closer if I expect to balance my budget.   _____

26. Di finds that she cannot write letters as easy as she can type them.   _____

27. The surf broke rough against the sea wall.   _____

28. Mr. Moseley, yours is a most unique hairpiece.   _____

29. The incident ended happy once Claudine discovered the keys in the depths of her purse.   _____

30. Weatherby strolled casually down the street, as if he had the whole day to himself.   _____

| Exercise 52 | ADJECTIVES AND ADVERBS |

Select the correct form of the words in parentheses, and write it in the space at the right.

EXAMPLE: Her fruitcake is (*some, somewhat*) better than mine.   _____*somewhat*_____

1. The two women chatted (*pleasant, pleasantly*) as they waited for the downtown bus.   _____

2. As Al hurried toward the gate, the scream of the factory whistle sounded (*shrill, shrilly*) in the morning stillness.   _____

3. My Uncle Alonzo speaks (*grand, grandly*) about his plans.   _____

4. Which of these three magazines do you like (*better, best*)?   _____

5. The Dallas Cowboys appear (*wary, warily*) of the Bears.   _____

6. The snow fell (*steady, steadily*) all day, finally covering the entire yard.   _____

7. I stared (*absent, absently*) out the window of the train.   _____

8. The boy darted (*quick, quickly*) across the street, trying to retrieve his papers.   _____

9. John and his brother from Denver debated (*vigorous, vigorously*) the subject of price supports.   _____

10. Capt. Cook remains (*vigorous, vigorously*) despite his seventy years.   _____

11. The wide brown river inched (*lazy, lazily*) toward the sea.   _____

12. Is your sister or your cousin the (*older, oldest*)?   _____

13. Early in December we were urged to mail our packages (*prompt, promptly*).   _____

14. Julia may have appeared (*calm, calmly*), but she had a bad case of stage fright.   _____

15. Hortense, this cough medicine doesn't taste (*bad, badly*).   _____

16. Molly smiled (*sweet, sweetly*) at Harold as she explained why she could not keep their date.   _____

17. My brother (*cautious, cautiously*) introduced the subject of buying a motorcycle.   _____

18. Grandfather says that this is the (*worse, worst*) winter he has seen since he was a boy in South Dakota.   _____

19. The figures on the gauge spun (*rapid, rapidly*) as I filled my tank with gasoline.   _____

20. The Dow Jones average gained (*significant, significantly*) after the President announced his new economic policy.   _____

21. Now when you slice the pie, Barbara, be sure to divide it (*fair, fairly*).   _____

22. Dolly felt (*ambitious, ambitiously*) once she had that first cup of coffee.   _____

23. The small boys steered their bicycles (*careful, carefully*) through the late afternoon traffic.   _____

24. Dudley called home (*frequent, frequently*) no matter how busy he was.   _____

25. The manager feels (*good, well*) about the April sales report.   _____

26. Although Marvin installed the storm windows (*easy, easily*), the job was difficult for me.   _____

27. Taking the windows down did not seem (*easy, easily*) either.   _____

28. The young salesman spoke (*enthusiastic, enthusiastically*) about the vacuum cleaner he was demonstrating.   _____

29. The former riverbed could be seen (*plain, plainly*) from the Piper Cub.   _____

30. Of the two newspapers this one has the (*more, most*) interesting feature articles.   _____

31. Clarence is one of those persons who laugh (*lusty, lustily*) at their own jokes.   _____

32. Mamie (*sure, surely*) seems interested in her job at the radio station.   _____

33. Mother had a virus and felt (*bad, badly*) all weekend.   _____

13

Tense, Voice, Mood

In Chapter 1 we found that a single verb may be classified according to **tense, voice,** and **mood**; therefore, it is not surprising that choosing the appropriate verb form occasionally presents difficulty.

13a Principal Parts of Verbs

We know that there are three **principal parts** of a verb. These are (1) **the first person singular, present indicative**; (2) **the first person singular, past indicative**; (3) **the past participle**. The first two of these provide the basic forms of the present, past, and future tenses; the third is used as the basis for the three perfect tenses:

PRINCIPAL PARTS:
begin, began, begun

Present:	I begin	
Past:	I began	
Future:	I shall (will) begin ———	(This form based on present tense *begin*)
Present Perfect:	I have begun	(These forms based on past participle *begun*)
Past Perfect:	I had begun	
Future Perfect:	I shall (will) have begun	

If you know the principal parts of a verb and the way to form the various tenses from them, you should never make a mistake such as the one contained in the following sentence: "The play had already began when I arrived." If the speaker had known that the principal parts of *begin* are *begin, began, begun* and that the past perfect tense is formed by using *had* with the past participle, he would have known that the correct form is *had begun*.

Regular verbs—that is, those verbs which form their past tense and past participle by adding *-d* or *-ed* to the present tense—rarely cause difficulty. It is the **irregular verbs** that are most frequently used incorrectly. When necessary, consult a dictionary for their principal parts. The following list contains the principal parts of certain especially troublesome verbs. Learn these forms:

Present	*Past*	*Past Participle*	*Present*	*Past*	*Past Participle*
ask	asked	asked	know	knew	known
bite	bit	bitten	lead	led	led
blow	blew	blown	ride	rode	ridden
break	broke	broken	ring	rang (rung)	rung
burst	burst	burst	run	ran	run
choose	chose	chosen	see	saw	seen
come	came	come	shake	shook	shaken
dive	dived (dove)	dived	sing	sang (sung)	sung
do	did	done	speak	spoke	spoken
drag	dragged	dragged	steal	stole	stolen
draw	drew	drawn	sting	stung	stung
drink	drank	drunk	suppose	supposed	supposed
drown	drowned	drowned	swim	swam	swum
eat	ate	eaten	swing	swung	swung
fall	fell	fallen	take	took	taken
fly	flew	flown	tear	tore	torn
freeze	froze	frozen	throw	threw	thrown
give	gave	given	use	used	used
go	went	gone	wear	wore	worn
grow	grew	grown	write	wrote	written

Note that the past tense and the past participle of the verbs *ask, suppose* and *use* are regularly formed by the addition of *-ed* (or *-d*) to the present tense. Possibly because the *d* is not always clearly sounded in the pronunciation of the past tense and the past participle of these verbs, people frequently make the mistake of writing the present-tense form when one of the other forms is required:

> I have *asked* (not *ask*) him to go with me.
>
> I was *supposed* (not *suppose*) to do that job.
>
> He *used* (not *use*) to be my best friend.

13b Two Troublesome Pairs of Verbs

Lie and *lay* and *sit* and *set* are frequent stumbling blocks to correct writing. These verbs need not be confusing, however, if the following points are remembered:

1. Each verb has a distinguishing meaning. *Lay* and *set*, for instance, are clearly distinguished from *lie* and *sit* by their meanings: both *lay* and *set* usually mean *place* and are correctly used when the verb *place* can be substituted for them.

2. *Lay* and *set* are always transitive verbs; that is, they require an object to complete their meaning when they are used in the active voice. *Lie* and *sit* are intransitive verbs and hence do not take an object.

3. Although *lay* and *lie* share the form *lay*, they use it in different tenses. The remaining principal parts are clearly distinguishable.

These three points may be graphically shown:

PRINCIPAL PARTS	
Intransitive (takes no object)	*Transitive (takes an object)*
lie lay lain, *recline, remain in position*	lay laid laid, *place*
sit sat sat, *be in a sitting position*	set set set, *place*

Let us look at a few sentences which illustrate these distinguishing characteristics. Should we say *I set the box on the table* or *I sat the box on the table*? To answer the question, we should try substituting *placed* for *set* and should also see whether there is a direct object following the verb. We can say *I placed the box on the table*; also, *box* is clearly the direct object of the verb. Therefore, the first sentence, employing *set*, is the correct one. But in the sentence *I left the box sitting on the table*, the correct form is *sitting*, not *setting*, since *placing* cannot be substituted for *sitting* and since there is no direct object after *sitting*:

I *laid* (that is, *placed*) the book by the bed and *lay* (past tense of *lie*) down to rest.

Do not fall into the error of thinking that only animate things can stand as subjects of intransitive verbs. Note the following sentences in which inanimate objects are used as subjects of the intransitive verbs:

The book *lies* on the table.

The house *sits* near the road.

13c Tense Sequence

Tense sequence demands that a logical time relationship be shown by the verbs in a sentence. Through force of habit we generally indicate accurate time relationships. A few cautions, however, should be stressed:

1. Use the present tense in the statement of a timeless universal truth or a customary happening:

   I wonder who first discovered that the sun *rises* (not *rose*) in the east. [The fact that the sun rises in the east is a universal truth.]

   Joe said that the class *begins* (not *began*) at 10:30. [The clause *that the class begins at 10:30* states a customary happening.]

2. Use the present tense of an infinitive or the present participle if the action it expresses occurs at the same time as that of the governing verb:

Yesterday I really wanted *to go.* [Not *to have gone.* The governing verb *wanted* indicates a past time. At that past time I wanted to do something *then* — that is, yesterday — not at a time prior to yesterday.]

Skipping along, she hummed a merry tune. The skipping and the humming occur at the same time.)

3. When necessary for clarity, indicate time differences by using different tenses:

INCORRECT: I told him that I *finished* the work just an hour before.

CORRECT: I told him that I *had finished* the work just an hour before. [The verb *told* indicates a past time. Since the work was finished before the time indicated by *told*, the past perfect tense *had finished* must be used.]

INCORRECT: *Making* my reservations, I am packing to go to Cape Cod.

CORRECT: *Having made* my reservations, I am packing to go to Cape Cod. [The perfect participle *having made* must be used to denote an action before the time indicated by the governing verb *am packing.*]

13d   Voice

Transitive verbs always indicate whether the subject is acting or is being acted upon. When the subject is doing the acting, the verb is said to be in the **active voice**:

I *laid* the book on the table. [*Laid* is in the active voice because the subject *I* is doing the acting.]

When the subject is being acted upon or receiving the action, the verb is in the **passive voice**:

The book *was laid* on the table. [*Was laid* is in the passive voice because the subject *book* is being acted upon.]

NOTE: The passive voice verb always consists of some form of the verb *to be* plus a past participle: *is seen, was laid, have been taken.*

In general, the active voice is more emphatic than the passive and therefore should normally be used in preference to the passive voice:

WEAK: The automobile *was driven* into the garage.

MORE EMPHATIC: She *drove* the automobile into the garage.

When, however, the receiver of the action should be stressed rather than the doer, or when the doer is unknown, the passive voice is appropriate:

Class officers *will be elected* next Thursday. [The receiver of the action should be stressed.]

The dog *was found* last night. [The doer is unknown.]

Generally speaking, one should not shift from one voice to the other in the same sentence:

AWKWARD: John *is* the best athlete on the team, and the most points *are scored* by him.

BETTER: John *is* the best athlete on the team and also *scores* the most points.

AWKWARD: After Dr. Lovett *was conferred* with, I *understood* the assignment.

BETTER: After I *conferred* with Dr. Lovett (OR After *conferring* with Dr. Lovett), I *understood* the assignment.

13e   The Subjunctive Mood

The **subjunctive mood** is most frequently used today to express a wish or to state a condition contrary to fact. In both types of statement the subjunctive *were* is used instead of the indicative *was*. Tenses in the subjunctive do not have the same meaning as they do in the indicative mood. For example, the past subjunctive form points toward the present or future, as seen in the sentence *If I WERE you, I would give his suggestion strong consideration.* The present subjunctive form usually points toward the future with a stronger suggestion of hopefulness than does the past subjunctive. (*I move that John Marshall BE named chairman of our committee.*) The present subjunctive form of the verb *to be* is invariably *be* for all persons, and the past subjunctive form of the verb *to be* is invariably *were.* In all other verbs the subjunctive form varies from the indicative only in that in the present tense the third person singular ending is lost, as in *I suggest that he TAKE the subway to his friend's house.* Note the following examples of verbs in the subjunctive mood:

I wish that I *were* (not *was*) going with you to Hawaii this summer.

If I *were* (not *was*) king, I couldn't be happier.

The subjunctive mood may also be used in the following instances:

If the report *be* true, we will have to modify our plans. [To express a doubt or uncertainty.]

She commanded that the rule *be* enforced. [To express a command.]

Even though he *disagree* with me, I will still admire him. [To express a concession.]

It is necessary that he *see* his parents at once. [To express a necessity.]

I move that the proposal *be* adopted. [To express a parliamentary motion.]

Exercise 53 | TWO TROUBLESOME PAIRS OF VERBS

Select the correct form of the verbs in parentheses, and write it in the space at the right.

EXAMPLE: Don't forget the packages (*lying, laying*) on the counter.   ___*lying*___

1. Please (*lie, lay*) your completed application form on the desk.   _____

2. The girl (*lying, laying*) at the end of the sundeck is going to be burned
   to a crisp.   _____

3. The construction crew which (*lain, laid*) the foundation for the field
   house has worked here before.   _____

4. To dust the shelves, I had no choice but to (*lie, lay*) the books on the floor.   _____

5. Claire (*lay, laid*) in the upper berth, listening to the clacking of the wheels
   on the track.   _____

6. The wet leaves were (*lying, laying*) in great heaps along the curb.   _____

7. The escape route (*lies, lays*) through the trap door and then goes into a
   tunnel to the riverbank.   _____

8. The pieces of the jigsaw puzzle were (*lying, laying*) scattered across the
   the card table.   _____

9. The scene of the opening act was (*lain, laid*) in Transylvania.   _____

10. Our calico cat has (*lain, laid*) most of the morning in the sunny patches on
    the kitchen floor.   _____

11. The soprano (*lay, laid*) dying in the tenor's arms for every bit of ten
    minutes.   _____

12. Totally relaxed, Snoopy (*lies, lays*) on the roof of his doghouse year in and
    year out.   _____

13. In Scotland motorists often come upon sheep (*lying, laying*) in the middle
    of the road.   _____

14. The men (*lain, laid*) the rolls of carpet, one on top of the other, in the
    storeroom.   _____

15. Every afternoon Bert folds the flag and (*lies, lays*) it on the same shelf in the
    the Post Office.   _____

16. Marilyn must (*sit, set*) out bulbs in the fall if she expects to have jonquils in the spring.   _____

17. My faithful Rabbit was (*sitting, setting*) in the driveway, waiting for the ice to thaw.   _____

18. (*Sit, Set*) the groceries on the kitchen table, and I will put them up.   _____

19. I don't know when I've had time to (*sit, set*) down and chat with Muriel.   _____

20. Here comes Alison with her tam (*sitting, setting*) at its usual rakish angle.   _____

21. The waitress (*sat, set*) the steaming platters of spaghetti before us.   _____

22. The boys have (*sat, set*) on the steps for almost an hour arguing over the President's defense budget.   _____

23. Having (*sat, set*) down the last figures in the ledger, Mr. Clinkscales climbed down from his stool and reached for his coat.   _____

24. (*Sitting, Setting*) in the choir loft, Mrs. Haskins kept a close watch on her half-dozen children.   _____

25. No matter what the circumstances, the six of them always (*sat, set*) in the same pew.   _____

26. Michael (*sat, set*) the clay on the potter's wheel.   _____

27. The trucker hurriedly (*sat, set*) out flares to warn passing motorists of the accident.   _____

28. Did you know that Judge Rodriguez has been (*sitting, setting*) on the bench for more than a quarter of a century?   _____

29. (*Sitting, Setting*) high in the holly bush, the bird plucked at the red berries.   _____

30. Has anyone (*sat, set*) a glass of water on the podium?   _____

Exercise 54 | TWO TROUBLESOME PAIRS OF VERBS

Underline any form of **lie, lay, sit,** or **set** that is incorrectly used. Then write the correct form in the space at the right. Write **C** if a sentence is correct.

EXAMPLE: I'll sit these geraniums in a sunny window.   _____*set*_____

1. After struggling up the stairs with the bookcase, Walter was relieved to sit
   it down.   _____

2. Once we had driven halfway up the mountain, we could see the red roofs of
   the village laying below.   _____

3. The landscape architect has suggested that boxwoods be sat out here.   _____

4. Sid must have lain his keys on the counter in the drug store when he was
   talking with Mr. Ash.   _____

5. The game was so exciting that we stood more often than we set.   _____

6. Norman is not one who enjoys setting through lengthy musical
   performances.   _____

7. After Luis rounded up the brush and the bucket of paint, he set the ladder
   in place.   _____

8. The workmen are already beginning to lie the gas line along the other side
   of the street.   _____

9. It was a cold November afternoon, and the plaid robe I had lain across my
   knees felt good.   _____

10. The broken kite laid stranded in the top of the maple tree.   _____

11. I finally found my blue suede shoes setting on the closet shelf.   _____

12. Once you cross Putnam Square, you will see the flower stand setting on
    the right.   _____

13. Behind us laid the lights of New York, ahead the dark Atlantic.   _____

14. Setting in the back booth eating pizza was Celeste, whom I had not seen for months. _____

15. Setting down ideas on paper was a slow, painful process for Kevin. _____

16. I believe that you will find your jacket laying across the back of the chair in my bedroom. _____

17. The class read literature from countries that lay on either side of the Sahara. _____

18. The graduate sat her mortar board squarely on her head and started down the aisle. _____

19. I think that I lain the morning mail on the coffee table. _____

20. Sylvester, who is an expert at laying tile, works at Dempsey's. _____

21. Only once have I set all night in an airport. _____

22. George, please lay some more wood on the fire. _____

23. The freighter is laying at Pier 20, waiting to be unloaded. _____

24. Setting in front of us at the movie was a woman with two boisterous little boys. _____

25. I wonder how many nights Mother has laid awake waiting for one of us to come in. _____

26. Mrs. Dilworth's red wig sets rather precariously on her head. _____

27. From his glider the pilot could see the mountain ridge laying below. _____

28. Let's sit the Christmas tree in the window that overlooks the street. _____

29. It is not unusual to see a flock of pigeons setting on the courthouse roof. _____

30. In Westerns bandits are forever lying in wait for the stagecoach. _____

| Exercise 55 | TENSE AND MOOD |

A. In the space at the right write the correct form of the verb that appears in parentheses.

EXAMPLE: After we gathered around the piano, we (*sing*) all the old
            favorites.   _____*sang*_____

1. The wind has (*blown*) the snow in drifts as high as the fence.   _____

2. Trying hard to keep up, Juan (*cling*) to his mother's hand.   _____

3. To enjoy the fields and woods, we have often (*take*) the back roads.   _____

4. I was (*shake*) up when Jan slammed on the brakes.   _____

5. They must have (*stand*) in line for half an hour, waiting for the Bijou
   to open.   _____

6. While looking for a shovel in the tool shed, Bill was (*sting*) by a wasp. _____

7. We are (*suppose*) to mail the check for our rent to Mrs. Tetley.   _____

8. Rankin (*burst*) into the room with the news that Ellen had agreed to
   begin to think about his proposal.   _____

9. Last summer the three of us often (*ride*) the Great Scream Machine
   at Six Flags.   _____

10. What name has Wilbur (*choose*) for his new truck?   _____

11. Despite all precautions the child had (*steal*) a glimpse of his birthday
    cake.   _____

12. Uncle Luke (*use*) to tell tall tales about his years in the Army.   _____

13. Francisco has (*fall*) in love more times than he cares to remember.   _____

14. Clara (*tear*) open the letter which contained a check for her trip
    to Colorado.   _____

15. Neither of us has (*swim*) much since last summer.   _____

B. Underline all verbs in the following sentences. Then write the past tense of the underlined
   verbs in the space at the right.

EXAMPLE: I often <u>see</u> Lucy at the mall.   _____*saw*_____

1. The telephone rings, but I scarcely hear it in the kitchen.   _____
   _____

2. The novelist writes a chapter at a time and then reads over it carefully.   _____
   _____

3. The candidate rises and speaks to the roomful of supporters.   _____
   _____

4. At the sound of the alarm Frank drags himself out of bed and eats a   _____
   breakfast of Wheaties.   _____

5. I hear that she wears only the best.   _____
   _____

C. Select the correct form of the verb in parentheses, and write in the space at the right.

EXAMPLE: I wish that I (*was, were*) able to take the ferry to Halifax.   ____*were*____

1. It is necessary that our signatures (*are, be*) witnessed by a notary.   _____

2. (*Passing, Having passed*) a car with a flat tire, the police officer turned
   around to offer help.   _____

3. I move that a committee (*is, be*) appointed to draw up the resolutions.   _____

4. If I (*was, were*) you, I would go by ship to Dakar.   _____

5. The schedule stated that the last bus regularly (*left, leaves*) at 11:50 p.m.   _____

Exercise 56	TENSE AND MOOD

Underline any verb that is incorrect. Then write the correct form in the space at the right. Write **C** if a sentence is correct.

EXAMPLE: How many times has the President <u>spoke</u> to this

organization? _____*spoken*_____

1. Gloria has wrote to Orson every day since the fleet left Hawaii. _____

2. Unfortunately the canvas was tore slightly when the painting was brought out of storage. _____

3. The Taylors often use to spend their summer holiday touring with their camper. _____

4. My nephew has swam since he was little more than an infant. _____

5. Fernando has never throwed a better fast ball than he did today. _____

6. We were told at the service station that it was at least fifty miles from Plattsburg to Saranac Lake. _____

7. Did you hear about the men who flown across the United States in a balloon? _____

8. I promise you that I have wore this suit for the last time. _____

9. In the future we are suppose to be able to do our shopping or to contact our representative on a computer. _____

10. Although the forester planted the seedlings only last year, I can see that they have already growed. _____

11. Have you ever swang from birches the way Robert Frost must have? _____

12. I wish I was not addicted to soap operas. _____

13. Have you drank any of the green tea that Eloise brought from China? _____

14. The art student has drawed sketches of several of the old houses that
line Green Street. _____

15. Going to bed early, Clifford did not know that the Dolphins had won
the game until he read the morning paper. _____

16. Neither of us has ate at the Sandwich Basket yet. _____

17. For several years Mrs. Pitts has gave books she no longer wanted to
our book fair. _____

18. She also loans books to neighbors and other friends. _____

19. Our plane was late in taking off because the runway was froze over. _____

20. When Sarah was in high school, her greatest desire was to have opened
a book shop. _____

21. Fortunately she did not do so: she knowed very little about running
a business. _____

22. Few of us appreciate Eastern music because few of us are accustom
to hearing it. _____

23. Because I had ran over some glass in the parking lot, I stopped to
have my tires checked. _____

24. The reason that Sawyer arrived late for dinner is that he taken
the wrong subway. _____

25. Mary Virginia drowned her sorrows in short order and is now dating
Henry. _____

26. Having fell numerous times, Warren has decided to give up skating. _____

27. Someone was ringing the doorbell at the same moment that the
telephone rung. _____

28. Adams has scarcely spoke to his brother since they argued over moving
the Dodgers back to Brooklyn. _____

29. It is urgent that we are at the airport an hour before flight time.   _____

30. Yesterday Harvey hoped to have finished the repairs on his car.   _____

31. After the boys drug the Christmas tree to the edge of the woods, they hoisted it into the back of the truck.   _____

32. Our friend Red has rode a little bit of everything: horses, motorcycles, and bobsleds.   _____

33. No one on my hall has seed the Playmakers' spring production.   _____

34. Did you read that someone had stole the mascot from the Naval Academy?   _____

35. The Speaker of the House recognized Miss Wells, who moved that the report be accepted.   _____

36. Receiving her bank statement, Pauline decided to forgo the trip to Calgary.   _____

37. We have got a cable from Maggie but not a letter.   _____

38. Years later the boys confessed that they had often dove from Thompson Bridge.   _____

39. If it was not for the computer, we could not complete the annual report by Friday.   _____

40. The heavy smog hanged over the city all weekend.   _____

41. Although Bill has often gave me perfume, it has never been Chanel.   _____

42. A great deal of our topsoil has been blowed away as a result of poor farming practices.   _____

43. It is so stuffy in here that I'm going to have to raise the window.   _____

44. Mary and Frances have ask their customers to drop by to see their redecorated shop.   _____

45. The sun had not broke through the mist until shortly before noon.   _____

46. I wish that I was the golf player that you are.   _____

47. We rang the doorbell at Celia's apartment several times, but no one answered.   _____

48. A young man at the service station shown us the way to the doctor's office.   _____

49. Jack has chose political science as his major.   _____

50. If the posse had caught the horse thief, I'm afraid he would have been hung from a cottonwood tree.   _____

| Exercise 57 | VOICE |

Revise the following sentences, using verbs in the active voice and eliminate unnecessary verbs.

EXAMPLE: The photograph was taken by Travis.

   Travis took the photograph.

1. The vegetables for the salad were chopped by Nan while the lasagna was prepared by Abe.

2. The first set was won by a seasoned tennis player, but the match was taken by a girl in her teens.

3. An old oak was toppled by the storm, and a few shingles were blown from our roof.

4. Two of the paintings which were auctioned yesterday by Christie's were bought by a bidder from Saudi Arabia.

5. The lamp in the living room had been turned off by David, but the front door had not been locked.

6. The trout that were caught by Ray were broiled for dinner by Mother.

7. The marriage contract was drawn up by a young attorney whose offices are located in the Mercer Building.

8. The dress that was being worn by the star of the movie had been designed by Maurice.

9. Jerusalem, which is divided into the Old City and the New City, is considered a religious shrine by Jews, Christians, and Muslims.

10. Trudy was hired by the supervisor of nurses and was assigned to work on the children's ward.

11. "The Murders in the Rue Morgue," which was written by Edgar Allan Poe, has been described by Howard Haycraft as the first detective story.

12. Prince Edward Island, which was named for Queen Victoria's father, was once inhabited only by the Micmac Indians.

13. Instructions for making overseas calls have been published in a pamphlet and have been distributed by the telephone company.

14. The bells of the Old North Church, which is located in Boston, are rung to welcome the New Year.

15. The children, who were taken to Kensington Gardens on Monday by their father, were shown the statue of Peter Pan, which was sculpted by Sir George Frampton.

14

Dangling Modifiers

A **modifier** must always have a word to modify. This fact seems almost too obvious to warrant discussion. And yet we frequently see sentences similar in construction to this one: "Hearing a number of entertaining stories, our visit was thoroughly enjoyable." *Hearing a number of entertaining stories* is a modifying phrase. But where in the sentence is there a word for it to modify? Certainly the phrase cannot logically modify *visit*: it was not our visit that heard a number of entertaining stories. Who did hear the stories? *We* did. Since, however, the word *we* does not appear in the sentence for the phrase to modify, the phrase is said to "dangle." Any modifier dangles, or hangs unattached, when there is no obvious word to which it is clearly and logically related. (Note the similarity of this problem of modifiers and the problem of pronouns and their antecedents.)

14a Recognizing Dangling Modifiers

It is important that you recognize dangling modifiers when you see them. Such modifiers usually appear as two types of constructions—as *verbal phrases* and as *elliptical clauses.* (An elliptical clause, as applicable to this lesson, is a dependent clause in which the subject and/or verb are omitted.)

> *Hearing a number of entertaining stories,* our visit was thoroughly enjoyable. [Dangling participial phrase.]
>
> *On entering the room,* refreshments were being served. [Dangling gerund phrase.]
>
> *To play tennis well,* the racket must be held properly. [Dangling infinitive phrase.]
>
> *When only three years old,* my father took me to a circus. [Dangling elliptical clause.]

In each of the examples given above, the dangling modifier stands at the beginning of the sentence. If the modifier were *not* dangling—that is, if it were correctly used—it would be

related to the subject of the sentence. In none of these sentences, however, can the introductory modifier logically refer to the subject. If the error is not immediately apparent, try
placing the modifier just after the subject. The dangling nature of the modifier becomes
easily recognizable because of the illogical meaning which results when you say, "Our visit,
hearing a number of entertaining stories, . . ." or "Refreshments, *on entering the room, . . ."*

Dangling modifiers frequently appear at the end as well as at the beginning of sentences.
The participial phrase dangles in the sentence "The dog had only one eye, *caused by an
accident."*

At this point an exception to the rules governing the recognition of dangling modifiers
should be noted: some introductory verbal phrases are general or summarizing expressions
and therefore need not refer to the subject which follows:

> CORRECT: *Generally speaking,* the boys' themes were more interesting than the girls'.

> CORRECT: *To sum up,* our vacation was a disaster from start to finish.

14b Correcting Dangling Modifiers

Sentences containing dangling modifiers are usually corrected in one of two ways. One way is
to leave the modifier as it is and to reword the main clause, making the subject a word to
which the modifier logically refers. Remember that when modifiers such as those discussed in
this lesson stand at the beginning of the sentence, they must always clearly and logically modify or be related to the subject of the sentence:

> Hearing a number of entertaining stories, *we* thoroughly enjoyed our visit.

> On entering the room, *I* found that refreshments were being served.

> To play tennis well, *one* must hold the racket properly.

> When only three years old, *I* was taken to a circus by my father.

You may test the correctness of these sentences, as you tested the incorrectness of the
others, by placing the modifier just after the subject. Then see whether the sentence reads
logically; if it does, the modifier has been correctly used. The following sentence, though
awkward, is clear and logical: "We, hearing a number of entertaining stories, thoroughly
enjoyed our visit."

The other way to correct sentences containing dangling modifiers is to expand the modifiers into dependent clauses:

> *Since we heard a number of entertaining stories,* our visit was thoroughly enjoyable.

> *When I entered the room,* refreshments were being served.

> *If one wishes to play tennis well,* he must hold the racket properly.

> *When I was only three years old,* my father took me to a circus.

| Exercise 58 | **DANGLING MODIFIERS** |

Rewrite in correct form all sentences containing dangling modifiers. Write **C** if a sentence is correct.

EXAMPLE: To wash these windows well, a sunny day is needed.

To wash these windows well, I need a sunny day.

1. Having dropped to a record low, boating on the lake became hazardous.

2. When rounding the curve, the tires of the police car screeched and squealed.

3. After using the adding machine, it should be returned to Betty's desk.

4. When playing for Coach Jacobs, fundamentals are always stressed.

5. Rowing against the tide, headway was made slowly by the crew of the small boat.

6. Played flawlessly by the young pianist, the critic praised her treatment of the waltzes.

7. When passing another car at King's Crossing, the road should be clear to the next hill.

8. After reading your instructions, there was no difficulty finding Skylake.

9. Brad, to insure that your tires wear evenly, it is a good idea to rotate them occasionally.

10. Having failed to deflect the puck, the score became 1 to 0.

11. By walking briskly, the campus can be reached in less than thirty minutes.

12. Though majoring in marketing, Coolidge's interest in finance persisted.

13. Generally speaking, our dogs prefer the out-of-doors.

14. When completed, the quickest and easiest way to reach downtown will be by the rapid transit system.

15. Staring out of the plane window, the town soon looked like a Monopoly board.

16. Though not an expert, playing the guitar has become Mason's favorite pastime.

17. A shiny glaze covered the tree limbs after dropping below freezing.

18. In choosing the paint, an effort was made to find a color that would make the room seem warmer.

19. Dejected by the 10 to 7 loss, it seemed a long way back to Brookville.

20. The debate could scarcely be heard when sitting at the back of the auditorium.

Exercise 59 | INTRODUCTORY MODIFIERS

Using the following phrases and elliptical clauses as introductory modifiers, write complete sentences.

EXAMPLE: Snowbound for a week, *we learned to enjoy beans for breakfast.* _____

1. Before polishing his car, _____

   _____

2. To learn something about computers, _____

   _____

3. Amazed at the final score, _____

   _____

4. By writing home once a week, _____

   _____

5. Though eighty years old, _____

   _____

6. Busily engaged in the study of fruit flies, _____

   _____

7. Having just begun to jog, _____

   _____

8. While hidden in the underbrush, _____

   _____

9. After walking three miles, _____

   _____

10. Pleased with the announcement, _____

   _____

11. Not having consulted a schedule, _____

_____

12. While clambering over the rocks, _____

_____

13. To attend the World's Fair, _____

_____

14. Collecting my gear, _____

_____

15. Having missed my flight, _____

_____

16. Racing after the bus, _____

_____

17. To sum up, _____

_____

18. After struggling into my bathing suit, _____

_____

19. Bursting into bloom, _____

_____

20. When stretched out on the beach, _____

_____

21. By setting my watch five minutes ahead, _____

_____

22. To balance my budget, _____

_____

23. Repeatedly asked about my future plans, _____

_____

24. In searching for an answer, _____

_____

25. To strengthen the party platform, _____

_____

15
Misplaced Modifiers

Modifiers must always be so placed that there will be no uncertainty about the words they modify. A modifier should, in general, stand as close as possible to the word that it modifies. This does not mean, however, that in every sentence there is only one correct position for a modifier. The following sentence, in which the adverb *today* is shifted from one position to another, is equally clear in any one of these three versions:

> *Today* she arrived in Chicago.
>
> She arrived *today* in Chicago.
>
> She arrived in Chicago *today*.

The position of the modifier *today* can be shifted because, no matter where it is placed, it clearly modifies the verb *arrived*.

15a Misplaced Phrases and Clauses

When, however, a modifier can attach itself to two different words in the sentence, the writer must be careful to place it in a position which will indicate the meaning intended:

> They argued the subject while I tried to study *at fever pitch*.

This sentence is illogical as long as the phrase *at fever pitch* seems to modify *to study*. The phrase must be placed where it will unmistakably modify *argued*:

> CORRECT: They argued the subject *at fever pitch* while I tried to study.
>
> ALSO CORRECT: *At fever pitch* they argued the subject while I tried to study.

A relative clause—that is, a clause introduced by a relative pronoun—should normally follow the word which it modifies:

ILLOGICAL: A piece was played at the dance *which was composed of dissonant chords.*

CORRECT: A piece *which was composed of dissonant chords* was played at the dance.

15b Ambiguous Modifiers

When a modifier is placed between two elements so that it may be taken to modify either element, it is **ambiguous**. These ambiguous modifiers are sometimes called **squinting modifiers**:

The girl who had been dancing *gracefully* entered the room.

Does the speaker mean that the girl had been dancing gracefully or that she entered the room gracefully? Either of these meanings may be expressed with clarity if the adverb *gracefully* is properly placed:

The girl who had been *gracefully* dancing entered the room. [*Gracefully* modifies *had been dancing.*]

The girl who had been dancing entered the room *gracefully.* [Here *gracefully* modifies *entered.*]

15c Misplaced Words Like *Only, Nearly,* and *Almost*

Words such as *only, nearly,* and *almost* are frequently misplaced. Normally these modifying words should immediately precede the word they modify. To understand the importance of properly placing these modifiers, consider in the following sentences the different meanings which result when *only* is shifted:

Only I heard John shouting at the boys. [*Only* modifies *I.* Meaning: I was the only one who heard John shouting.]

I *only* heard John shouting at the boys. [*Only* modifies *heard.* Implied meaning: I heard but didn't see John shouting.]

I heard *only* John shouting at the boys. [*Only* modifies *John.* Meaning: John was the only one whom I heard shouting.]

I heard John *only* shouting at the boys. [*Only* modified *shouting.* Possible implied meaning: I didn't hear John hitting the boys—I heard him only shouting at them.]

I heard John shouting at the boys *only.* [*Only* modifies *boys.* Possible implied meaning: The boys were the ones I heard John shouting at—not the girls.]

Misplacing *only, nearly,* or *almost* will frequently result in an illogical statement:

ILLOGICAL: The baby *only* cried until he was six months old.

CORRECT: The baby cried *only* until he was six months old.

ILLOGICAL: Since his earnings amounted to $97.15, he *nearly* made a hundred dollars.

CORRECT: Since his earnings amounted to $97.15, he made *nearly* a hundred dollars.

ILLOGICAL: At the recent track meet Ralph *almost* jumped six feet.

CORRECT: At the recent track meet Ralph jumped *almost* six feet.

15d   Split Infinitives

A **split infinitive** is a construction in which the sign of the infinitive *to* has been separated from the verb with which it is associated. *To vigorously deny* and *to instantly be killed* are split infinitives. Unless emphasis or clarity demands its use, such a construction should be avoided:

> AWKWARD: He always tries *to efficiently and promptly do* his work.

> CORRECT: He always tries *to do* his work *efficiently and promptly*.

> CORRECT: We expect *to more than double* our sales in April. [Placing the modifiers *more than* anywhere else in this sentence would result in ambiguity or changed meaning.]

Exercise 60	MISPLACED MODIFIERS

Place **M** or **C** in the space at the right to indicate whether each sentence contains a misplaced modifier or is correct. Underline the misplaced words and indicate their proper position by means of a caret (∧). Use additional carets if there is more than one correct position.

EXAMPLE: Jeff <u>nearly</u> kicked the ball ∧ sixty yards.   <u>M</u>

1. Dennis helped me carry the sacks up the back stairs filled with groceries.   _____

2. The brick building was designed by a famous architect standing on the corner of North Avenue and Second Street.   _____

3. Baxter's recipe only calls for the juice of one lemon.   _____

4. I pulled my car over to the shoulder of the road, which was not running at all well.   _____

5. The train which had been moving slowly came to a stop.   _____

6. Our lost collie is wearing a collar around his neck made of red leather.   _____

7. The slim silver pocket watch still kept good time, which Grandfather had always enjoyed.   _____

8. The dry cleaner told Oscar that it would be possible to completely remove the spot.   _____

9. The students celebrated after the game in the streets.   _____

10. I believe that we nearly have enough snow for skiing.   _____

11. The marshal galloped into town on his faithful horse, wearing his silver star and white Stetson.   _____

12. The traffic light could only be seen dimly through the heavy fog.   _____

13. We have been making plans to tour the Northwest for a long time.   _____

14. Phil read almost the entire novel on one rainy afternoon.   _____

195

15. The law clerk was relieved to at last finish the brief that she had been working on.   _____

16. The rain was the result of a storm in the Gulf, which poured all morning.   _____

17. We had just walked a short distance before we came upon the restaurant that you had recommended.   _____

18. The boy that was holding the frightened kitten carefully came down the ladder.   _____

19. We visited the house where Emerson lived during the summer of 1981.   _____

20. Please get the morning paper for your father on the front steps.   _____

Exercise 61 | MISPLACED MODIFIERS

Place **M** or **C** in the space at the right to indicate whether each sentence contains a misplaced modifier or is correct. Underline the misplaced words and indicate their proper position by means of a caret (∧). Use additional carets if there is more than one correct position.

EXAMPLE: Hyman has <u>about</u> swum∧twenty laps.   *M*

1. The ordinance was only passed by a one-vote margin.   _____

2. The truck pulled up beside the all-night diner with its heavy load of pulpwood.   _____

3. The radio announcer who dashed into the studio breathlessly reported the fire.   _____

4. It is difficult for Garrison not to greatly exaggerate any story he tells.   _____

5. My chief interest became playing the flute in the seventh grade.   _____

6. The song reminded me of an old friend being played by the band.   _____

7. I discovered Barbara Pym's novels when turning through a publisher's catalogue, all of which I have now read.   _____

8. Even though he dropped his baton, the drum major hardly missed a step.   _____

9. She recorded the events that took place as she sailed up the Nile in a journal.   _____

10. I can't believe that he has just found a little information on the subject of consumerism.   _____

11. That dress has influenced the design of countless other dresses, chosen by the princess for her wedding.   _____

12. The student who was listening to the French tapes carefully took notes.   _____

13. One day last week my psychology professor discussed Freud's theories about dreams in class.   _____

14. Dick and I nearly listened to all of the President's press conference.   _____

15. To never know the pleasure of a good book is no small tragedy.   _____

16. Scoured by one storm after another, the barrier island gradually disappeared
    into the sea.   _____

17. The philosophy text is published by Rinehart Press, which James Christian
    has written.   _____

18. Even the want-ads are read by my grandfather appearing in the Sunday *Times*. _____

19. We were late getting to the theater and hardly heard any of Conley's songs. _____

20. We looked forward to seeing the room in which George Washington slept
    during spring holidays.   _____

16

Parallelism

Frequently in our writing and speaking we need to indicate equality of ideas. To show this equality, we should employ **parallel** grammatical constructions. In other words, we should convey parallel thought in parallel language; and conversely, we should use parallel language only when we are conveying parallel thoughts.

16a Coordinate Elements

In employing parallelism, we should balance nouns against nouns, infinitives against infinitives, prepositional phrases against prepositional phrases, adjective clauses against adjective clauses, etc. We should never make the mistake of saying, "I have always liked *swimming* and *to fish*." Since the object of *have liked* is two parallel ideas, we should say:

I have always liked *swimming* and *fishing*. (*And* joins two gerunds.)

OR

I have always liked *to swim* and *to fish*. (*And* joins two infinitives.)

Parallel prepositional phrases are illustrated in the following sentence. The parallel elements appear immediately after the double bar:

Government ‖ of the people,
‖ by the people,
and ‖ for the people   shall not perish from the earth.

Next we see an illustration of parallel noun clauses:

He said ‖ that he would remain in the East,
‖ that his wife would travel through the Northwest,
and ‖ that his son would attend summer school in the South.

199

The following sentence contains parallel independent clauses:

‖ I came;
‖ I saw;
‖ I conquered.

Parallel elements are usually joined either by simple coordinating conjunctions or by (tive conjunctions. The most common coordinating conjunctions used with parallel co_____tions are *and, but, or.* Whenever one of these connectives is used, you must be careful to see that the elements which are being joined are coordinate or parallel in construction:

FAULTY: Ann is a girl with executive ability and who therefore should be elected class president.

This sentence contains faulty parallelism, since *and* is used to join a phrase (*with executive ability*) and a dependent clause (*who therefore should be elected class president*). To correct the sentence, (1) expand the phrase into a *who* clause, or (2) make an independent clause of the *who* clause:

CORRECT: Ann is a girl ‖ who has executive ability
       and ‖ who therefore should be elected class president.

NOTE: A safe rule to follow is this: *And who* or *and which* should never be used unless preceded by another *who-* or *which-*clause.

ALSO CORRECT: ‖ Ann is a girl with executive ability;
        ‖ she therefore should be elected class president.

A common error results from making a construction appear to be parallel when actually it is not:

Mr. Lee is honest, intelligent, and works hard.

The structure of the sentence suggests an *a, b,* and *c* series; yet what we have is not three parallel elements but two adjectives (*honest, intelligent*) and a verb (*works*). The sentence can be corrected in two ways: we can use three adjectives in a series or two independent clauses in parallel construction, thus:

CORRECT: Mr. Lee is ‖ honest,
            ‖ intelligent,
       and ‖ industrious.

ALSO CORRECT: ‖ Mr. Lee is honest and intelligent,
          and ‖ he works hard.

16b   Use of Correlative Conjunctions

Correlative conjunctions are used in pairs: *either . . . or . . . ; neither . . . nor . . . ; both . . . and . . . ; not only . . . but also . . . .* When these conjunctions are employed in a sentence, they must be followed by parallel constructions:

INCORRECT: I hope *either* to spend my vacation in Mexico *or* Cuba. [In this sentence *either* is followed by an infinitive, *or* by a noun.]

CORRECT: I hope to spend my vacation either ‖ in Mexico
or ‖ in Cuba.

ALSO CORRECT: I hope to spend my vacation in either ‖ Mexico
or ‖ Cuba.

INCORRECT: She knew *not only* what to say, *but also* she knew when to say it.

CORRECT: She knew not only ‖ what to say
but also ‖ when to say it.

16c Repetition of Certain Words

In order to make parallel constructions clear, you must sometimes repeat an article, a preposition, an auxiliary verb, the sign of the infinitive (*to*), or the introductory word of a dependent clause. Three of these types of necessary repetition are illustrated in the sentences which follow:

OBSCURE: He must counsel all employees who participate in sports and also go on recruiting trips throughout the Southwest.

CLEAR: He must counsel all employees who participate in sports and *must* also go on recruiting trips throughout the Southwest.

OBSCURE: The instructor wants to meet those students who enjoy barber-shop harmony and organize several quartets.

CLEAR: The instructor wants to meet those students who enjoy barber-shop harmony and *to* organize several quartets.

OBSCURE: He thought that economic conditions were improving and the company was planning to increase its dividend rate.

CLEAR: He thought that economic conditions were improving and *that* the company was planning to increase its dividend rate.

16d *Than* and *As* in Parallel Constructions

Than and *as* are frequently used to join parallel constructions. When these two connectives introduce comparisons, you must be sure that the things compared are similar. Don't compare, for instance, a janitor's salary with a teacher. Compare a janitor's salary with a teacher's salary:

INCORRECT: A janitor's salary is frequently larger than a teacher.

CORRECT: ‖ A janitor's salary is frequently larger
than ‖ a teacher's (salary).

16e Incorrect Omission of Necessary Words

A very common kind of faulty parallelism is seen in the following sentence:

I always have and always will *remember* to send my first-grade teacher a Christmas card.

In this sentence *remember* is correctly used after *will*, but after *have* the form needed is *remembered.* Consequently, *remember* cannot serve as the understood participle after *have*:

CORRECT:　I ‖ always have *remembered*
　　　　　and ‖ always will remember　to send my first-grade teacher
　　　　　　　　a Christmas card.

Other sentences containing similar errors are given below:

INCORRECT:　I *was* mildly surprised, but all of my friends gravely shocked. [After *all of my friends* the incorrect verb form *was* seems to be understood.]

CORRECT:　I was mildly surprised, but all of my friends *were* gravely shocked.

INCORRECT:　He gave me an apple and pear. [Before *pear* the incorrect form *an* seems to be understood.]

CORRECT:　He gave me an apple and *a* pear.

INCORRECT:　I was interested and astounded *by* the story of his latest adventure.

CORRECT:　I was ‖ interested *in*
　　　　　and ‖ astounded by　the story of his latest adventure

INCORRECT:　She is as tall if not taller *than* her sister.

CORRECT:　She is as tall *as* her sister, if not taller. [The reader understands *than her sister.*]

ALSO CORRECT:　She is as tall *as*, if not taller than, her sister.

16f　Correct Use of "Unparallel" Constructions

A caution should be added to this lesson. Parallelism of phraseology is not always possible. When it is not, do not hesitate to use natural, "unparallel" constructions:

CORRECT THOUGH "UNPARALLEL":　He spoke *slowly* and *with dignity.*

Here *slowly* and *with dignity* are parallel in a sense: they are both adverbial modifiers.

Exercise 62   PARALLELISM

Rewrite in correct form all sentences that contain faulty parallelism. Write **C** if a sentence is correct.

EXAMPLE: The District Attorney stood up, removed her glasses, and then she turned to the jury.

The District Attorney stood up, removed her glasses, and then turned to the jury.

1. Tony is tall, dark, and drives a Corvette.

2. Steve hoped to find tickets to the Super Bowl and that he could take two days of his vacation for the game.

3. The miners not only were interested in higher pay but also better working conditions.

4. The girl at the circulation desk was wearing green corduroy knickers, a blue sweater, and she had auburn hair.

5. Tacked on Angela's walls were an old poster of the Beatles, a Picasso print, and Sierra calendar.

6. Murphy always has and always will spend most of his summer fishing from the pier.

7. The pamphlet explains solar energy and how one can build a solar heating system.

8. My youngest brother wants to be a beachcomber but the other two corporation presidents.

9. The old man on the park bench is enjoying his pipe, his newspaper, and he occasionally feeds the pigeons.

10. I have read neither the book by Thomas Mann nor seen the film based on it.

11. The candidate must speak to her supporters who appear at the airport and meet with members of the local media.

12. You must go home, take off those wet shoes, and have a cup of hot chocolate.

13. Dr. Hyde is an excellent dentist but who asks questions when there is no way for me to answer them.

14. The discount store's prices are not always as low as Anderson.

15. We found the ballet to be colorful, exciting, and it was beautifully performed.

16. The French film is as fine if not finer than any other film produced this year.

17. Richard Chase not only collects folktales, but he also tells them.

18. Mother's cake seems to have risen higher than Aunt Fran.

19. My brother is amazed and concerned about my difficulty in finding an apartment.

20. Mr. Brandeis said that the roads will be cleared by tomorrow and the divisional managers are going to the seminar.

| Exercise 63 | PARALLELISM |

Complete each of the following sentences by adding a construction that is parallel to the *italicized* construction.

EXAMPLE: The boy at the door was *small, cold,* and __dirty._____

1. I wonder *how my old friend Will is* and _____

_____

2. Mr. Foster is not only *an excellent barber* but also _____

_____

3. The file folders slipped *out of Wilson's arms* and _____

_____

4. The parade is *to begin at city hall* and _____

_____

5. We will either have to *open a window* or _____

_____

6. At the back of the tool shed were *the sled, two pairs of skates,* and _____

_____

7. Pierre *allowed the cakes to cool* and then _____

_____

8. Not only *does the book deal with witchcraft in Europe,* but also_____

_____

9. Our newspaper comes neither *regularly* nor _____

_____

10. The stars are a subject *with which humans have been fascinated for centuries* and _____

_____

17

Subordination

Parallelism enables you to indicate equality of ideas. More often, however, your writing will include sentences in which some ideas are more important than others. The main device for showing the difference between major and minor emphasis is **subordination**: we reserve the independent clause for the main idea and use dependent clauses, phrases, and single words to convey subordinate ideas:

> In our garden there is a birdbath *which is carved from marble*. [Subordinate idea placed in a dependent clause.]

> In our garden there is a birdbath *carved from marble*. [Subordinate idea reduced to a participial phrase.]

> In our garden there is a *marble* birdbath. [Subordinate idea reduced to a one-word modifier.]

17a   Primer Style

It is necessary to understand the principle of subordination, for without subordination you would be unable to indicate the relative importance of ideas or their various shades of emphasis in your thinking. The following group of sentences is both childish and monotonous because six dissimilar ideas have been presented in six simple sentences and thus appear to be of equal importance:

> A pep meeting was held last Friday night. Memorial Stadium was the scene of the meeting. The meeting was attended by thousands of students. Over a hundred faculty members were there too. It rained Friday night. There was also some sleet.

As you know, coordinating conjunctions are used to join ideas of equal importance. Consequently, the six sentences given above would not be improved if they were joined by such conjunctions. As a matter of fact, a type of sentence which you should avoid is the long, stringy one which is tied together by *and, but, so,* or *and so*. Instead of using this kind of sentence, weigh the relative importance of your several ideas, and show their importance by the use of main and subordinate sentence elements. Notice how the six ideas can be merged into one clear sentence:

> Despite rain and some sleet the pep meeting held last Friday night at Memorial Stadium was attended by thousands of students and over a hundred faculty members.

In combining the six sentences, the writer has chosen to use the fact about student and faculty attendance as the main idea. Another writer might have chosen otherwise, for there will not always be complete agreement as to which idea can be singled out and considered the most important. You may be sure, however, that if your sentence reads with emphasis and effectiveness you have chosen a correct idea as the main one.

17b   Upside-down Subordination

When there are only two ideas of unequal rank to be considered, you should have no difficulty in selecting the more important one:

1. He showed some signs of fatigue.
2. He easily won the National Open Golf Tournament.

Of these two sentences the second is undoubtedly the more important. Hence, when the two sentences are combined, the second should stand as the independent clause, and the first should be reduced to a dependent clause or even a phrase. If you made an independent clause of the first sentence and a subordinate element of the second, your sentence would contain upside-down subordination:

> FAULTY (upside-down subordination):   Though he easily won the National Open Golf Tournament, he showed some signs of fatigue.
>
> CORRECT: Though he showed some signs of fatigue, he easily won the National Open Golf Tournament.

17c   Choice of Subordinating Conjunctions

In introducing a subordinate element, be sure that you choose the right subordinating conjunction. The following sentences illustrate the correct use of certain conjunctions:

> I don't know *whether* (or *that*; not *as* nor *if*) I can see you tomorrow.
>
> *Although* (not *while*) she isn't a genius, she has undeniable talent.
>
> I saw in the autobiography of the actor *that* (not *where*) there is a question about the exact date of his birth.

(See Chapter 22, Glossary of Faulty Diction, for further discussion of accurate word choice.)

Exercise 64 | SUBORDINATION

Combine the ideas in each of the following groups of sentences into one effective simple or complex sentence.

EXAMPLE: Celestine Sibley is a newspaperwoman.
             She writes a column.
             It appears several times a week in the Atlanta *Constitution.*

Celestine Sibley is a newspaperwoman, whose column appears several times a week in the Atlanta Constitution.

1. Mack Sennett was a film director and producer.
   He worked in Hollywood.
   He is chiefly noted for his slapstick comedies.

2. John Ringling organized a circus.
   He had the help of four of his brothers.
   The circus became known as the "Greatest Show on Earth."

3. Cluny is a town in France.
   A famous abbey was located there.
   The abbey remained in use for over eight hundred years.

4. Edmund Hoyle was an Englishman.
   He wrote books containing rules for games.
   The expression "according to Hoyle" alludes to him.

5. Germans immigrated to southern Chile in 1850.
   Most of them settled on small farms.
   They raised cattle and wheat.

6. Pawtucket is a town in Rhode Island.
   Its name is derived from an Algonquin word.
   In English the word means *little falls* or *falls at the mouth of a river.*

7. Hamilton Fish served as Secretary of State.
   He served under President Ulysses S. Grant.
   Fish served during both of Grant's terms of office.

8. In Greek mythology there are three Fates.
   The Fates are goddesses.
   One spins the web of life.
   Another determines its length.
   The third cuts it.

9. Marco Polo traveled to China.
   He spent seventeen years there.
   Afterward he wrote a book.
   It proved to be a valuable source of information about the Far East.

| Exercise 65 | SUBORDINATION |

Combine the ideas in each of the following groups of sentences into one effective simple or complex sentence.

EXAMPLE: Flag Day is observed on June 14.
This date marks the anniversary of the adoption of the United States flag.

Flag Day, which is observed on June 14, marks the anniversary of the adoption of the United States flag.

1. Frances Perkins served as Secretary of Labor.
   She served under President Franklin D. Roosevelt.
   She was the first woman to serve as a Cabinet member.

2. Hawaii consists of more than twenty islands.
   It was once called the Sandwich Islands.
   It was named the Sandwich Islands in honor of the fourth Earl of Sandwich.
   He was first lord of the British admiralty.

3. Ring Lardner began his career as a sports writer.
   He is remembered for his short stories.
   His first collection is entitled *You Know Me Al.*

4. Graham Greene wrote the script for the film *Our Man in Havana.*
   The film was based on his novel.
   The novel was first published in 1958.

5. The Falkland Islands lie east of the southern tip of South America.
   They are also known as Las Islas Malvinas.
   Great Britain claims them.
   Argentina also claims them.

6. Isabella Hardenburgh was a black American.
   She became known as Sojourner Truth.
   She advocated the abolition of slavery.
   She spoke out for women's rights.

7. Muslims fast from dawn to dark during Ramadan.
   Ramadan is a holy month.
   It commemorates the revelation of the Koran.
   Mohammed received this revelation from Allah.

8. Friedrich Engels was a German socialist.
   He and Karl Marx were close associates.
   He shared Marx's views.
   He gave financial support to Marx's research.

9. The hot dog is an American invention.
   No one knows positively where it was first served.
   Mitford Mathews' historical dictionary quotes a source that identifies Coney Island as its
   place of origin.

Exercise 66	SUBORDINATION

The following sentences contain upside-down subordination or too much coordination. Rewrite each sentence to make it an effective simple or complex sentence.

EXAMPLE: We went to Caldecott's for lunch, and we saw Mr. Morse, and we asked him to join us.

When we went to Caldecott's for lunch, we saw Mr. Morse, whom we asked to join us.

1. Avoiding the stalled car, Phil swerved to the right.

2. We arrived in Ft. Lauderdale on Thursday, and it was raining, but the sun came out Friday afternoon.

3. When the sailor finally saw land on the horizon, he was standing in the crow's-nest.

4. John Maynard Keynes was an English economist, and he was a capitalist, but he advocated government participation in economic planning.

5. The small velvet box, which contained the diamond ring, was slowly opened by Ted's fiancée.

6. Racing across the goal line, Walker was trailed by a host of tacklers.

7. The first woman to be elected on her own as governor of a state, Ella Grasso was a Democrat from Connecticut.

8. I left the library at eight o'clock, and I went straight home, and I was able to see all the hockey game.

9. Skidding to the bottom of the hill, Bud rounded the icy curve in his old truck.

10. Searching for the underground stream, Stanley used a divining rod.

18

Illogical Comparisons and Mixed Constructions

Correctness and clarity are essential to good writing. To reach these goals, you must know the rules of grammar and punctuation. But further, you must think logically and find the exact words in which to express your thoughts. Nothing is more bothersome to a reader than inexact, illogical, or confusing sentences. Some of the lessons which we have already studied have stressed means of avoiding certain errors which produce vagueness or confusion in writing; among these errors are faulty reference of pronouns, dangling or misplaced modifiers, and upside-down subordination. This lesson will consider certain other errors which obstruct clarity of expression.

18a Illogical Comparisons

When you make comparisons, you must be sure not only that the things compared are similar (a matter considered in the lesson on parallelism) but that all necessary elements of the comparison are included.

Note the following sentence:

> Harold is taller than any boy in his class.

Since *Harold*, the first term of the comparison, is included in the classification *any boy in his class*, the comparison is obviously illogical: the sentence might be interpreted to mean *Harold is taller than Harold*. Therefore, the first term of the comparison must be compared with a second term or classification which excludes the first term, thus:

> CORRECT: Harold is taller than any *other* boy in his class.

> ALSO CORRECT: Harold is taller than any *girl* in his class.

It should also be pointed out that when the superlative is followed by *of,* the object of *of* must be plural:

ILLOGICAL: Harold is the tallest of any other boy in his class.

CORRECT: Harold is the tallest of *all the boys* in his class.

ALSO CORRECT: Harold is the *tallest boy* in his class.

Ambiguity results from a comparison like this one:

I helped you more than Jim.

Does the sentence mean *I helped you more than I helped Jim* or *I helped you more than Jim did*? The writer should use one sentence or the other, according to whichever meaning is intended.

The type of incomplete comparison illustrated by the following vague sentences is particularly popular with writers of advertising copy and with careless speakers:

VAGUE: Eastern Rubber Company makes a tire which gives twenty percent more mileage.

CLEAR: Eastern Rubber Company makes a tire which gives twenty percent more mileage *than any tire it made ten years ago.*

ALSO CLEAR: Eastern Rubber Company makes a tire which gives twenty percent more mileage *than any other tire made in the United States.*

VAGUE: Litter is more of a problem in cities.

CLEAR: Litter is more of a problem in cities *than in small towns.*

ALSO CLEAR: Litter is more of a problem in cities *than it used to be.*

18b   Mixed on Confused Constructions

Mixed constructions are frequently the result of some sort of shift in a sentence. Through ignorance or forgetfulness the writer starts a sentence with one type of construction and then switches to another. Notice the shift of construction in the following sentence:

She bought an old, dilapidated house which by having it extensively repaired converted it into a comfortable home.

The sentence reads correctly through the realtive pronoun *which*. The reader expects *which* to introduce an adjective clause; however, he is unable to find a verb for *which*. Instead, he finds that the sentence is completed by a construction in which a gerund phrase stands as the subject of the verb *converted*. The sentence may be corrected in various ways. Two correct versions are:

She bought an old, dilapidated house which after extensive repairs was converted into a comfortable home.

By means of extensive repairs she converted into a comfortable home an old, dilapidated house which she had bought.

Other examples of mixed constructions are given below:

MIXED: Bob realized that during the conference how inattentive he had been. [This sentence is confusing because *that* as used here is a subordinating conjunction and should introduce a noun clause. However, the *that*-construction is left incomplete. Futher on, *how* introduces a noun clause. What we find then is only one noun clause but two words, *that* and *how*, used to introduce noun clauses. Obviously, only one such word should introduce the one dependent clause.]

CORRECT: Bob realized that during the conference he had been inattentive.

ALSO CORRECT: Bob realized how inattentive he had been during the conference.

MIXED: Because she had to work in the library kept her from attending the party. [A dependent clause introduced by *because* is always adverbial; hence such a clause can never be used as the subject of a sentence.]

CORRECT: Having to work in the library kept her from attending the party.

ALSO CORRECT: Because she had to work in the library, she could not attend the party.

MIXED: He pulled a leg muscle was why he failed to place in the broad jump. [He *pulled a leg muscle* is an independent clause standing as the subject of *was*. An independent clause, unless it is a quotation, can never be used as the subject of a sentence.]

CORRECT: Because he pulled a leg muscle, he failed to place in the broad jump.

MIXED: By attending the reception as a guest rather than as a butler was a new experience for him. [The preposition *by* introduces a modifying phrase, and a modifying phrase can never be used as the subject of a sentence.]

CORRECT: Attending the reception as a guest rather than as a butler was a new experience for him.

ALSO CORRECT: By attending the reception as a guest rather than as a butler, he enjoyed a new experience.

MIXED: A pronoun is when a word is used in the place of a noun. [Never use *is when* or *is where* in defining a word. Remember that a *when*- or *where*-clause which is clearly adverbial cannot be used as a predicate nominative.]

CORRECT: A pronoun is a word used in the place of a noun.

MIXED: I was the one about whom she was whispering to my father about. [To correct this sentence, omit either *about*.]

MIXED: We know that if he were interested in our offer that he would come to see us. [To correct this sentence, omit the second *that*. The first *that* introduces the noun clause *that . . . he would come to see us. If he were interested in our offer* is an adverbial clause within the noun clause.]

| Exercise 67 | ILLOGICAL COMPARISONS AND MIXED CONSTRUCTIONS |

The following sentences contain illogical or ambiguous comparisons and mixed constructions. Rewrite each sentence in a correct form. (Notice that some sentences permit more than one correct interpretation.)

EXAMPLE: Injustice is when one is treated unfairly.

   Injustice is unfair treatment.

1. Agnes is the best cook; you should taste her pound cake.

2. After running around in the rain without a raincoat was what caused Sydney's sore throat.

3. Jamie says he feels like that he is the only person who is really behind the team one hundred percent.

4. Lulu really believes that her new car gets better gas mileage.

5. Mary told Sam that Father gave her more money than Mother.

6. Aunt Evie is always talking about when she was a little girl, how poor her family was.

7. Jonathan Reilly has a bigger house than any man in this section of the state.

8. Haven't you sometimes felt like that you would like to get away from it all?

9. A euphemism is where one uses a term that is less disagreeable than the direct expression would be.

10. By trying to avoid doing any work was how Fred got himself into this difficulty.

11. Old Mrs. Magillicuddy is the most delightful person!

12. If you will use real butter in your icing, it will be creamier.

13. After hearing that Mr. Jones was running for mayor was when I knew that it would be a tight race.

14. Lonnie admitted that after eating two slices of watermelon what a terrible stomach ache he had.

15. We tried to get the old car started but which even after we added water and gas, it would not start.

16. Laurie is the prettiest of any girl I know.

17. I soon realized that until I got a good typewriter that it would be impossible for me to turn out decent copy.

18. Harry certainly looks more like his father than his sister.

19. I found an old table in the cellar and which when I refinished it turned out to be solid mahogany.

20. Knoxville is where the World's Fair will be held and which is a lovely city in Tennessee.

21. Isn't it surprising that Mrs. Tucker's salary is larger than her husband?

22. Sue says that she buys this brand of canned beans because it is cheaper.

23. Forgiveness is when someone is willing to give up the desire for punishment.

24. The beer that advertises that it has fewer calories doesn't appeal to me.

25. I have just received the most beautiful sweater; it was knitted by my sister.

19
Punctuation

Punctuation depends largely upon the grammatical structure of a sentence. In order to punctuate correctly, you must therefore have an understanding of grammatical elements. For this reason, rules of punctuation in this text have been correlated, whenever applicable, with your study of grammar and sentence structure. You learned, for instance, how to punctuate certain phrases when you studied the phrase as a sentence unit.

In order that this chapter may present a reasonably complete treatment of punctuation, you will find here, along with additional rules, a summary of the rules already studied and reference to the chapters in which they are discussed. The rules given below have become to a large extent standardized; hence they should be clearly understood and practiced. Following the principle of punctuating "by ear" or of using a comma wherever there is a vocal pause results in an arbitrary and frequently misleading use of punctuation.

19a Terminal Marks

The terminal marks of punctuation—that is, those marks used to end a sentence—are the period, the question mark, and the exclamation mark.

Use a period after a declarative sentence, an imperative sentence, or an indirect question:

DECLARATIVE: John answered the telephone.

IMPERATIVE: Answer the telephone.

INDIRECT QUESTION: She asked whether John had answered the telephone.

NOTE: A request which is stated as a polite question should be followed by a period. Such a request frequently occurs in business correspondence:

Will you please send me your special summer catalogue.

Use a period also after most abbreviations:

Mr., Ms., Dr., B.S., Jr., *i.e.*, viz., etc., A.D., B.C., A.M., P.M.

Use three periods to indicate an omission of a word or words within a quoted sentence, three periods plus a terminal mark to indicate an omission at the end of a quoted sentence:

"Fourscore and seven years ago our fathers brought forth . . . a new nation . . . ."

Use a question mark after a direct question:

Did John answer the telephone?

"Have you finished your work?" she asked.

Use an exclamation mark after an expression of strong feeling. This mark of punctuation should be used sparingly:

"Halt!" he shouted.

How disgusting!

There goes the fox!

19b   The Comma

1. Use a comma to separate independent clauses when they are joined by the coordinating conjunctions *and, but, or, nor, for, so,* and *yet.* (See Chapter 6.)

The game was over, but the crowd refused to leave the park.

If the clauses are long or are complicated by internal punctuation, a semicolon should be used instead of a comma. (See 19c, Rule #3.)

2. Use a comma to separate words, phrases, and clauses written as a series of three or more coordinate elements. This rule covers short independent clauses when used in a series, as shown in the third example sentence below.

A trio composed of Marie, Ellen, and Frances sang at the entertainment.

Jack walked into my office, took off his hat, and sat down.

I washed the dishes, I dried them, and I put them away.

3. Use a comma to separate two or more coordinate adjectives that modify the same noun:

The noisy, enthusiastic freshman class assembled in Section F of the stadium. [*Noisy* and *enthusiastic* are coordinate adjectives; therefore they are separated by a comma. But *freshman*, though an adjective, is not coordinate with *noisy* and *enthusiastic*; actually *noisy* and *enthusiastic* modify not just *class* but the word group *freshman class*. Hence no comma precedes *freshman*.]

To determine whether adjectives are coordinate, you may make two tests: if they are coordinate, you will be able (1) to join them with *and* or (2) to interchange their positions in the sentence. You can certainly say *the noisy and enthusiastic freshman class* or *the enthusiastic, noisy freshman class*; thus *noisy* and *enthusiastic* are clearly coordinate. However, to say *the noisy and freshman class* or *the freshman noisy class* would be absurd; thus *freshman* is not structurally parallel with *noisy*:

a blue wool suit [Adjectives not coordinate.]

an expensive, well-tailored suit [Adjectives coordinate.]

a new tennis court [Adjectives not coordinate.]

a muddy, rough court [Adjectives coordinate.]

4. Use a comma to separate sharply contrasted coordinate elements:

He was merely ignorant, not stupid.

5. Use commas to set off all nonessential modifiers. Do not set off essential modifiers. (See Chapter 7 for a discussion of essential and nonessential clauses.)

NONESSENTIAL CLAUSE: Sara Sessions, *who is wearing red shorts today*, was voted the most versatile girl in her class.

NONESSENTIAL PHRASE: Sara Sessions, *wearing red shorts today*, was voted the most versatile girl in her class.

ESSENTIAL CLAUSE: The girl *who is wearing red shorts today* is Sara Sessions.

6. Use a comma after an introductory adverbial clause, verbal phrase, or absolute phrase. (See Chapter 7 for a discussion of dependent clauses, Chapter 5 for a discussion of phrases).

INTRODUCTORY ADVERBIAL CLAUSE: *When he arose to give his speech*, he was greeted with thunderous applause.

INTRODUCTORY PARTICIPIAL PHRASE: *Being in a hurry*, I was able to see him only briefly.

INTRODUCTORY GERUND PHRASE: *On turning the corner*, Tom ran squarely into a a police officer.

INTRODUCTORY INFINITIVE PHRASE: *To get a seat*, we have to arrive by 7:30 P.M.

INTRODUCTORY ABSOLUTE PHRASE: *My schedule having been arranged*, I felt like a full-fledged college freshman.

7. Use commas to set off nonesssential appositives. (See Chapter 5.)

Tom, *the captain of the team*, was injured in the first game of the season.

Sometimes an appositive is so closely "fused" with the word which it follows that it constitutes an essential element in the sentence and thus is not set off by commas:

William *the Conqueror* died in 1087.

The poet *Keats* spent his last days in Italy.

The word *bonfire* has an interesting history.

8. Use commas to set off items in dates, geographical names, and addresses and to set off titles after names:

July 22, 1977, was a momentous day in his life.

Birmingham, Alabama, gets its name from Birmingham, England.

Do you know who lives at 1600 Pennsylvania Avenue, Washington, D.C.?

Alfred E. Timberlake, Ph.D., will be the principal speaker.

9. Use commas to set off words used in direct address:

It is up to you, *Dot*, to push the campaign.

I think, *sir,* that I am correct.

You, *my fellow Americans,* must aid in the fight against inflation.

10. Use a comma after a mild interjection and after *yes* and *no*:

Oh, I suppose you're right.

Yes, I will be glad to go.

11. Use a comma to separate an independent clause from a question dependent on the clause:

You will try to do the work, won't you?

12. Use commas to set off expressions like *he said* or *she replied* when they interrupt a sentence of direct quotation. (But see rule 1 under The Semicolon, below.)

"I was able," *she replied,* "to build the bookcase in less than an hour."

13. Use commas to set off certain parenthetic elements:

I was, *however,* too tired to make the trip.

My hopes, *to tell the truth,* had fallen to a low ebb.

14. Use a comma to prevent the misreading of a sentence:

Above, the mountains rose like purple shadows.

To John, Harrison had been a sort of idol.

19c   The Semicolon

1. Use a semicolon to separate independent clauses when they are not joined by *and, but, or, nor, for, so,* or *yet.* (See Chapter 6.)

Wade held the ball for an instant; then he passed it to West.

"He is sick," she said; "therefore, he will not come."

2. Use a semicolon to separate coordinate elements which are joined by a coordinating conjunction but which are internally punctuated:

His tour included concert appearances in Austin, Texas; Little Rock, Arkansas; Tulsa, Oklahoma; and Kansas City, Kansas.

3. Use a semicolon to punctuate independent clauses which are joined by a coordinating conjunction in sentences which are heavily punctuated with commas internally:

I invited Sara, Susan, Leon, and John to the party; but Joe, Robert, and Charles also dropped in.

19d   The Colon

1. Use a colon after a clause which introduces a formal list. Do not use a colon unless the words preceding the list form a complete statement:

INCORRECT: The poets I like best are: Housman, Yeats, and Eliot.

CORRECT: The poets I like best are these: Housman, Yeats, and Eliot.

ALSO CORRECT: The poets I like best are Housman, Yeats, and Eliot.

INCORRECT: The basket was filled with: apples, oranges, and bananas.

CORRECT: The basket was filled with the following fruits: apples, oranges, and bananas.

ALSO CORRECT: The basket was filled with apples, oranges, and bananas.

2. Use a colon after a statement which introduces an explanation or amplification of that statement:

One characteristic accounted for his success: complete honesty. [A dash, which is less formal than the colon, may be substituted for the colon in this sentence.]

There was only one way to solve the mystery: we had to find the missing letter.

3. Use a colon after expressions like *he said* when they introduce a long and formal quotation:

The speaker rose to his feet and said: "Students and teachers, I wish to call your attention to . . . ."

4. Use a colon after the formal salutation of a letter, between the hour and minute figures in time designations, between a chapter and verse reference from the Bible, and between a title and subtitle:

Dear Sir:

8:40 P.M.

John 3:16

Victorian England: Portrait of an Age

19e   The Dash

1. Use a dash to indicate an abrupt shift or break in the thought of a sentence or to set off an informal or emphatic parenthesis:

Harvey decided to go to—but you wouldn't be interested in that story.

Mary told me—would you believe it?—that she preferred a quiet vacation at home.

At the age of three—such is the power of youth—Mary could stand on her head.

2. Use dashes to set off an appositive or a parenthetic element which is internally punctuated:

Her roommates—Jane, Laura, and Ruth—are spending the weekend with her.

19f   Quotation Marks

1. Use quotation marks to enclose direct quotations, but do not use them to enclose indirect quotations:

INCORRECT: He said that "I was old enough to know better."

CORRECT: He said, "You are old enough to know better."

ALSO CORRECT: He said that I was old enough to know better.

If a direct quotation is interrupted by an expression like *he said*, use quotation marks to enclose only the quoted material. This necessitates the use of two sets of quotation marks:

> INCORRECT: "It's just possible, Mary responded, that I'll get up before six in the morning."
>
> CORRECT: "It's just possible," Mary responded, "that I'll get up before six in the morning."

If there are two or more consecutive sentences of quoted material, use only one set of quotations marks to enclose all the sentences, not one set for each sentence:

> INCORRECT: Ruby shouted, "Wait for me." "I'll be ready in two minutes."
>
> CORRECT: Ruby shouted, "Wait for me. I'll be ready in two minutes."

Use single marks to enclose a quotation with a quotation:

> The instructor asked, "Who said, 'Change the name of Arkansas? Never!'?"

Place the comma and the period inside the quotation marks, the semicolon outside. Place the question mark and exclamation mark inside the quotation marks when they apply to the quoted material, outside when they apply to the entire sentence:

> "Of course," he replied, "I remember you." [Comma and period inside the quotation marks.]
>
> Her favorite poem was Kipling's "If."
>
> Several times the witness said, "I swear to the truth of my statement"; yet the jury remained unconvinced. [Semicolon outside the quotation marks.]
>
> He asked, "Where are you going?" [The question mark comes within the quotation marks because only the quoted material is a question.]
>
> Did she definitely say, "I accept your invitation"? [The question mark comes outside the quotation marks because the entire sentence is a question.]

2. Use quotation marks to enclose the titles of short works (short stories, short poems, articles, one-act plays, songs, and speeches) and of smaller units of books. (See Rule 3 under Italics, Chapter 20, Section b.)

> Benét's story "The Devil and Daniel Webster" was first published in the *Saturday Evening Post*.
>
> The kindergarten children sang "America" for us.
>
> "Who Will Be the New Bishop?" is the title of the first chapter of *Barchester Towers*.

3. Use quotation marks to enclose words taken from special vocabularies or used in a special sense:

> All the money he had won on the quiz program was invested in "blue chips."
>
> In certain sections of the United States a man who is both honest and good-natured is known as a "clever man."

19g Parentheses

Use parentheses to enclose certain parenthetic elements. From a study of the preceding marks of punctuation you will remember that commas and dashes are also used to set off parenthetic material. There are no clearly defined rules by which you can always determine which marks to use. In general, however, commas are used to set off a parenthetic element which is fairly closely connected with the thought of the sentence. Dashes are used to set off a loosely connected element such as an abrupt break in the thought of the sentence; they tend to emphasize the element set off. Parentheses are used to enclose (1) material that is supplementary or explanatory and (2) figures repeated to insure accuracy or used to designate an enumeration. An element enclosed by parentheses is usually even more loosely connected with the sentence than one set off by dashes; and parentheses, unlike dashes, tend to minimize the element set off:

> The *Ville de Nantes* (see Plate 5) is a large, semidouble, red and white camellia.
>
> I am enclosing a check for thirty-five dollars ($35.00).
>
> Please write on the card (1) your full name, (2) your home address, and (3) a parent's or guardian's full name.

19h Brackets

Use brackets to enclose any interpolation, or insertion, which you add to material that is being quoted. (You will note that in this text brackets are used to enclose explanations which follow illustrative sentences.)

> In September, 1793, Robert Burns wrote a letter which included this sentence: "So may God ever defend the cause of truth and liberty as he did that day [the day of Bruce's victory over Edward II at Bannockburn]."

If one parenthetical expression falls within another, then brackets replace the inner parentheses:

> Thomas Turner, a member of the Class of 1981, (Mr. Turner was his class valedictorian [See Athens *Banner-Herald* story, May 16, 1981] and class president) has been named a Rhodes Scholar.

| Exercise 68 | THE COMMA |

In the following sentences insert commas wherever they are needed. If a sentence is punctuated correctly, mark it **C**.

EXAMPLE: Yes,∧ thank you,∧ I will have more chocolate pudding.

1. Gloria please remember to leave the key under the mat for Uncle Rob who is arriving at midnight.

2. Pretending that she knew nothing of the missing diary Roberta managed to avoid close questioning.

3. The word *flaunt* is often misused to mean *flout.*

4. Margie called "I've been looking everywhere for you Frances!"

5. While I was reading Carrie's letter came in the afternoon mail.

6. Honestly I can hardly believe that we are finally here in Nome Alaska.

7. The plaintive wailing call of the screech owl came to us as we sat close together around the campfire.

8. Jerry looks as though he will soon be six feet tall doesn't he?

9. I looked cautiously up and down the street and then crossed safely to the other side.

10. To Miriam Marshall appeared haughty and aloof.

11. John is however not prepared to undertake this trip without the support of the entire group.

12. Having been ready for hours Nora paced the floor and fumed with exasperation.

13. To be sympathetic and practical at the same time is often difficult.

14. In the distance the skyline of the city appeared; above the dark clouds of a thunderstorm hovered menacingly.

15. I must renew my five-year driver's license on July 15 1984.

16. "You are mistaken" she replied "in assuming that I will readily agree to your proposal."

17. After he had arranged for Margaret to take care of his goldfish Charlie left for Edinburgh Scotland.

18. Jane was terribly hurt when Oliver rejected her proposal of marriage.

19. Working hard in order to be a successful salesman Harry found little time for a social life.

20. Shakespeare's play *Much Ado about Nothing* is a fast-moving rollicking comedy.

21. Before they left for the theater Henry and his wife Joan put the baby to bed and walked the dog.

22. The beds were made the dishes were washed and dried the cat was fed and I was ready for a nap.

23. I could see that he was unwilling to hear my argument; moreover I was afraid that he was prejudiced against me.

24. In the quiet dusk the only sound was that of the katydids.

25. The four boys — Jim Steve Bud and Tommy — decided to go out for their school's soccer team.

26. Frankly I believe that you have gained weight again this summer.

27. Norman my friend who lives in Dothan Alabama is coming for a visit in November.

28. The hot dry summer has given way to a raw drizzly fall.

29. Bursting into tears he tried desperately to explain the reason for his broken promise.

30. Before you came we were trying to decide where to go for lunch.

31. To catch a fish one must have the proper equipment.

32. To catch a fish is an exhilarating experience.

33. We lay in the sun on the warm lake shore; throughout the day had been a perfect one.

| Exercise 69 | THE COMMA |

In the following sentences insert commas wherever they are needed. If a sentence is punctuated correctly, mark it **C**.

EXAMPLE: Joe∧ Dave∧ and Ben are heading for Springfield∧ Illinois.

1. I would not please believe me want to see you drop out of college in mid-quarter.

2. The house that stands on the corner belongs to Mrs. Delaney a retired actress.

3. I wanted to try on the coat that was in Burdine's window because I have always like purple.

4. Jonathan asked "When have you last seen our friend Frances?"

5. Before you set the table Martha wash the goblets and the silver.

6. The delicious warmth of the soft lightweight down comforter made me drift quickly off to sleep.

7. As many have said before me it was the humidity not the heat that made us uncomfortable.

8. Working manfully in spite of the driving rain were three men in ankle-length raincoats and knee boots.

9. Well∧ you don't need me to tell you that you did a stupid thing Jacqueline.

10. George walked the two miles to his office this morning but he was too tired to walk home.

11. Writing my essay in longhand I developed writer's cramp after the first five hundred words.

12. Writing my essay in longhand made me realize that I needed a typewriter.

13. Yes I did agree to drive you to the campus but I didn't know that you planned to wash your hair first.

14. Jack who considers himself an excellent cook can never seem to master the mysteries of the microwave oven.

15. As the Prince's rich elegant gold carriage came into view the two children danced with excitement.

16. In our family it is a tradition to spend Thanksgiving at my grandparents' home which is in Pennsylvania.

17. Dora and Lydia two girls whom I met at camp last summer are going to be my college roommates.

18. We all agreed that Tyler's speech was disorganized uninteresting and outrageously long.

19. So far you have been doing well in school Matthew; nevertheless you cannot relax your efforts until the end of the year.

20. In the middle of the examination Charlotte developed a headache and did poorly on the rest of the test.

21. The thread that I used to mend your torn pocket was not the right color unfortunately.

22. The book a stinging satiric indictment of modern society has received excellent reviews from the critics.

23. While we were watching two deer walked majestically into the clearing.

24. Tony was amazed to put it mildly that Elise had never been to New York.

25. My but I wish I had an appetite like yours Mr. McGregor.

26. Terence was reading the Flannery O'Connor novel *Wise Blood* when Mother called him to dinner.

27. Thinking that I would surprise Martin with a party I was disappointed that Joe gave the secret away.

28. I need a new ribbon for my typewriter so I will buy one tomorrow.

29. "Let me know what time you want to go skating today " said Penelope.

30. Just for Suzanne Milton was willing to drive twenty miles back to pick up the sweater she had left behind.

| Exercise 70 | THE COLON AND THE DASH |

In the following sentences insert colons and dashes wherever they are needed. If a sentence is correctly punctuated, mark it **C**.

EXAMPLE: There is one game that I have never understood: backgammon.

1. Marianne, please bring my red jacket that's hanging in the oh, never mind; here it is in the kitchen.

2. Rose said that she plans to take the 9 45 plane from Indianapolis to Detroit.

3. Here is a list of the people who will go on the skiing trip with us Mary Horton, George Sanderson, Millie Thomas, Frank O'Neill, and Bob Allen.

4. Jacob Fitzsimmons has written a new book entitled *The Conservatives   A Portrait of the Far Right.*

5. Of the three names mentioned as possible candidates Leo Martinez, Greg Northrup, and Charles Wilkins only one was familiar to me Leo Martinez.

6. I think that now is a good time for us don't interrupt me while I'm talking, Sandra to wash the blankets and put them away for the summer.

7. Suddenly I remembered an important clue to Mr. Rathbone's disappearance the mysterious woman in black who had followed him home.

8. She never complained such was her easy nature about having to do all the housework while her two sisters lay about and read silly novels.

9. Those present at our big family reunion included my great-grandfather, his brother Amos, and his sister Amelia.

10. Hugh's letter to the editor began as follows "Dear Sir Please cancel my subscription to your paper, which I consider a striking example of yellow journalism."

11. Henry had left his tools a rake, a hoe, a spade, and a garden hose scattered all over the yard.

12. For her birthday Jenny received a bottle of perfume, a pair of earrings, a lavender sweater, and a generous check from Aunt Maude.

13. When we finally found him, Joe was entangled in briars, and his face can you imagine it? was scratched and bleeding.

14. Many trees in the woods behind our house dogwood, maple, hickory, and sweet gum turn beautiful colors in autumn.

15. My advice to you is to take an expert Don Lopez, for instance the first time you hike the Appalachian Trail.

16. In our Shakespeare class we studied only these plays *King Lear, Macbeth, Othello,* and *Hamlet.*

17. Dorothy said, "We will just have to start the meeting without well, at last you're here, James."

18. All the refreshments for the party were provided by Mrs. Sanders, Mrs. Harrison, and Mrs. Tupper.

19. The new club handbook listed all the important events for the coming year installation of officers, club picnic, field trip to Savannah, Christmas party, and attic sale.

20. Mrs. Muse, usually a quiet and retiring person, stood up and shouted we were all stunned that the basketball coach should be fired.

| Exercise 71 | QUOTATION MARKS |

In the following sentences insert quotation marks wherever they are needed. If a sentence is correctly punctuated, mark it **C**.

EXAMPLE: The excited driver shouted, ⱽYes, officer, I am on my way to a
fire.ⱽ

1. Mother has an old recording of Louis Armstrong singing Honeysuckle Rose.

2. Frankly, said David, I'd like to see someone other than the Yankees win the American League pennant.

3. Are you certain that it was General Sherman who said, War is hell ?

4. I don't know when I have enjoyed a short story as much as I did Eudora Welty's Why I Live at the P.O.

5. In the Southern United States a burlap bag is sometimes called a croker sack.

6. I believe, Lucile told me, that you are heading for disaster on that ski slope.

7. Sadie told Mark that he didn't deserve another piece of cake.

8. Did you know that William Faulkner wrote a short mystery story entitled Smoke ?

9. I am surprised, said Mrs. Franklin, that not one of you knows all the words to The Star-Spangled Banner.

10. Pierce said that it took him two months to finish reading Tolstoy's great novel *War and Peace.*

11. After spending the summer in Mexico, Kay went around calling everybody amigo.

12. When will you learn, groaned Father, that I am not made of money ?

13. Horace and Jennie drove to the party in the old car that they call their rattletrap.

14. When Fred kept talking about goobers, I didn't know that he was referring to peanuts.

15. One of the first poems that I ever memorized was William Cullen Bryant's To a Waterfowl.

16. Please tell me, said Thomas, why Nora said to me, You have made a terrible mistake.

17. Aunt Nellie has been poring over *Southern Living* for hours; she's copying recipes from an article called Squash Surprises.

18. Although Alice is eighteen years old now, her father still refers to her as Baby Dumpling.

19. Jack exclaimed, I think that the Reverend Mr. Booth was quoting a line from Milton's sonnet On His Blindness !

20. Yes, replied Joan, it was the last line: They also serve who only stand and wait.

| Exercise 72 | REVIEW OF PUNCTUATION |

In the following sentences insert all necessary punctuation marks. If a sentence is correctly punctuated, mark it **C**.

EXAMPLE: "Violence," says Terkel," is the seed of drama — and, by natural extension, of film and television."

1. I had no hammer or pliers so I couldn't repair the lock on our pantry door.

2. I understand that the winters in Boise Idaho are cold and long but that otherwise it is a fine city.

3. Here is Martha Harcourt's address 455 Longstreet Avenue Clemson South Carolina.

4. Carefully turning the eggs in the skillet Kitty cooked them without breaking a single yolk.

5. My mother's brother Harrison Dunbar lives all year round in a small cottage on the coast of Maine.

6. Catherine Mercer a child psychiatrist will speak tonight to a group of interested parents the title of her talk is Children's Fears.

7. That is an attractive girl whom Bart brought to the square dance however I hear that she is engaged to Frank Morris.

8. The smooth grassy knoll was a perfect spot for a picnic and we were delighted that there was not an ant in sight.

9. Those two pretty blonde girls are cousins not sisters Eileen.

10. Gloria simply refused to learn trigonometry in the tenth grade consequently she had to take it over the next year.

11. Norma is sure insisted Mr. Franklin that she left her glasses in the back seat of Dorothy's car.

12. In Kathy Norman's humorous book *Cats and Their Owners* the first chapter is called Myths and Facts about Cats.

13. Inside the old mansion was dusty and dank the empty rooms echoed strangely as we whispered to each other.

14. Arthur's youngest brother Bill wants to be a professional baseball player as soon as he finishes college.

15. Ruth said to Naomi Entreat me not to leave you.

16. The woman who sells tickets at the Roxy Theater is my nextdoor neighbor.

17. Jerry please wipe your feet before oh goodness you've already left mud on the carpet.

18. You are planning to help Todd make the casserole for supper aren't you Marcia?

19. Peggy has often told me that her future husband must be handsome rich and witty.

20. The popular Professor Sargent camellia see Figure 2 usually blooms in late February.

21. Jessica ran upstairs she closed her door and she took out the velvet box containing the diamond necklace.

22. Well I do believe that this is the place we have been searching for Walter's Cove.

23. This is the new book by Foster Stearns the title is *William Shakespeare A Study of the Man and His Work*.

24. The four of us Harry Joe Don and Rob hope to find summer jobs in Oregon.

25. The cat said Lucy is trying to get in the back door.

| Exercise 73 | REVIEW OF PUNCTUATION |

In the following sentences insert all necessary punctuation marks. If a sentence is correctly punctuated, mark it **C**.

EXAMPLE: He began to compose⌒chamber music,^ songs,^ piano pieces,^ an octet⌒ and his schoolmates chipped in to buy him music paper.

1. Here is the problem Rosemary wants us to stay overnight with her but we must be back in Nashville by 9 30 tomorrow morning.

2. Most of the so-called Watergate plumbers have now been released from jail.

3. Jane Jenkins president of Jenkins Incorporated is a graduate of the Massachusetts Institute of Technology.

4. Follow these simple directions to start the dishwasher 1 Put dishwasher powder into the receptacle in the door; 2 shut the dishwasher door and secure the latch; and 3 press the button marked *Full Cycle* on the control panel.

5. You see don't you Katie that I cannot go shopping with you until the baby has been put to bed?

6. Jasper has named his favorite cities as follows Asheville North Carolina Houston Texas Savannah Georgia and London England.

7. For her trying to learn Latin grammar was the most difficult task of her life.

8. Alice thought and thought and finally decided that she would make chess pie for dessert.

9. Being ready to begin the trip I was impatient that my fellow-travelers were late.

10. Being ready on time to begin a trip can be frustrating if one's fellow-travelers are late.

11. Patricia's lovely apple-green chiffon dress complemented her delicate fair-haired beauty.

12. Joanna Whitman standing at the podium read the minutes of the last meeting.

13. On January 3 1984 my parents will observe their thirtieth wedding anniversary.

14. The English poet A. E. Housman has written several poems containing a grim sort of humor.

15. The bus having left without me I called Father to pick me up.

16. While watching the dreary incessant rain I thought sadly of my disrupted plans and I finally broke down and wept bitterly.

17. The word *fond* no longer means what it meant in the sixteenth century.

18. Only we two Frank Cartwright and I thought that Jed would be good in the part of Willy Loman.

19. I want to be in the front pew of the church said Mother when Janet gets married.

20. Mr. Morrison said that he thought I was doing the right thing to hand in my resignation.

21. Yes you should write your name and address on the application your age however is not required.

22. Robert announced The polls will close at 7 00 P.M. as usual David however did not hear him.

23. I understand that Coach Riley has called Tim the backbone of the team.

24. Whenever I eat pumpkin pie I remember the wonderful Thanksgiving dinners we used to have at Aunt Annie's.

25. Dr. Felton asked Who wrote the poem that begins O Rose, thou art sick! ?

20

Mechanics: Capital Letters, Italics, the Apostrophe, the Hyphen

20a Capital Letters

1. Capitalize the first word of a sentence, of a line of traditional poetry, and of a direct quotation:

> All the students attended the meeting.

> Under a spreading chestnut-tree
> The village smithy stands.

> He said, "She does not wish to see you."

2. Capitalize proper nouns, words used as proper nouns, and adjectives derived from proper nouns:

> Great Britain, William, the Bible

> President, Senator, Captain, University (when these are used with or substituted for the name of a particular president, senator, captain, or university), and similarly

> Mother, Grandfather, Uncle (as in *We told Mother to go to bed, We bought Grandfather a bicycle,* and *We buried Uncle in Arlington Cemetery,* but not in *My mother is ill, His grandfather is eighty-two,* and *Our uncle was wounded at Gettysburg*)

> British, Shakespearean, Biblical, Scandinavian

3. Capitalize the names of days, months, and holidays:

> Monday, February, Fourth of July, Ash Wednesday, Veterans Day

4. Capitalize the names of historical periods and events:

> The Middle Ages, the French Revolution, the Battle of the Bulge, the Reformation

5. Capitalize the first word in the titles of books, chapters, essays, short stories, short

poems, songs, and works of art. Capitalize also all other words in these titles except articles, prepositions, and conjunctions:

> *The Last of the Mohicans,* "Without Benefit of Clergy," "Ode to the West Wind," "Only a Bird in a Gilded Cage," El Greco's *View of Toledo*

6. Capitalize names of the Deity, religions, and religious organizations:

> Jehovah, God, the Redeemer, Buddhism, Church of England, Society of Jesus, Order of St. Francis

7. Capitalize the names of governing bodies, political parties, governmental agencies, and civic and social organizations:

> The House of Commons, the Senate, the Democratic Party, the Internal Revenue Department, the Chamber of Commerce, Daughters of the American Revolution

8. Capitalize the points of the compass when they refer to a specific region but not when they indicate direction:

> He lived in the East all his life.
>
> They traveled west for about a hundred miles and then turned south.

9. Capitalize the names of studies only if they are derived from proper nouns or are the names of specific courses of instruction:

> He was studying physics, chemistry, and German.
>
> He failed in Mathematics 101 and in Human Biology 1.

10. Capitalize personfications:

> O wild West Wind, thou breath of Autumn's being.
>
> Daughters of Time, the hypocritic Days.
>
> Be with me, Beauty, for the fire is dying.

20b Italics

1. Italicize words that you wish to emphasize. (In manuscript indicate italics by underlining.)

> Do you mean to say that she ate them *all*?
>
> It could hardly have been *the* Robert Frost.

NOTE: Use this device sparingly. Frequent use of italics for emphasis is a sign of an immature style.

2. Italicize numbers, letters, and words referred to as such:

> He made his *7* and his *9* very much alike.
>
> She has never yet learned to pronounce *statistics.*
>
> In his handwriting he employs the old-fashioned *s.*

3. Italicize the names of books, magazines, and newspapers. (Smaller units of books, such as chapters, stories, essays, and poems, are usually set in quotation marks.)

A Tale of Two Cities, the *Atlantic Monthly,* the Atlanta *Journal*

NOTE: In the names of newspapers or magazines it is not always necessary to italicize the definite article or the name of a city.

4. Italicize the names of ships, trains, and airplanes:

The *Queen Elizabeth,* the *Twentieth-Century Limited,* the *Spirit of St. Louis*

5. Italicize foreign words and phrases in an English context:

The *coup d'état* led to his becoming emperor.

6. Italicize the titles of paintings, statues, and other works of art:

Gainesborough's *Blue Boy,* Rodin's *The Thinker*

20c The Apostrophe

1. Use the apostrophe and *s* to form the possessive case of singular nouns:

The boar's head, Mary's lamb, the boss's orders

NOTE: Proper names ending in *s* may form the possessive by adding *'s* if the resulting word is not unpleasant or difficult to sound:

Keats's poems, Charles's work, *but* Ulysses' return

2. Use an apostrophe without *s* to form the possessive of plural nouns ending in *s:*

Soldiers' quarters, boys' clothes

3. Use an apostrophe and *s* to form the possessive of plural nouns not ending in *s:*

Men's coats, children's shoes, the alumni's contributions

4. The possessive of words indicating time is formed like the possessive of other nouns:

A week's delay, a day's journey, *but* a two days' visit

5. The apostrophe is frequently omitted in the names of organizations and institutions:

The Farmers Hardware Company, Boys High School, State Teachers College

6. In forming the possessives of compounds, use the apostrophe according to the meaning and the logic of the construction:

Beaumont and Fletcher's plays [Plays written by Beaumont and Fletcher jointly.]
Smith's and Jones's children [The children of Smith and the children of Jones.]
John and Mary's house [The house belonging to John and Mary.]
Somebody else's business [The business of somebody else.]

7. Use an apostrophe to indicate the omission of letters in contractions and of digits in numerals:

Isn't, don't, 'tis
The cat's had kittens.
The Class of '23

NOTE: Be sure that the apostrophe is placed at the exact point where the letter or digit is omitted. Do not write *is'nt, do'nt.*

8. Use an apostrophe and *s* to indicate the plural of letters, numerals, signs, and words used as such:

Dot your *i*'s and cross your *t*'s.

His telephone number contains four *8*'s.

In your next theme omit the *&* 's.

He uses too many *so*'s.

20d The Hyphen

In English, compounds are made in three ways:

(1) by writing the words solid (*bedroom, watchmaker, starlight*),

(2) by writing them separately (*ice cream, motion picture, mountain lion*), or

(3) by separating the words with a hyphen (*name-caller, ne'er-do-well, finger-paint*).

The resulting confusion, like so much confusion in English, lies in the fact that the language is constantly changing. A compound may begin its career as two words; then it may move on to the form with a hyphen; and finally it may end as a solid formation—its destiny accomplished, as it were. So we have *bedroom* (written solid) but *dining room* (two words). We have the noun *bluepoint* to refer to an oyster, but we use the two words *blue point* to describe a Siamese cat. A decision may be *far-reaching,* but a forecaster is *farseeing.* The only solution to this confusing problem is to consult a dictionary. But this authority is not always satisfactory because many compounds are made for the occasion and are not in the dictionary— and dictionaries may disagree. Furthermore, a compound with a hyphen may be correct in one part of a sentence and incorrect in another, or it may be correct as a noun and incorrect as a verb. The stylebook of one publisher says, "If you take hyphens seriously, you will surely go mad." Nevertheless, there is a sort of logic in the use of the hyphen, as well as a kind of common sense; furthermore, one can learn some of the pitfalls to avoid.

Consider the following sentences:

He is a great admirer of Henry Kissinger, the ex-Republican Secretary of State. [Is Mr. Kissinger no longer a Republican? The phrase should read *the former Republican Secretary of State.*]

The parents enjoyed their children's recreation of the first Thanksgiving. [In this sentence *re-creation* is the appropriate word, and the hyphen distinguishes it from *recreation.*]

I would think that your sixteen year old brother could scramble an egg. [In this sentence *sixteen, year,* and *old* form a compound modifier and should be hyphenated. The phrase should read *your sixteen-year-old brother.*]

He introduced me to his uncle, an old car enthusiast. [Is his uncle old? Or is his uncle interested in old cars? The phrase is clarified with a hyphen: *an old-car enthusiast.*]

Did you hear the reporter's interview with the singing whale authority? [Did the reporter interview a whale authority who sings or an authority on singing whales? Appropriate hyphenation clears up the confusion; the phrase should read *with the singing-whale authority.*]

The following rules indicate common practice and are fairly reliable:

1. Compound numerals (*twenty-one* through *ninety-nine*) are always written with a hyphen:

> Twenty-six, forty-eight, fifty-two

2. Fractions are written with a hyphen if they are adjectival:

> His speech was one-third fact and two-thirds demagoguery.
> *But*   Three fourths of the apples are rotten.

3. Compounds with *self* are written with a hyphen:

> Self-styled, self-taught, self-centered

Note the exceptions *selfsame, selfhood, selfless.*

4. The hyphen is used in certain expressions of family relationship:

> Great-grandfather, great-aunt

5. Most compounds beginning with *ex, pre,* and *pro* are written with a hyphen:

> Ex-president, pre-Christian, pro-British

6. The hyphen is commonly used with compounds with prepositional phrases:

> Mother-in-law, stick-in-the-mud, heart-to-heart

7. One of the commonest uses of hyphens is to form compound modifiers for nouns and pronouns:

> An eight-year-old child, a well-done steak, a blue-green sea

NOTE: Such compounds are hyphenated when they immediately precede the word they modify, but frequently they are not hyphenated when they are used predicatively:

> His well-spoken words pleased the audience [*but* His words were well spoken].
> She made a number of off-the-record comments [*but* Her comments were made off the record].

8. Hyphens are used in coined or occasional compounds:

> She gave him a kind of you-ought-to-know-better look.
> Her bird-on-the-nest hat was sensational.

9. The hyphen is used in compound nouns that name the same person in two different capacities:

> Author-publisher, musician-statesman, tycoon-playboy

10. The hyphen is frequently used to avoid confusion between words:

> Re-claim [to distinguish from *reclaim*]
> Re-cover [to distinguish from *recover*]

11. Hyphens are used to avoid clumsy spellings:

Bull-like, semi-independent, ante-election, pre-empt

NOTE: *Cooperate* and *coordinate* are common enough to be accepted.

12. The hyphen is used at the end of a line of writing to indicate the division of a word continued on the next line. The division must always come at the end of a syllable. Do not divide words of one syllable:

PROPER DIVISIONS: con-tin-ued, in-di-cate, au-di-ence

IMPROPER DIVISIONS: wo-rd, laugh-ed, comp-ound

NOTE: If you are uncertain about the division of a word, consult your dictionary.

| Exercise 74 | CAPITALS |

In the following sentences change the small letters to capital letters wherever necessary and vice versa. If a sentence is correct as it stands, mark it **C**.

EXAMPLE: Uncle f̶red has gone on an a̶frican s̶afari and plans to return home by way of s̶outh America.

(with corrections: F, A, S, S marked above the letters)

1. When I was a Freshman in college, I used a poetry text called *Sound And Sense.*

2. Although English and French are easy for me, I have always had trouble with Mathematics.

3. Being over ninety years old, my Grandfather now plays golf only four times a week instead of six.

4. Ernie is my first cousin, and Sam is Ernie's first cousin, but Sam and I are not related.

5. Theo's sunday school teacher asked each student to recite his favorite verse from the bible.

6. Moving Eastward, the heavy thunderstorm struck our area at about midnight.

7. Browsing through the attic the other day, I came upon a copy of that old Zane Grey classic *Riders Of The Purple Sage.*

8. Although she has lived in the north most of her life, Susan has picked up a southern drawl very quickly.

9. My drama teacher is an englishwoman, and naturally her favorite plays are the shakespearean ones.

10. Harvey made an unforgivable error in our history 155 class today; he said that the norman conquest took place in 1076.

11. Formosa is the former name of taiwan, which is located off the coast of the chinese mainland.

12. My Mother and Father love to dance to the old Benny Goodman records; one of their favorites is "A String Of Pearls."

13. I believe that Frances is President of her Garden Club.

14. Sidney Lanier's poem "Song of the Chattahoochee" was written about the Chattahoo-

chee river.

15. When we were in London, we visited the English houses of parliament and saw the famous

clock big ben.

| Exercise 75 | ITALICS |

In the following sentences underline all words that should be *italicized.* If a sentence is correct as it stands, mark it **C.**

EXAMPLE: After reading <u>Gone with the Wind,</u> I wished that Margaret Mitchell had written other novels.

1. Do you think that the crossword puzzles in the Baltimore Sun are hard?

2. Last summer the Faulkners cruised around the British Isles on a ship called Regina Maris.

3. The word ski originated in Norway.

4. I have always admired Tennyson's imagery in his poem "The Eagle."

5. Arthur Miller has written numerous plays, but my favorite is still Death of a Salesman.

6. Aunt Margaret has given Mother a subscription to the beautiful magazine Architectural Digest for her birthday.

7. When you arrive in Barcelona, Bridget, be sure to mind your p's and q's.

8. As we departed on our journey, the old priest whispered to us, "Deus vobiscum."

9. I hope that you can visit the Louvre Museum when you are in Paris; you will enjoy seeing the famous sculpture Venus de Milo.

10. Mr. Karloff, did you know that the poet Shelley's wife, Mary, wrote the horror novel Frankenstein?

11. Apparently your definition of the word happiness and mine are not the same, Millicent.

12. I will try—please remember that I said try—to get us two tickets to the Army-Navy game.

13. I felt definitely de trop as I entered the room and saw that the situation was quite tense.

14. Have you seen all the episodes of the Masterpiece Theater production A Town like Alice?

15. A print of Titian's painting Lavinia hangs over the sideboard in the Walkers' dining room.

16. She was interested to learn that there are two operas based on Shakespeare's Othello.

17. The Latin term amicus curiae is applied to a person who advises or is asked to advise a court on a pending case to which he is not a party.

18. It is hard to believe that Bart was reluctant—no, unwilling—to help us change the flat tire.

19. The 7 in this check that you gave me looks too much like a 1.

20. Becky says that it is now de rigueur among her friends to have cheese for dessert instead of a sweet.

| Exercise 76 | THE APOSTROPHE |

In the following sentences underline all words that should have apostrophes and all those that have apostrophes incorrectly used; then write the word(s) correctly in the space at the right. If a sentence is correct, mark it **C**.

EXAMPLE: I cant believe that Frances didn't pass French 102.   *can't*

1. The waiter says therell be a fifteen-minute wait for a table.   _____

2. The Smiths little girl was born on the Fourth of July.   _____

3. Sara says that my new blazer is prettier than her's.   _____

4. Please do'nt walk on my newly planted grass, Don.   _____

5. In the new department store the boys clothing is just next to the
    men's clothing.   _____

6. An hours relaxation in peace and quiet will do you good.   _____

7. The closet space in Mary and Lillie's apartment leaves something to
    be desired.   _____

8. The dog ran away quickly with it's tail between it's legs.   _____

9. Its amazing that Tommy ate his lemon pie in about two minutes after
    dawdling over his spinach.   _____

10. Whats going to be done about the terrible traffic problem caused by
    the collapsed bridge?   _____

11. The class's decision to sponsor a car-wash was made after long and
    heated discussion.   _____

12. Theres' no way that I know of to prevent Ellen's using the hair dryer
    just when I need it most.   _____

13. The womens soccer game last Saturday was just as exciting as Agnes
    had said it would be.   _____

14. I believe that thats a new skirt Joanna is wearing, Mabel, and it's just
    like your's.   _____

15. The Wilson's are planning to give a party on New Years Eve.   _____

16. Gilbert's and Robert's new puppy is a Golden Labrador, and they've
    named him Brandy.   _____

17. We are all fervently hoping that Johnny will graduate in the Class
    of 83.   _____

18. Marty said, "Last night I really found out that threes a crowd."   _____

19. Tony's going to lend us his flashlight because our's has a dead battery. _____

20. We all sat quiet as Grandfather began reading the familiar words:
    "Twas the night before Christmas . . . ."   _____

Exercise 77	THE HYPHEN

In the sentences below underline the incorrect compounds and write the correct forms at the right. If a sentence is correct, mark it **C**. Some sentences contain more than one error.

EXAMPLE: The noted <u>author critic</u> will review current fiction
in his weekly column.   *author-critic*

1. Joan is taking a three month leave of absence in order to
   make a leisurely tour of Europe.   _____

2. I stood and gazed at the ivy covered walls of the decaying
   old mansion.   _____

3. Aline is well known in our community for her historic
   preservation activities.   _____

4. It is a shame that you had to return empty handed from
   the search for your lost wallet.   _____

5. The protest march by the anti nuclear demonstrators was
   carried out with respect for law and order.   _____

6. Valerie walked into the living room, sat down on the love
   seat, and calmly announced that she and Tom were married. _____

7. I have lived in Texas for twenty three years and in Arkansas
   for only three.   _____

8. William gave Mike a terrible tongue lashing for failing to
   keep their appointment on time.   _____

9. I think that Donald is a good choice for master of cere-
   monies; he has the know how to do the job splendidly.   _____

10. There is a falllike nip in the air tonight though it is still
    only August.   _____

11. Jennie is a gentle person, who has a peace at any price
    attitude.   _____

12. Virginia has a job as sales clerk in the ladies' ready to wear department of a new shop.

_____

13. The masons had to relay the brick walk because it was uneven at first.

_____

14. My fifteen year old sister is a self taught dressmaker.

_____

15. Tony is pleased that he was recently given a cost of living raise.

_____

16. Ronnie told the selfsame half truths that he has been telling for years.

_____

17. My parttime job has very good hours, so I often have a little rest and relaxation period in the afternoons.

_____

18. Jack's newest form of recreation is reading one of those cloak and dagger novels far into the night.

_____

19. Television's recreation of the King Edward Mrs. Simpson story is an intriguing drama.

_____

20. Marie's great grandmother was born in France but came to the United States when she was twenty one.

_____

| Exercise 78 | **REVIEW OF MECHANICS** |

Underline the errors in mechanics in the following sentences, and then write the correct forms in the spaces at the right. If a sentence is correct, mark it **C**.

EXAMPLE: Mother and Father took us to the San Diego <u>Zoo,</u>   _____*Zoo*_____

which is known to be one of the best in the <u>Nation.</u>   _____*nation*_____

1. I'll never forget Gilberts diving from the high board when the rest of us were afraid to try it. _____

2. Traveling Northeastward from Detroit, we hoped to reach Toronto by nightfall. _____

3. A seven hour flight across the Atlantic ocean is a pleasant way to get to London. _____ _____

4. The emeraldlike green of the grass is a lovely setting for that white house. _____

5. I think that the Smith's were hoping that the lucky lottery ticket would be their's. _____ _____

6. Nick had told his Mother that he would study his Economics last night, but he went to the skating rink instead. _____ _____

7. Robert squandered two months salary on a stereo that he never has time to enjoy. _____

8. Janet, do you fully understand Keats poem "Ode On A Grecian Urn"? _____ _____

9. Mr. Jackson, an ex football player, is coaching a group of teen age boys in the afternoons. _____ _____

10. After having lived in Germany for several years, Mark always says, "Auf Wiedersehen" when leaving his friends. _____

11. The wind had scattered the pages of his manuscript far and wide, and it took us an hour to recollect them. _____

12. Marjorie and Vic spent hours arguing about whether the first c _____
in the word arctic is pronounced. _____

13. Robbie says that his Grandfather still favors turn of the century _____
music, clothing, and manners. _____

14. Quincy is serving as pro tempore head of the group, but we
must soon elect a permanent chairman. _____

15. Harry says that he wo'nt be able to join us at daytona beach _____
until Tuesday. _____

16. Have you ever read John Crowe Ransoms poem "Bells for John _____
Whiteside's daughter"? _____

17. My professor in Horticulture 101 is a Japanese bonsai
enthusiast. _____

18. Most of Socrates philosophic sayings are still true in the
modern world. _____

19. Do you know when the legal voting age was reduced from
twenty-one to eighteen? _____

20. Our voyage on the Queen Elizabeth II has been cancelled. _____

21

Use of the Dictionary

A convenient and valuable source of linguistic information is a standard dictionary. It is easy to use, and, if used intelligently, very informative. Many people do not realize that a dictionary contains important facts far beyond simple definitions and guides to pronunciation and spelling. One of the best investments that a college student can make is the purchase of a standard collegiate dictionary. Frequent use of a good dictionary is a necessary step toward the development of an effective vocabulary, but more importantly it is essential to any reader's understanding of the material he encounters daily. In any college course, in the newspapers, and in regular communication with others, the student will read and hear unfamiliar words. An alert student's desire to learn the meaning, spelling, and pronunciation of a new word will lead him to a dictionary that can provide this information along with other facts such as the derivation of the word, its level of usage, discussions of its synonyms, and frequently an antonym which will illuminate still further its precise shade of meaning.

The best dictionaries have taken years of preparation by hundreds of workers directed by the finest scholars of the time. Unabridged dictionaries are absolutely comprehensive in their explanations and descriptions of words, containing thousands more entries than the more commonly used desk dictionary. In the United States perhaps the best-known unabridged dictionary is *Webster's Third New International Dictionary of the English Language*, often called simply *Webster's Third*. It was published by the G. & C. Merriam Company of Springfield, Mass., in 1961; there have been several subsequent printings with minor additions and changes. This work, though it is too bulky to be used as a casual desk dictionary (and for most purposes unnecessary), may be found when you need it in your college library.

Any one of several extremely reliable collegiate dictionaries is the best choice for the college student. Severely abridged paperback editions of these dictionaries are a poor substitute, as they do not contain the detailed information which students may find necessary for specialized assignments in their courses. Most language authorities recommend the following standard college dictionaries: *Webster's Eighth New Collegiate Dictionary,* published by

G. & C. Merriam Co., Springfield, Mass.; *Webster's New World Dictionary of the American Language*, Simon and Schuster, New York; *The American Heritage Dictionary of the English Language*, The American Heritage Publishing Co., Inc., and Houghton Mifflin Co., Boston; *The Random House Dictionary of the English Language*, Random House, New York; *Funk and Wagnall's Standard Collegiate Dictionary*, Harcourt, Brace and World, Inc., New York.

Select one of these dictionaries and buy it as soon as you get to college, and then follow the list of suggestions given below in order to familiarize yourself with the dictionary and the ways in which you can get the maximum use from this very handy and easy-to-use reference work.

1.   Read all the introductory material in the front of the dictionary, because this explains what information the book has to offer. If some of it seems too scholarly for you to understand, read on, and at least find out what it is mainly concerned with and what you can expect to find in its entries.

2.   Study carefully the key to pronunciation, and check it with words that you know so that you will be sure of understanding it. A need for guidance in pronunciation is one of the most common reasons for consulting a dictionary.

3.   Refer often to the table of abbreviations which is most likely to be found inside the front cover of your dictionary. To save space, dictionaries necessarily use many abbreviations, and these are explained in the table. Become familiar with these abbreviations so that no piece of information escapes your notice.

4.   Examine the appendixes to learn what information is given in them. Some dictionaries list biographical and geographic information in their appendixes; others list them in the main entries in the book. Other information often found in the appendixes of a dictionary includes tables of interpretations of various specialized symbols, like those connected with mathematics, chemistry, music, chess, medicine, and pharmacy; a directory of colleges and universities; a table of weights and measures; a dictionary of English given names, etc.

One of the most important things a dictionary can tell you is the *level of usage* of a given term. The English language, ever-changing and full of colorful informality, functions on many levels. Young people may use the expression *laid back* to describe a person who has a relaxed, uncomplicated approach to life. Politicians and reporters use the term *bottom line* to mean the end result of something. An educated adult may in conversation refer to *lots of trouble*. And an editor of a magazine may write of the *dichotomy between work and leisure classes* or, in a book review, of an *involuted search for self*. Each of these expressions is in a sense proper in its own context. Judgment of a term as "good English" is usually determined by the level on which it is used. The magazine editor would not in a formal article use the term *laid back*; the youth of today would hardly think or write using terms like *dichotomy*. Your dictionary will tell you whether the use of a word in a particular sense is slang, informal (colloquial), dialectal, archaic, obsolete, or none of these, i.e., Standard English.

Slang is the term used to describe the spontaneous, vivid, and sometimes racy inventions used frequently in the speech and writings of groups like teen-agers, gangsters, popular musicians, soldiers, and sports writers—not that these groups necessarily have anything else in common. The life of a slang expression is usually short, but sometimes, if it is striking enough and colorful enough, it may gain universal usage and become at least an informal part of the national vocabulary.

The term *informal* or *colloquial* is applied to words or expressions which are acceptable in the speech of the educated but not in formal writing. It is all right to say, "He's going to have *lots of trouble* explaining his whereabouts on the night of June third," but it is not Standard English to write this statement formally.

Dialect, another usage label, means that a word or expression is common to the speech of a particular group or geographical region. *Archaic* means that the word or term is rarely used today except in certain contexts like church ritual, but that it may be found fairly frequently in early writings. *Obsolete* means that the term is no longer used, but may be found in early writings. In addition, as a part of its usage discussion, a dictionary will inform you if a word or term is commonly considered obscene, vulgar, or profane.

To see how a dictionary presents its information, consider now the following entry from *The Random House Dictionary of the English Language*:*

bur·den[1] (bûr'dᵊn), *n.* **1.** that which is carried; load: *a horse's burden of rider and pack.* **2.** that which is borne with difficulty; obligation or trouble: *the burden of leadership.* **3.** *Naut.* **a.** the weight of a ship's cargo. **b.** the carrying capacity of a ship: *a ship of a hundred-tons burden.* **4.** *Mining.* the earth or rock to be moved by a charge of explosives. **5.** *Accounting.* overhead (def. 6). —*v.t.* **6.** to load heavily. **7.** to load oppressively; trouble. [ME, var. of *burthen.* OE *byrthen;* akin to G *Bürde,* Goth *baurthei;* see BEAR[1]] —**bur'den·er,** *n.* —**bur'den·less,** *adj.* —**Syn. 1.** See **load.** **2.** weight, encumbrance, impediment.

Here we are given the correct spelling of the word *burden* and its proper division into syllables. The small numeral[1] after the entry word indicates that this is the first of two or more words which have the same spelling but which differ radically in meaning and derivation and are therefore listed separately. Next the proper pronunciation is given. It becomes clear immediately that you need to learn the significance of the signs, called diacritical marks, that are used to indicate pronunciation. In this entry the first five numbered definitions are preceded by *n* (for *noun*) and the last two by *v.t.* (for *verb, transitive*). After 3, *Naut.* (*Nautical*) means that the definitions given under 3 are special technical senses of the word as used in shipping. The same interpretation is true of definitions 4 and 5. The information in brackets gives the derivation or origin of the word. It tells that *burden* is a variant form of the older word *burthen,* which is derived from the Old English form *byrthen,* and that the word is linguistically akin to the word *bear* as described in the first *bear* entry elsewhere in the dictionary. Finally we learn that the synonyms of *burden*[1] are discussed under the entry *load.* The second entry, *burden*[2], is arranged on the same principles.

---

*Reproduced by permission from *The Random House Dictionary of the English Language,* The Unabridged Edition. Copyright ©1981 by Random House, Inc.

Consider now the following entry from *Webster's New World Dictionary of the American Language*:*

> **drunk** (druŋk) [ME. *dronke* < *drunken*: see DRUNKEN] *pp.* &
> *archaic pt.* of DRINK —*adj.* [*usually used in the predicate*] **1.**
> overcome by alcoholic liquor to the point of losing control
> over one's faculties; intoxicated **2.** overcome by any
> powerful emotion [*drunk* with joy] **3.** [Colloq.] *same as*
> DRUNKEN (sense 2) —*n.* [Slang] **1.** a drunken person **2.** a
> drinking spree
> *SYN.*—**drunk** is the simple, direct word, usually used in the
> predicate, for one who is overcome by alcoholic liquor [he is
> *drunk*]; **drunken**, usually used attributively, is equivalent to
> **drunk** but sometimes implies habitual, intemperate drinking of
> liquor [a *drunken* bum]; **intoxicated** and **inebriated** are euphe-
> misms, the former often expressing slight drunkenness and the
> latter, a state of drunken exhilaration; there are many euphemistic
> and slang terms in English expressing varying degrees of drunken-
> ness: e.g., **tipsy** (slight), **tight** (moderate, but without great loss
> of muscular coordination), **blind** (great), **blotto** (to the point
> of unconsciousness), etc. —*ANT.* **sober**

Here we learn that the adjective *drunk*, with the specific meanings that follow, is the past participle and was formerly a past tense of the verb *to drink*. Two definitions are given: the first of these is the common one; the second is often used figuratively. The discussion of synonyms gives us the fine shades of distinction among a group of words that mean essentially the same thing. In addition, one antonym, or word of opposite meaning, is given. The final part of the entry, defining *drunk* as a noun, explains that when the word is used as a noun, meaning a person in a drunken condition, or a period of heavy drinking, the word is slang.

The kind of knowledge that a good dictionary can give you far exceeds what has been discussed here. Every good dictionary, for instance, pays special attention to biography and geography. One can learn when Beethoven died and the name of the capital of Peru. One can find the height of Mount Everest and the approximate number of islands in the Philippines. Literature, mythology, and particularly science are well covered in the modern dictionary. Finally, special appendixes sometimes include such miscellaneous information as the meanings of common Christian names, foreign words and phrases, abbreviations, and the symbols used in the preparation of copy for the printer and in proofreading. Some books even contain a dictionary of rhymes. The following exercises illustrate the variety of information one may obtain from a good dictionary.

---

*By permission. From *Webster's New World Dictionary of the American Language*, Second College Edition. Copyright © 1982 by Simon and Schuster, Inc.

| Exercise 79 | WORD ORIGINS |

After each of the following words indicate in the first space at the right the first systematical-
ly recorded language from which the word is derived, and in the second space the meaning
of the source word.

	LANGUAGE	MEANING
EXAMPLE: nature	*Latin*	*born + act, process, or result of*
1. invade		
2. girdle		
3. flexible		
4. euphoria		
5. exalt		
6. enigma		
7. spirit		
8. supervise		
9. ruby		
10. mystery		
11. myriad		
12. nicotine		
13. noon		
14. noodle		
15. opal		
16. endorse		
17. bizarre		

18. brogue   _____   _____

19. bronco   _____   _____

20. cyclone   _____   _____

21. democracy   _____   _____

22. elope   _____   _____

23. every   _____   _____

24. false   _____   _____

25. human   _____   _____

Exercise 80	**BRITISH AND AMERICAN USAGE**

The following words illustrate differences between British and American usage. Write the equivalents of these British terms:

EXAMPLE: ironmonger   *hardware dealer*

 1. biscuit   _____

 2. bonnet   _____

 3. bounder   _____

 4. bowler   _____

 5. chemist   _____

 6. corn (n.)   _____

 7. draper   _____

 8. dustman   _____

 9. gaol   _____

10. geyser   _____

11. lift (n.)   _____

12. lorry   _____

13. pasty (n.)   _____

14. petrol   _____

15. pillarbox   _____

16. post (v.)   _____

17. pub   _____

18. queue (n.)   _____

19. rates   _____

20. removal   _____

21. roundabout (n.)   _____

22. sieve (v.)   _____

23. spanner   _____

24. sultanas   _____

25. sweet (n.)   _____

26. tin (n.)   _____

27. tipping (n.)   _____

28. torch   _____

29. underground (n.) or tube   _____

30. verge   _____

| Exercise 81 | PLURALS |

Write the plural form of each of the following nouns:

EXAMPLE: crisis   *crises*

1. tomato   _____

2. wolf   _____

3. bench   _____

4. month   _____

5. solo   _____

6. mouthful   _____

7. spy   _____

8. studio   _____

9. alumna   _____

10. woman   _____

11. donkey   _____

12. century   _____

13. fish   _____

14. knife   _____

15. phenomenon   _____

16. parenthesis   _____

17. Chinese   _____

18. maid-of-honor   _____

19. species   _____

20. echo   _____

21. soprano   _____

22. roof   _____

23. chimney   _____

24. calf   _____

25. goose   _____

26. lens   _____

27. cargo   _____

28. brush   _____

29. lieutenant colonel   _____

30. sister-in-law   _____

31. Englishman   _____

32. series   _____

33. tornado   _____

34. army   _____

35. trout   _____

| Exercise 82 | LEVELS OF USAGE |

After each of the following sentences indicate the level of usage of the *italicized* words or expressions, using these abbreviations:

A	for archaic,	**I**	for informal or colloquial,
D	for dialectal,	**S**	for slang.

NOTE: Most standard collegiate dictionaries agree in the classification of these words and expressions. Other dictionaries may differ in their classifications (or show none at all), so use a reliable collegiate dictionary when you need information about the usage level of an expression.

Dictionary used for this exercise: _____

EXAMPLE: We all had *ferocious* appetites after skating all day on the frozen pond.   *I*

1. Frank says that the boys cooked steaks and *spuds* over a campfire when they went on their overnight hike.   _____

2. Dianne reports that the dress that she will wear to the wedding is *"super."*   _____

3. The bank *heist* that took place last night was committed by two *guys* in stocking masks.   _____

4. Take *ahold* of that rope, Foster, and help me tie the Christmas tree to the top of the car.   _____

5. Aunt Janie says that we're invited to her house for Thanksgiving turkey and all the *fixings.*   _____

6. We heard that the police had *nabbed* a man and charged him with robbing a convenience store.   _____

7. You and your *folks* will be more comfortable here on the sofa, Vivian, than you will be on those hard chairs.   _____

8. Well, I'm tired and sleepy, so I think I'll go upstairs and *hit the sack.*   _____

9. Alas and *alack,* I cannot find my beautiful antique silver locket.   _____

10. Did you hear Mr. Gloucester say that the used-car salesman had *ripped him off?*   _____

11. Terry's story about being offered a big promotion turned out to be *baloney.*   _____

12. Gene said that he'd *swap* me his camera for my stereo.   _____

13. Harry vows that the best part of a mess of turnip greens is the *pot liquor* that he eats along with cornbread. _____

14. Robert really *lit into* Mariana about *standing him up* for their date. _____

15. Those *hoods* that stole Susie's hubcaps ought to be put in jail. _____

16. I hope that you were only *kidding* when you told me that you are quitting school. _____

17. Father says that his new secretary is young, ambitious, and *on the ball.* _____

18. Rachel was *plenty* angry when she saw the mess we had left in her kitchen. _____

19. Two boys on our baseball team had a *row* over who had more hits for the season. _____

20. You *dudes* give a *holler* when you're ready for lunch. _____

21. The two tramps were last seen on a south-bound *rattler* headed toward New Orleans. _____

22. It was Queen Gertrude in Shakespeare's *Hamlet* who said, "The lady *doth* protest too much." _____

23. We spent the afternoon *goofing off,* and now Mother is *fit to be tied.* _____

24. Irene tried to persuade Sally to go to Canada with her, but it was *no go.* _____

25. "I wish that you would *attend* me when I am speaking to you," said Miss Martin to her class. _____

| Exercise 83 | GENERAL INFORMATION |

Refer to your dictionary for the information you will need to fill in the blanks below.

EXAMPLE: Date of the Boston Tea Party: _____ *1773* _____

1. Area and population of the island of Crete: _____

2. Pursuits for which John James Audubon is notable: _____

   _____

3. Family of birds to which the bittern belongs: _____

4. Constellation in which the star Arcturus is seen: _____

5. Conference that took place at Bretton Woods, New Hampshire, in 1944: _____

   _____

6. Date of the annual Michaelmas celebration in England: _____

7. Pseudonym of Charles Lutwidge Dodgson and the work for which he is most famous: ___

   _____

8. Chief characteristics of the legendary Don Juan: _____

   _____

9. Word for which the letters EKG are used: _____

10. Ingredients in egg foo yong: _____

11. Location of the Gallipoli Peninsula: _____

   _____

12. Game in which the term *game point* is most frequently used: _____

13. Danish spelling of Copenhagen: _____

14. Location and name of the mountain range of which Mount McKinley is a part: _____

   _____

15. Name of the forest where Robin Hood and his followers lived: _____

16. Date of and price paid for the Louisiana Purchase: _____

17. Nationality of the composer Dmitri Shostakovich: _____

18. Name of the place of which Manxmen and Manxwomen are natives or inhabitants: _____

_____

19. Birth and death dates of Mao Tse-tung: _____

20. Country of which the koala is a native: _____

Exercise 84 | BORROWED FOREIGN EXPRESSIONS

The following words and expressions occur frequently in our everyday speech and writing.
They have been borrowed in their original forms from languages other than English and have
in most instances become integral parts of our language. After consulting your dictionary,
write the meaning of each expression and the language from which it has been borrowed.

EXAMPLE: blitzkrieg *sudden, swift offensive in war intended to gain quick victory (German)*

1. en masse _____

2. *Gesundheit* _____

3. desperado _____

4. non compos mentis _____

5. caballero _____

6. bamboo _____

_____

7. smorgasbord _____

8. crescendo _____

9. nabob _____

10. kayak _____

_____

11. luau _____

12. caveat emptor _____

13. sauerkraut _____

14. denouement _____

15. *carpe diem* _____

16. gendarme _____

_____

17. sombrero _____

18. faux pas _____

19. nolo contendere _____

_____

20. nom de plume _____

22
Diction

Diction is one's choice of words in the expression of ideas. Because one speaks and writes on various levels of usage, the same expression may be appropriate to one level but not to another. The diction, for instance, of formal writing seems overprecise in informal conversation, and the acceptable diction of everyday speech seems out of place in serious, formal composition. But on all levels of speech and writing, faulty diction appears—in wordiness, in trite expressions, and in faulty idiom.

22a Wordiness

Wordiness is the use of too many words—more words, that is, than are necessary to express an idea correctly and clearly. Many sentences written by college students may be greatly improved by reducing the number of words. The following kind of sentence is common in student themes:

> WORDY: There is a man in our neighborhood, and he has written three novels.
>
> BETTER: A man in our neighborhood has written three novels.
>
> A neighbor of ours has written three novels.

What is called **excessive predication** is responsible for a common type of wordiness. Usually this fault results from the too frequent use of *and* and *but*. It may usually be remedied by proper subordination:

> WORDY: The test was hard, and the students were resentful, and their instructor was irritated.
>
> BETTER: Because the students resented the hard test, their instructor was irritated.

Another kind of wordiness originates in the desire to impress but ends in pretentious nonsense. It is the language of those persons who refer to bad weather as the "inclemency of the elements," who speak of "blessed events" and "passing away" instead of birth and death. Following are further examples of this kind of wordiness:

> Our horse Hap has gone to the big round-up in the sky.
>
> *Our horse Hap has died.*
>
> Due to the fact that he was enamored of Angela, Thomas comported himself in such a way as to appear ridiculous.
>
> *Because he was in love with Angela, Thomas behaved foolishly.*
>
> I regret extremely the necessity of your departure.
>
> *I am sorry you must go.*

Sometimes, of course, expressions like these are used facetiously. But do not make a habit of such usage.

Recently a new kind of wordiness has become popular, probably because it is believed to make its users appear knowledgeable. It is the jargon of government officials, social workers, educators on all levels, and others. Its basic principles seem to be these: Never use one word where two or more will do the work. Never use a concrete expression if it is possible to use an abstract one. Never be plain if you can be fancy. The clear sign of this kind of writing and speaking is seen in the repeated use of such phrases as *frame of reference, in terms of, point in time,* and compounds formed with the suffix *-wise.* The writers of this new jargon never simply look at the budget; they "consider the status budget-wise." They don't study crime among the young; they "examine social conditions in terms of juvenile delinquency." They "evaluate," they "utilize," they "expedite," and they "finalize." They speak of the "culturally deprived," the "classroom learning situation," "meaningful experiences," "togetherness," and "lifestyle." All these expressions reflect a desire to be a part of the "in group" (another example of this jargon) by picking up catchwords that seem to show a certain sophistication; what they really show is a failure to use precise language and a lack of judgment.

Redundancy, or unnecessary repetition, is another common type of wordiness, due to carelessness or ignorance of the meanings of certain words. Note the following examples of redundancy:

> Repeat that again, please. [Why *again*?]
>
> His solution was equally as good as hers. [Why *equally*?]
>
> The consensus of opinion of the group was that Mrs. Jacobs will make a good mayor. [Use either *consensus of the group* or *the opinion of the group.*]
>
> This location is more preferable to that one. [The word *preferable* means "more desirable"; therefore the word *more* is unnecessary. The sentence should read *This location is preferable to that one.*]
>
> The union continues to remain at odds with factory management. [*Continues* and *remain* mean essentially the same thing. Say, *The union continues at odds with factory management* or *The union remains at odds with factory management.*]
>
> It was a dog large in size and brown in color. [*It was a large brown dog.*]
>
> Mrs. Frost rarely ever wears her fur coat. [*Mrs. Frost rarely wears her fur coat.*]

22b Vagueness

A general impression of vague thinking is given by the too frequent use of abstract words instead of concrete words. Note especially the vagueness of such common words as *asset, factor, phase, case, nature, character, line,* and *field.* All these have basic meanings and should be used cautiously in any other sense. The following examples show that the best way to treat these words is to get rid of them:

> In cases where a person receives a ticket for speeding, he must pay a fine of fifty dollars. [*In cases where* can be replaced with the single word *if.*]

> Industry and intelligence are important assets in business success. [Omit *assets* and the sense remains the same.]

> The course is of a very difficult nature. [*The course is very difficult.*]

> Jerry was aware of the fact that he was risking his savings. [*Jerry was aware that he was risking his savings.*]

Whenever you are tempted to use such words, stop and ask yourself just what you are trying to say. Then find the exact words to say it, cutting out all the "deadwood."

22c Triteness

Trite means worn. Certain phrases have been used so often that they have lost their original freshness. Oratory, sermons, newspaper headlines and captions, and pretentious writing in general are frequently marred by such diction. Expressions of this kind are often called **clichés**. The following list is merely illustrative; you can probably think of numerous ones to add to these:

upset the applecart	proud possessor
an ace up his sleeve	nipped in the bud
dull thud	few and far between
one fell swoop	on pins and needles
up on Cloud Nine	make one's blood boil
grim reaper	eat one's heart out
last but not least	having a ball
face the music	as luck would have it
as straight as a die	quick as a wink
bitter end	gung ho

Avoid also quotation of trite phrases from literature and proverbs. Expressions like the following have already served their purpose:

a lean and hungry look

a sadder but wiser man

a rolling stone

those who live in glass houses

the best laid plans of mice and men

where angels fear to tread

love never faileth

to be or not to be

22d Euphemisms

Euphemisms are expressions used to avoid the outright statement of disagreeable ideas or to give dignity to something essentially lowly or undignified. The Victorians were notoriously euphemistic: they called their legs "limbs," and instead of the accurate and descriptive terms *sweat* and *spit*, they substituted the vague but more delicate words "perspire" and "expectorate." Unfortunately, the Victorians were not the last to use euphemisms. While we cannot admire or condone some of today's obscenely explicit language, there is little justification for the fuzzy-minded delicacy of euphemisms. There is a decided difference between the choice of an expression which offers a tactful connotation rather than a hurtful one and that of an expression which is deliberately misleading. The condition of pregnancy is euphemistically referred to as "expecting"; a garbage collector is a "sanitation engineer"; a janitor is a "superintendent," etc. *Death*, of course, has numerous euphemistic substitutes such as "passing on," "going to his reward," and many others.

   Again, it should be emphasized that the laudable wish to spare the feelings of others is not to be confused with the sort of prudery or false sense of gentility that most often produces euphemisms. Unless the desire to use a euphemism is inspired by the necessity to soften a blow or avoid offensiveness, the more factual term is to be preferred. Ordinarily, avoid euphemisms—or change the subject.

22e Idiom

Construction characteristic of a language is called **idiom**. The established usage of a language, the special way in which a thing is said or a phrase is formed, must be observed if writing is to be properly idiomatic. In English the normal sentence pattern has the subject first, then the verb, and then the direct object. In French, if the direct object is a pronoun, it usually (except in the imperative) precedes the verb. In English an adjective that directly modifies a noun usually precedes it. In French the adjective usually follows the noun. In English we say, "It is hot." The French say, "It makes hot." Such differences make it hard to learn a foreign language.

   Another meaning of the word *idiom* is somewhat contrary to this one. The word is also used for all those expressions that seem to defy logical grammatical practice, expressions that cannot be translated literally into another language. "Many is the day" and "You had better" are good examples. Fortunately idioms of this sort cause little trouble to native speakers.

   In English, as in most modern European languages, one of the greatest difficulties lies in the idiomatic use of prepositions after certain nouns, adjectives, and verbs. Oddly enough, one agrees *with* a person but *to* a proposal, and several persons may agree *upon* a plan. One may have a desire *for* something but be desirous *of* it. One is angry *at* or *about* an act but *at* or *with* a person. These uses of prepositions may seem strange and perverse. But they are part of the idiomatic structure of English and must be learned. Good dictionaries frequently indicate correct usage in questions of this kind. Do not look up the preposition but rather the word with which it is used. The definition of this word will usually indicate the correct preposition to use with it.

22f Connotation

In selecting words that will express their thoughts accurately, careful writers pay attention to the **connotations** of certain expressions. *Connotation* is the associative meaning, or what the word suggests beyond its literal definition.

Through popular usage certain terms convey favorable or unfavorable impressions beyond their literal meanings; they frequently have emotional or evaluative qualities that are not part of their straightforward definitions. Careless use of a word with strong connotations may cause faulty communication of your ideas. On the other hand, skillful use of connotation can greatly enrich your ability to communicate accurately. For example, you would not refer to a public figure whom you admire and respect as a "politician," a term which suggests such qualities as insincerity and conniving for personal gain. The word *childish* is inappropriate when you mean "childlike"; and the adjective *thin* suggests something scanty or somehow not full enough (especially when describing a person's figure), but *slim* and *slender*, two words close to *thin* in literal meaning, imply grace and good proportion.

Again, your dictionary can provide these shades of meaning that will keep you from writing something far different from your intention and will help you develop a vocabulary you can use accurately.

GLOSSARY OF FAULTY DICTION

The following glossary should help you rid your speech and writing of many errors. The term **colloquial** means that an expression is characteristic of everyday speech. **Dialectal** means that an expression is peculiar to a particular place or class.

NOTE: Remember that colloquialisms, that is the language we use in our everyday conversations with friends and associates, are perfectly acceptable in informal writing and speech. The purpose of this Glossary of Faulty Diction is to point out expressions which should be avoided in formal writing of any kind.

Above. Avoid the use of *above* as a modifier in such phrases as *the above reference, the above names.* An exception to this rule is that the word is proper in legal documents.

Accept, Except. *To accept* is *to receive; to except* is *to make an exception of, to omit. Except* (as a preposition) means *with the exception of.*

Accidently. There is no such word. The correct form is *accidentally,* based on the adjective *accidental.*

A.D. This is an abbreviation of *Anno Domini* (in the year of our Lord). Strictly considered, it should be used only with a date: *A.D. 1492.* But it has recently come to mean *of the Christian era*, and expressions like *the fifth century A.D.* have become common. Here logic has bowed to usage.

Administrate. There is no such word. The verb is *administer*; the noun formed from it is *administration.*

Adverse, Averse. *Adverse* means *unfavorable: The weatherman forecast adverse conditions for the yacht race. Averse* means *opposed to: Mother was averse to our plans for ice skating at midnight.*

Affect, Effect. In common usage *affect* is a verb meaning *to influence, to have an effect upon* or *to like to have or use* (He *affects* a gold-headed cane) or *to pretend* (She *affects* helplessness). *Effect* is both verb and noun. *To effect* is *to produce, to bring about.* The noun *effect* is a *result*, a *consequence.*

Aggravate. Colloquial when used to mean *provoke* or *irritate. Aggravate* means to make worse (*The rainy weather aggravated his rheumatism*).

Agree to, Agree with. One agrees *to* a proposal but *with* a person. (*We agree to his suggestion that we go,* but *The boy did not agree with his father.*)

Ain't. This form is occasionally defended as a contraction of *am not*, but even those who defend it do not use it in writing.

Alibi. Colloquial for *excuse*. In formal usage *alibi* has legal significance only and means a confirmation of one's absence from the scene of a crime at the time the crime was committed.

All ready, Already. *All ready* means simply that all are ready (*The players were all ready*). *Already* means *previously* or *before now* (*He has already gone*).

All together, Altogether. *All together* means all of a number taken or considered together (*She invited them all together*). *Altogether* means *entirely, completely* (*He was altogether wrong*).

Allusion, Illusion. An *allusion* is a casual or indirect reference to something, usually without naming the thing itself (*The quotation in her speech was an allusion to Shakespeare's* Macbeth). An *illusion* is a false or unreal impression of reality (*After his unkind treatment of the puppy Mildred lost her illusions about Arthur*).

Alright. This is not an acceptable alternate spelling for the words *all right*.

Alumnus, Alumna. *Alumnus* is masculine and has the plural *alumni. Alumna* is feminine and has the plural *alumnae.*

Among, Between. The common practice is to use *between* with two or more persons or objects (*between a rock and a hard place*) and *among* with more than two (*The crew quarreled among themselves*). Exception: *The plane traveled between New York, Chicago, and Miami.* Here *among* would be absurd.

Anyone, Any One. *Anyone*, the indefinite pronoun, is one word. *Any one*, meaning any single person or any single thing, should be written as two words (*Any one of your friends will be glad to help you.*)

Any place, No place. Dialectal corruptions of *anywhere* and *nowhere.*

Apt, Liable, Likely. *Apt* means *suitable, appropriate, tending to,* or *inclined to* (*an apt phrase, a man apt to succeed*). *Liable* means *exposed to something undesirable* (*liable to be injured, liable for damages*). *Likely* means *credible, probable, probably* (*He had a likely excuse*). It can also overlap to some extent with *apt* in its sense of probability (*It is likely— or apt—to rain today*).

As far as. This expression is frequently misused when it is not followed by a clause (*As far as her ability she is perfectly able to do the work*). It should always function as a subordinating conjunction, introducing both a subject and a verb (*As far as her ability is concerned, she is perfectly able to do the work.*)

Asset. In its essential meaning this word is used in law and accounting (*His assets exceeded his liabilities*). But it seems to have established itself in the meaning of *something useful or desirable.* When used in this sense, it is frequently redundant.

Attend, Tend. *Attend* means *to be present at.* When meaning *to take care of,* it is followed by *to* (*He attends to his own business*). *Tend* without a preposition also means *to take care of* (*He tends his own garden*). *Tend to* means *to have a tendency to* (*She tends to become nervous when her children are noisy*).

Author, Host, Chair, Position. These nouns are frequently misused as verbs (*She has authored three best sellers, The Joneses plan to host a party for their friends, The woman who chairs the committee is a lawyer, Please position the chairs around the table.*). In these four sentences there are perfectly adequate verbs that should be used: *written, give, is* chairwoman of, and *place.*

Awful, Awfully. Either of these is colloquial when used to mean *very*.

Awhile, A While. *Awhile* is used as an adverb (*They stayed **awhile** at their friend's house*). When used after the preposition *for, while* is a noun, the object of the preposition (*I thought for **a while** that you were going to miss the plane*). The adverb is written as one word; the object of the preposition and its article are written as two.

Bad, Badly. *Bad* is an adjective, *badly* an adverb. Say *I feel **bad**,* not *I feel **badly**,* if you mean *I am ill* or *I am sorry.*

Balance. Except in accounting, the use of *balance* for *difference, remainder, the rest* is colloquial.

Being As. Dialectal for *since* or *because.*

Beside, Besides. *Beside* is a preposition meaning *by the side of* (*Along came a spider and sat down **beside** her*). *Besides* is a preposition meaning *except* (*He had nothing **besides** his good name*) and an adverb meaning *in addition, moreover* (*He received a medal and fifty dollars **besides***).

Blame On. Correct idiom calls for the use of *to blame* with *for,* not *on.* (*They **blamed** the driver **for** the accident,* not *They **blamed** the accident **on** the driver.*) *Blame on* is colloquial.

Boyfriend, Girlfriend. These two terms are colloquial, meaning *a favored male or female friend, a sweetheart.* If no other term seems appropriate, write them as two words: *boy friend, girl friend.*

Burst, Bursted, Bust. The principal parts of the verb *burst* are *burst, burst,* and *burst.* The use of *bursted* or *busted* for the past tense is incorrect. *Bust* is either sculpture or a part of the human body. Used for *failure* or as a verb for *burst* or *break,* it is slang.

But What. Use *that* or *but that* instead of *but what* (*They had no doubt **that** help would come*).

Calvary, Cavalry. Mistakes here are chiefly a matter of spelling, but it is important to be aware of the difference: *Calvary* is the name of the hill where Jesus was crucified; *cavalry* refers to troops trained to fight on horseback, or more recently in armored vehicles.

Cannot. This word is the negative form of *can.* It is written as one word.

Cannot Help But. This is a mixed construction. *Cannot help* and *cannot but* are separate expressions, either of which is correct (*He **cannot but** attempt it,* or *He **cannot help** attempting it*).

Capital, Capitol. *Capital* is a city; *capitol* is a building. *Capital* is also an adjective, usually meaning *chief, excellent.*

Case. This is a vague and unnecessary word in many of its common uses today. Avoid *case* and seek the exact word.

Chairperson. Use the terms *chairman* and *chairwoman* in preference to *chairperson,* which should be used only if it is an official title in an organization or if you are quoting directly someone who has used the term.

Claim. Do not use simply to mean *say.* In the correct use of *claim* some disputed right is involved (*He **claims** to be the heir of a very wealthy man*).

Complement, Compliment. In its usual sense *complement* means *something that completes* (*Her navy blue shoes and bag were a **complement** for her gray suit*). A *compliment* is an expression of courtesy or praise (*My **compliments** to the chef*).

Connotate. There is no such verb as *connotate;* the verb is *connote,* and its noun form is *connotation.*

Considerable. This word is an adjective meaning *worthy of consideration, important* (*The idea is at least **considerable***). When used to denote a great deal or a great many, *considerable* is colloquial or informal.

Contact. Colloquial and sometimes vague when used for *see, meet, communicate with*, as in *I must **contact** my agent.*

Continual, Continuous. *Continual* means *repeated often* (*The interruptions were **continual***). *Continuous* means *going on without interruption* (*For two days the pain was **continuous***).

Convince, Persuade. Do not use *convince* for *persuade* as in *I **convinced** him to wash the dishes.* *Convince* means *to overcome doubt* (*I **convinced** him of the soundness of my plan*). *Persuade* means *to win over by argument or entreaty* (*I **persuaded** him to wash the dishes*).

Couple. This word, followed by *of* is informal for *two* or *a few.*

Credible, Creditable. *Credible* mean *believable* (*His evidence was not **credible***). *Creditable* means *deserving esteem or admiration* (*The acting of the male lead was a **creditable** performance*).

Critique. This word is a noun, not a verb; it means a critical review or comment dealing with an artistic work. The verb form is *criticize.*

Cupfuls, Cupsful. The plural of cupful is *cupfuls,* not *cupsful.*

Data. *Data* is the plural of *datum, something given or known.* It usually refers to a body of facts or figures. It normally takes a plural verb (*These **data** are important*). At times, however, *data* may be considered a collective noun and used with a singular verb.

Definitely. This is frequently used to mean *very* or *quite.* It is a trite expression and should be avoided for this reason as well as for its lack of accuracy.

Different Than. Most good writers use *different from*, not *different than.*

Disinterested. Often confused with *uninterested. Disinterested* means *unbiased, impartial; uninterested* means *lacking interest in.*

Don't. A contraction of *do not.* Do not write *he, she,* or *it don't.*

Drapes. Incorrect when used as a noun to mean *curtains. Drape* is the verb; *draperies* is the correct noun form.

Due To. Do not use *due to* for *because of* as in ***Due to** a lengthy illness, he left college. Due to* is correctly used after a noun or linking verb (*His failure, **due to** laziness, was not surprising. The accident was **due to** carelessness*).

Dyeing, Dying. *Dyeing* refers to the coloring of materials with dye. Do not omit the *e,* which would confuse the word with *dying,* meaning *expiring.*

Emigrant, Immigrant. A person who moves from one place to another is both an *emigrant* and an *immigrant*, but he emigrates *from* one place and immigrates *to* the other.

Enthuse, Enthused. These words are colloquial and always unacceptable in writing.

Equally As. Do not use these two words together; omit either *equally* or *as.* Do not write *Water is **equally** as necessary as air*; write *Water is **as** necessary as air* or *Water and air are **equally** necessary.*

Etc. An abbreviation of Latin *et* (*and*) and *cetera* (*other things*). It should not be preceded by *and*, nor should it be used as a catch-all expression to avoid a clear and exact ending of an idea or a sentence.

Everyday, Every day. When written as one word (*everyday*), this expression is an adjective (*Mother's **everyday** china is ironstone*). When used adverbially to indicate how often something happens, it is written as two words (***Every day** at noon I eat an apple and drink a glass of milk*).

Exam. A colloquial abbreviation for *examination.* Compare *gym, dorm, lab,* and *prof.*

Expect. This word means *to look forward to* or *foresee.* Do not use it to mean *suspect* or *suppose.*

Fact That. This is an example of wordiness, usually amounting to redundancy. Most sentences can omit the phrase *the fact that* without changing the sense of what is said (***The fact that*** *he wanted a new bicycle was the reason why he stole the money* may be effectively reduced to *He stole the money because he wanted a new bicycle*). Whenever you are tempted to use this expression, try rewording the sentence without it, and you will have a more concise and a clearer statement.

Farther, Further. The two words are often confused. *Farther* means *at or to a more distant point in space or time; further* means *to a greater extent, in addition.* One says *It is **farther** to Minneapolis from Chicago than from here*, but *We will talk **further** about this tomorrow.*

Faze. Colloquial for *to disturb* to *to agitate.* Most commonly used in the negative (*Mother's angry looks didn't **faze** Jimmy*).

Feel. *Feel* means to perceive through the physical senses or through the emotions. This word should not be used as a careless equivalent of *think* or *believe,* both of which refer to mental activity.

Fellow. Colloquial when used to mean a *person.*

Fewer, Less. Use *fewer* to refer to a number, *less* to refer to amount (*Where there are **fewer** persons, there is **less** noise*).

Fine. Colloquial when used as a term of general approval.

Fix. *Fix* is a verb, meaning *to make firm or stable.* Used as a noun meaning *a bad condition* or a verb meaning *to repair,* it is colloquial.

Flaunt, Flout. *Flaunt* means *to exhibit ostentatiously, to show off* (*She **flaunted** her new mink coat before her friends*). *Flout* means to show *contempt for, to scorn* (*Margaret often **flouts** the rules of good sportsmanship*).

Forego, Forgo. *Forego* means to *precede* or *go before* (*The **foregoing** data were gathered two years ago. Forgo* means *to give up, reliquish* (*I am afraid I must **forgo** the pleasure of meeting your friends today*).

Formally, Formerly. *Formally* means *in a formal manner* (*He was **formally** initiated into his fraternity last night*). *Formerly* means *at a former time* (*They **formerly** lived in Ohio*).

Gentlemen, Lady. Do not use these words as synonyms for *man* and *woman.*

Got. This is a correct past participle of the verb *to get* (*He had **got** three traffic tickets in two days*). *Gotten* is an alternative past participle of *to get.*

Guess. Colloquial when used for *suppose* or *believe.*

Guy. Slang when used for *boy* or *man.*

Hanged, Hung. *Hanged* is the correct past tense or past participle of *hang* when capital punishment is meant (*The cattle rustlers were **hanged** at daybreak*). *Hung* is the past tense and past participle in every other sense of the term (*We **hung** popcorn and cranberries on the Christmas tree*).

Hardly, Scarcely. Do not use with a negative. *I **can't hardly** see it* borders on the illiterate. Write *I **can hardly** see it* or (if you cannot see it at all) *I **can't** see it.*

Healthful, Healthy. Places are *healthful* if persons may be *healthy* living in them.

Hopefully. This word means *in a hopeful manner* (*She **hopefully** began getting ready for her blind date*). Do not use this modifer to mean *it is hoped* or *let us hope* (***Hopefully***, *the new rail system for Atlanta will be completed within five years*).

If, Whether. In careful writing do not use *if* for *whether.* *Let me know **if** you are coming* does not mean exactly the same thing as *Let me know **whether** you are coming.* The latter leaves no doubt that a reply is expected.

Imply, Infer. *Imply* means *to suggest, to express indirectly. Infer* means *to conclude,* as on the basis of suggestion or implication. A writer *implies* to a reader; a reader *infers* from a writer.

Incidently. There is no such word. The correct form is *incidentally*, based on the adjective *incidental.*

Into, In To. *Into* is a preposition meaning *toward the inside* and is followed by an object of the preposition. Do not use the one-word form of this expression when the object of the preposition is the object of *to* only, and *in* is an adverbial modifier. Say *He went **into** the building* but *The men handed their application forms **in to** the personnel manager.*

Irregardless. No such word exists. *Regardless* is the correct word.

Its, It's. The form *its* is possessive (*Every dog has **its** day*). *It's* is a contraction of *it is* (***It's** a pity she's a bore*).

It's Me. Formal English requires *It is I. It's me* is informal or colloquial, perfectly acceptable in conversation but not proper for written English. Compare the French idiom *C'est moi.*

Kid. Used to mean a child or young person, *kid* is slang.

Kind, Sort. These are singular forms and should be modified accordingly (*this kind, that sort*). *Kinds* and *sorts* are plural, and they, of course, have plural modifiers.

Kind Of, Sort Of. Do not use these to mean *rather* as in *He was **kind of** (or **sort of**) lazy.*

Last, Latest. *Last* implies that there will be no more. *Latest* does not prevent the possibility of another appearance later. The proper sense of both is seen in the sentence *After seeing his **latest** play, we hope that it is his **last**.*

Lend, Loan. The use of *loan* as a verb is incorrect. *Loan* is a noun. The distinction between the two words may be seen in the sentence *If you will **lend** me ten dollars until Friday, I will appreciate the **loan**.*

Like, As. Confusion in the use of these two words results from using *like* as a conjunction. The preposition *like* should be followed by an object (*He ran **like** an antelope*). The conjunction *as* is followed by a clause (*He did **as** he wished, He talked **as** though he were crazy*). The incorrect use of *as* as a preposition is a kind of reaction against the use of *like* as a conjunction. Consider the sentence: *Many species of oaks, **as** the red oak, the white oak, the water oak, are found in the Southeast.* Here the correct word is *like*, not *as*.

Literally. The word means *faithfully, to the letter, letter for letter, exactly.* Do not use in the sense of *completely,* or *in effect.* A sentence may be copied *literally*; but one never, except under extraordinary circumstances, **literally** *devours a book.* Frequently, the word *virtually*, meaning *in effect or essence, though not in fact,* is the correct word.

Lot, Lots. Colloquial or informal when used to mean *many* or *much.*

Mad. The essential meaning of *mad* is *insane.* When used to mean *angry*, it is informal.

May Be, Maybe. *May be* is a verb phrase (*It **may be** that you are right*). *Maybe* used as an adverb means *perhaps* (***Maybe** you are right*).

Mean. Used for disagreeable (*He has a **mean** disposition, He is **mean** to me*), the word is informal or colloquial.

Media. *Media* is the plural of *medium, a means, agency,* or *instrumentality.* It is often incorrectly used in the plural as though it were singular, as in *The **media** is playing an important role in political races this year.*

Midnight, Noon. Neither of these words needs the word *twelve* before it. They themselves refer to specific times, so *twelve* is redundant.

Most. Do not use for *almost.* ***Almost** all of them are here* or ***Most** of them are here* is correct. ***Most** all of them are here* is incorrect.

Muchly. There is no such word as *muchly. Much* is both adjective and adverb (***Much** water has flowed over the dam, Thank you very **much***). Compare *thusly.*

Mutual. The use of *mutual* for *common* is usually avoided by careful writers. ***Common** knowledge, **common** property, **common** dislikes* are things shared by two or more persons. ***Mutual** admiration* means *admiration of each for the other.*

Myself. Colloquial when used as a substitute for *I* or *me*, as in *He and **myself** were there.* It is correctly used intensively (*I **myself** shall do it*) and reflexively (*I blame only **myself***).

Nice. *Nice* is a catch-all word that has lost its force because it has no clearcut, specific meaning as a modifier. When writing in praise of something, select an adjective that conveys more specific information than *nice* does.

Of. Unnecessary after such prepositions as *off, inside, outside* (not *He fell **off** of the cliff* but *He fell **off** the cliff*).

On Account Of. Do not use as a conjunction; the phrase should be followed by an object of the preposition *of* (***on account of** his illness*). *He was absent **on account of** he was sick* is bad grammar.

Oral, Verbal, Written. Use *oral* to refer to spoken words (*An **oral** examination is sometimes nerve-wracking for a student*); use *verbal* to contrast a communication in words to some other kind of communication (*His scowl told me more than any **verbal** message could*); use *written* when referring to anything put on paper.

Orientate. There is no such word. The verb is *orient*, meaning *to cause to become familiar with or adjusted to facts or a situation* (*He **oriented** himself by finding the North Star*). The noun is *orientation.*

Over With. The *with* is unnecessary in such expressions as *The game was **over with** by five o'clock.*

Party. Colloquial when used to mean *a person.* Properly used in legal documents (***party of the first part***).

Peeve. Either as a verb or noun, *peeve* is informal diction.

Personally. This word is often redundant and is a hackneyed, sometimes irritating expression, as in ***Personally**, I think you are making a big mistake.*

Plan On. Omit *on.* In standard practice idiom calls for an infinitive or a direct object after *plan. They **planned** to go* or *They **planned** a reception* are both correct usage.

Plenty. This word is a noun, not an adverb. Do not write *He was **plenty** worried.*

Pore, Pour. *Pore,* meaning *to meditate* or *to study intently and with steady application,* is a verb used with the preposition *over.* (*She **pored over** her chemistry assignment for several hours.*) It should not be confused with *pour,* meaning *to set a liquid flowing or falling.* (*They **poured** the tea into fragile china cups.*)

Principal, Principle. *Principal* is both adjective and noun (***principal** parts, **principal** of the school, **principal** and interest*). *Principle* is a noun only (***principles** of philosophy, a man of **principle***).

Pupil, Student. Schoolchildren in the elementary grades are called *pupils*; in grades nine through twelve *student* or *pupil* is correct; for college the term must always be *student.*

Quote, Quotation. *Quote* is a verb and should not be used as a noun, as in *The **quote** you gave is from Shakespeare, not the Bible.*

Real. Do not use for *really. Real* is an adjective; *really* is an adverb (*The **real** gems are **really** beautiful*).

Reason Is Because. This is not idiomatic English. The subject-linking verb construction calls for a predicate nominative, but *because* is a subordinating conjunction that introduces an adverbial clause. Write *The reason I was late is that I had an accident,* not *The reason I was late is because I had an accident.*

Respectfully, Respectively. *Respectfully* means *with respect,* as in *The young used to act respectfully toward their elders. Respectively* is a word seldom needed; it means *in the order designated,* as in *The men and women took their seats on the right and left respectively.*

Reverend. This word, like *Honorable,* is not a noun, but an honorific adjective. It is not a title like *doctor* or *president.* It is properly used preceding *Mr.* or the given name or initials, as in *the Reverend Mr. Gilbreath, the Reverend Earl Gilbreath, the Reverend J. E. Gilbreath.* To use the word as a title as in *Reverend, will you lead us in prayer?* or *Is there a Reverend in the house?* is plainly absurd. *Reverend Gilbreath* instead of *the Reverend Mr. Gilbreath* is almost as bad.

Right. In the sense of *very* or *extremely, right* is colloquial. Do not write (or say) *I'm right glad to know you.*

Same. The word is an adjective, not a pronoun. Do not use it as in *We received your order and will give same immediate attention.* Substitute *it* for *same.*

Savings. This word is frequently misused in the plural when the singular is the correct form. It is particularly puzzling that many people use this plural with a singular article, as in *The ten per cent discount gives you a savings of nine dollars. A saving* is the proper usage here. Another common error occurs in reference to *Daylight Saving Time;* the right form again is *Saving,* not *Savings.*

Shape. In formal writing do not use *shape* for *condition* as in *He played badly because he was in poor shape.* In this sense *shape* is informal.

Should Of, Would Of. Do not use these terms for *should have, would have.*

Situation. This is another catch-all term, frequently used redundantly, as in *It was a fourth down situation.* Fourth down *is* a situation, so the word itself is repetitious. This vague term can usually be omitted or replaced with a more specific word.

So. Avoid the use of *so* for *very,* as in *Thank you so much. So* used as an adverb means *thus* or *like this.*

Some. Do not use for *somewhat,* as in *She is some better after her illness.*

Species. This word is both singular and plural. One may speak of *one species* or *three species.* The word usually refers to a kind of plant or animal.

Sprightly, Spritely. *Sprightly* means *animated, vivacious, lively.* There is no such word as *spritely,* but many people use this term, probably because it suggests the word *sprite,* an *elf* or *fairy.* Do not write *her spritely conversation was fascinating.*

Stationary, Stationery. *Stationary* means *fixed, not moving.* Remember that *stationery,* which is paper for writing letters, is sold by a *stationer.*

Statue, Stature, Statute. A *statue* is a piece of sculpture. *Stature* is bodily height, often used figuratively to mean *level of achievement, status,* or *importance.* A *statute* is a law or regulation.

Strata. This is the plural of the Latin *stratum.* One speaks of *a stratum* of rock but of *several strata.*

Super, Fantastic, Incredible, etc. When used to describe something exciting or marvelous, these overworked words actually add little to our everyday conversation because they have lost their original force. At any rate, they must never be a part of written formal English, as they are simply slang, and trite slang at that.

Suppose, Supposed. Many people incorrectly use the first form *suppose* before an infinitive when the second form *supposed* is needed, as in *Am I suppose to meet you at five o'clock?* The past participle *supposed* must go along with the auxiliary verb *am* to form the passive voice. This error almost certainly arises from an inability to hear the final *d* when it precedes the *t* in the *to* of the infinitive. The correct form is *Am I supposed to meet you at five o'clock?*

Sure, Surely. Do not use the adjective *sure* for the adverb *surely*. *I am sure that you are right* and *I am surely glad to be here* are correct.

Trustee, Trusty. The word *trustee* means *a person elected or appointed to direct funds or policy* for a person or an institution, as in *Mr. Higginbotham is a trustee on the bank's board of directors*. A *trusty*, on the other hand, is a prisoner granted special privileges because he is believed trustworthy, as in *Although he was a trusty, Harris escaped from prison early today*.

Too. *Too* means *in addition,* or *excessively.* It is incorrect to use the word to mean *very* or *very much*, as in *I was not too impressed with her latest book* or *I'm afraid I don't know him too well.*

Try And. Use *try to*, not *try and*, in such expressions as *Try to get here on time* (not *Try and get here on time*).

Type. Colloquial in expressions like *this type book;* write *this type of book.*

Undoubtably, Undoubtedly. There is no such word as *undoubtably*. The correct word is *undoubtedly*.

Unique. If referring to something as the only one of its kind, you may correctly use *unique*. (*The Grand Canyon is a unique geological formation.*) The word does not mean *rare, strange,* or *remarkable,* and there are no degrees of *uniqueness;* to say that something is *the most unique* thing one has ever seen is faulty diction.

Use (Used) To Could. Do not use for *once could* or *used to be able to.*

Very. Do not use as a modifier of a past participle, as in *very broken.* English idiom calls for *badly broken* or *very badly broken.*

Wait For, Wait On. *To wait for* means *to look forward to, to expect* (*For two hours I have waited for you*). *To wait on* means *to serve* (*The butler and two maids waited on the guests at dinner*).

Want In, Want Off, Want Out. These forms are dialectal. Do not use them for *want to come in, want to get off, want to get out.*

Way. Colloquial when used for *away* as in *Way down upon the Swanee River.*

Ways. Colloquial when used for *way* as in *a long ways to go.*

Whose, Who's. The possesive form is *whose* (*Whose book is this?*). *Who's* is a contraction of *who is* (*Who's at the door?*). The use of *whose* as a neuter possessive is confirmed by the history of the word and the practice of good writers. *The house whose roof is leaking* is more natural and less clumsy than *the house the roof of which is leaking.*

Your, You're. The possessive form is *your* (*Tell me your name*). *You're* is a contraction of *you are.*

Exercise 85 | DICTION

Rewrite the following sentences, reducing wordiness. Be careful that your reduction does not lead to a series of short, choppy declarative sentences, sometimes called "primer style."

EXAMPLE: To make a long story short, we waited and waited, and Abigail never did come to meet us, and finally we realized that she wasn't coming, so we talked it over and decided that we would go on to the Astrodome without her.

After waiting for Abigail and finally realizing that she was not coming, we decided to go to the Astrodome without her.

1. Marty is a girl who is always cheerfully optimistic, and honesty-wise, she can always be counted on to tell the true facts of a situation.

2. The important and vital message that Mr. Langdon meant to imply is that in cases where there is a question as to whether students are required to pre-register, they must consult the handbook and look up the information there.

3. The fact of the matter is that Turner is still in the process of revising his novel over again, and I really cannot say, in the final analysis, when he will be finished.

4. It appears to be a well-known fact that John is quite proud of the achievements that he has accomplished, and although he is my personal friend, I must point out that he is an individual of a most conceited nature.

5. The main protagonist of the drama is a man who falls into serious trouble because of the fact that his true identity is not known to his neighbors on the street where he lives, and they finally come to the conclusion that he is an escaped convict with a past history of arrest.

6. My new evening skirt, which is a beautiful pink color, is made of a taffeta fabric, and it will go nicely with my blouse, which is black velvet.

7. Our party that we had last night was such a success that all our guests continued to stay for hours, and they kept on eating until all the food was gone.

8. Salary-wise, my job is not of the type that I have always considered that a good job should be, but nevertheless, in my opinion, one sometimes has to make occasional sacrifices in order to use the talents that he has.

9. Normally, I would usually give you the opportunity to make a choice between selecting the blue dress or the green dress, but at this point in time, I have decided to let you have both dresses.

10. In a situation where the terrible weather conditions will not permit students to get safely to their classes without danger involved, the school administration is prepared to issue excuses for any unavoidable absences.

| Exercise 86 | Diction |

Rewrite the following sentences, reducing wordiness. Be careful that your reduction does not lead to a series of short, choppy declarative sentences, sometimes called "primer style."

EXAMPLE: Allowing for the fact that she is very small in size, Martha has demonstrated her physical strength by showing how strong she is in endurance swimming.

Although Martha is small, she has demonstrated her strength in endurance swimming.

1. Imogene cordially invited us in a most friendly way to come to dinner at her apartment and to share the evening meal with her.

2. While I was sleeping last night, I dreamed that, in company with some people whom I knew on friendly and congenial terms, I took a long journey that took us far away from our homes.

3. It is absolutely necessary that you understand completely the need for our cooperating together in this project that we have undertaken.

4. In my opinion, I believe that your car is equally as fine as Tom's in terms of its beauty, economy, and dependability.

5. Pete found that he had been erroneously misinformed by the airport information service, which told him that Gloria's plane would be arriving at 8 P.M. at night.

6. The irate owner of the property was angry that the young children were illegally trespassing on his land, and he refused to accept their apology that they were sorry.

7. I have heard a rumor concerning the fact that Mr. Knight is considering possibly writing an autobiography of his life.

8. In our conversation we exchanged opinions with each other, and we found that frequently our views were identically the same.

9. Dorothy was surprised to find that, amazingly, she was able to revert back to her childhood skills that she had had as a child and could ride a bicycle equally as well as she ever had.

10. The stingy old miser thought to himself that he would put the gold in a hiding place of a very unique type, but in the final analysis, he realized that the situation involved dangerous factors that he had not at first considered.

Exercise 87 | DICTION

A. The following sentences contain one or more trite expressions or euphemisms. Underline the trite and euphemistic phrases and for each one write either **T** or **E** in the space at the right.

EXAMPLE: <u>Let's face it</u>, Nick; <u>it's later than you think</u>.　　　　　*T, T*

1. Ginny was as sweet as pie to Sam until she realized that his presence was a real fly in the ointment.　　　_____

2. When all is said and done, it is not surprising that at ninety-five Mr. Thomas has gone to meet his maker.　　　_____

3. Charles, you will have better posture if you hold your shoulders up and your tummy in.　　　_____

4. Those two girls are babes in the woods when it comes to living in a city like Chicago.　　　_____

5. Lady Luck certainly smiled on you when you were born with curly hair.　　　_____

6. A group of senior citizens held a rally to protest the proposed closing of their meeting place at the Community Center.　　　_____

7. When the chips are down, I can always count on my brother Eliott to work like a beaver to help me.　　　_____

8. Ralph has bought a reconditioned typewriter, which he plans to use when he starts college next year.　　　_____

9. I was as sick as a dog after eating lobster last night, but every cloud has a silver lining: I didn't have to keep my dental appointment this morning.　　　_____

10. Father Time has taken his toll in the past twelve months: both my grandmother and my grandfather have passed away.　　　_____

11. Bill was arrested Saturday night and booked for driving under the influence.　　　_____

12. Martha was really stunned when she was asked for her resignation, but I suppose there's no use crying over spilt milk.　　　_____

13. The rumor has spread like wildfire that Tad and Elaine have eloped and are living in a honeymoon cottage in Wyoming.   _____

14. We got up at the crack of dawn to begin our trip and started on our way as happy as larks.   _____

15. I had always believed Roger to be as honest as the day is long, but I have discovered that he is not above a slight distortion of the truth.   _____

16. In Hong Kong our guide took us through an extremely disadvantaged area, where people often live ten or twelve to a single room.   _____

17. Those zinnias that have been in the crystal vase for two weeks are as dead as doornails.   _____

18. The goalie on our hockey team is as fast as greased lightning, and he is worth his weight in gold to the team.   _____

19. The maintenance engineer in our apartment building is a hard worker; he keeps things in apple-pie order.   _____

20. Dr. Parke and I had a meaningful dialogue about Southern literature; although he is in his golden years, he is sharp as a tack.   _____

B. Select ten of the above sentences and rewrite them below, replacing the trite expressions and euphemisms with more suitable diction.

1. _____

_____

2. _____

_____

3. _____

_____

4. _____

_____

5. _____

_____

6. _____

_____

7. _____

_____

8. _____

_____

9. _____

_____

10. _____

_____

Exercise 88 | DICTION

The following sentences contain unidiomatic uses of prepositions. Underline each preposition that is incorrectly used and write the correct form at the right.

EXAMPLE: I have been standing at this stop for forty-five minutes
waiting <u>on</u> a bus.   _____*for*_____

1. Jeanne wanted to listen at the symphony that was on the radio, but Sharon wanted to watch a re-run of *Ironside*.   _____

2. Mr. Burns is better with telling jokes than anyone else I know.   _____

3. Aunt Isabel was averse to our plans to go to Norway in winter; she said that we should wait to spring.   _____

4. They finally agreed with a plan that incorporated everybody's favorite idea.   _____

5. Myrtle and Susie are both angry at Penny because she left for town without them.   _____

6. Father says that Frank and I can decide among ourselves whether to go to camp this summer.   _____

7. Mrs. Murchison told us to get off of her land.   _____

8. Harriet ran in the room, sank in the big easy chair, and burst into tears.   _____

9. The crowd roared in laughter as the clown squirted water in the ringmaster's face.   _____

10. I cannot agree with your suggestion that we postpone the test to Friday.   _____

11. Mr. Morris asked Fred what goal he was working to in planning his college courses.   _____

12. In all my friends you are the only one who agrees with me about the horrid taste of turnips. _____

13. I believe that Jack's coat is different than Jimmy's. _____

14. Rain fell into our area for three days without stopping. _____

15. The house that stands just besides ours was built in 1800. _____

Exercise 89 | DICTION

The following exercises (89–92) are based on the Glossary of Faulty Diction in Chapter 22. Underline all errors and colloquialisms (informal expressions) and write the correct or preferred forms at the right.

EXAMPLE: I hope that you will <u>except</u> my apology for being late,

Mrs. Thorpe.   *accept*

1. The rotunda of our nation's capital is an impressive architectural feature of the building.   _____

2. My uncle Sammy is an alumni of four universities.   _____

3. I'm not enthused about staying up to see the sun rise.   _____

4. Harris tried hard to convince Mary that he really did have a creditable excuse for missing their date.   _____

5. Hopefully, Dot and Joanne will let me know if they can meet me out   _____
   at the lake.   _____

6. I don't honestly believe that there are less calories in mayonnaise than in butter.   _____

7. I expect that you think this data is incomplete.   _____
                                                              _____

8. Madge, if you will loan me your red plaid skirt, I'll try and get it back   _____
   to you the first thing tomorrow.   _____

9. I am surprised that your willing to get up at six o'clock to see the boys off on the plane.   _____

10. The reason that I went home early is because I was expecting Theo to drop in at five.   _____

11. I sure am happy that Rosie and myself are going to room together   _____
    next year.   _____

12. The quote that he used in his speech was kind of silly, don't you   _____
    think?   _____

13. We all feel that the examination was not only unfair but also
    irrelevant.   _____

14. Mrs. Walker's tarts are so delicious; I understand that she makes the   _____
    filling with two cupsful of butter.   _____

15. I cannot begin to tell you the terrible affect that this damp weather
    has on my sinuses.   _____

Exercise 90	DICTION

Underline all errors and colloquialisms in the following sentences and write the correct or preferred forms at the right.

EXAMPLE: Gertrude says that she expects to make <u>lots</u> of
money in her catering business.   _____*a great deal*_____

1. My principle reason for declining your invitation is that I
   cannot get my vacation until July.   _____

2. Nancy turned her request for a loan into the bank
   manager, but she was sort of dubious about her chances.   _____
   _____

3. "I'm sure Mr. Roberts will say it's alright for us to pick
   some of his apples," William said hopefully.   _____

4. Your comments infer that you thoroughly approve of
   Laura's fiancé.   _____

5. Mrs. Merriweather is eager to chair the social committee
   of our club, because she loves to give parties.   _____

6. Remember I had warned you, Josephine, that dying your
   hair would make you look older, not younger.   _____

7. Harley says that Marilyn treated him so bad that he can't   _____
   hardly bear to think about the experience.   _____

8. Frances says that irregardless of the weather, departure
   time is 7 A.M. tomorrow, being as we must be in Seattle   _____
   by Friday.   _____

9. I hope that you can stay and visit with us for awhile,   _____
   Reverend Marshall.   _____

10. Brad claims that he will graduate first in his class next   _____
    June, and I can't help but think that he is right.   _____

11. As far as nerve is concerned, Betsy has plenty, but she
aggravates some people.

   _____

   _____

12. Rena is a fine cook, but she can't make muffins like her
mother.

   _____

   _____

13. We are muchly impressed with Thomas's new job as a
computer programmer; I hear that the company plans on
promoting him soon.

   _____

   _____

14. The media has such influence on the public's thinking
about various issues that it should strive for accuracy and
objectivity at all times.

   _____

   _____

15. You would of died laughing if you could of seen Daisy
and Jim doing that old dance their mother taught them.

   _____

   _____

16. Dorothy had all ready left for Columbus before I remembered that I didn't have the address of the people who's
home she would be visiting.

   _____

   _____

17. You are undoubtably right, Garfinkle, when you say that
Annie is a fantastic show.

   _____

   _____

18. Tina was real glad when she came in and found Earl
pouring over his French grammar book.

   _____

   _____

19. Peg was aware of the fact that she must forego some of
her prejudices.

   _____

   _____

20. The party who painted that so-called "art" in the new
airport ought to be hung.

   _____

   _____

Exercise 91	DICTION

Underline all errors, colloquialisms, and trite expressions. Then write the correct or preferred forms at the right.

EXAMPLE: Robert was <u>awful</u> disappointed at losing the
game, but Coach Magill told him to <u>keep a</u>   *very much*
<u>stiff upper lip.</u>   *not to be discouraged*

1. Cathy seems to be in a no-win situation as far as Kevin's
   noticing her.

2. The elegant wedding announcement, engraved on creamy
   stationary, was a bolt from the blue for all of Louisa's
   other admirers.

3. Take your clothes, your cosmetics, your books, and etc.
   over to Aunt Hattie's for the weekend.

4. That man really turns me off; his last escapade was
   inexcusable.

5. Anyone of the books that I received for Christmas could
   turn up on the best seller lists this year.

6. Last week I had to miss a couple of days of classes on
   account of I had a toothache.

7. Sonny accidently stepped on the dog, making it howl
   to high heaven.

8. It was hard to orientate myself in the dark, and I was on
   pins and needles for fear that the sinister-looking woman
   would find me.

9. There are numerous short stories that would make good
   television plays, as "Revelation" by Flannery O'Connor,
   for example.

10. Steve told Ellis to get his act together and not blame his _____
troubles on bad luck. _____

11. Her soft blue eyes were a compliment to her black hair _____
and fair skin; Billy thought she was a raving beauty. _____

12. The postman past our house again today without leaving
anything; I'm going to have a bone to pick with Harry if _____
he doesn't write soon. _____

13. The Martins have hosted our annual club picnic at their
lake house for the past three years, putting the rest of us _____
to shame with their hospitality. _____

14. Have you heard that the gentleman who cut our grass all
last summer is a bank robber? _____

15. I guess it's time to lay the cards on the table; in a nutshell, _____
I'm planning to resign. _____
_____

16. Although the author was somewhat prepared for unen-
thusiastic reviews, he felt that the man who had critiqued _____
his novel was unqualified. _____

17. Grace and Margaret tried to contact us before the ice storm
began; they had heard a warning about it on the radio. _____

18. Although Jerry is pleasant most all the time, he can _____
literally be a monster when he loses his temper. _____

19. Saying that she wasn't too impressed with the new drapes, _____
Marguerite implied that she thought Gloria had no taste. _____

20. The people who formally lived next door were all ears _____
when we told them the latest neighborhood gossip. _____

| Exercise 92 | DICTION |

Underline all errors and colloquialisms. Then write the correct or preferred form at the right.

EXAMPLE: Prison authorities had given Jones <u>trustee</u> status,
but he betrayed their trust by aiding in a daring
escape.   *trusty*

1. Dolly, aren't you suppose to be working out in the gym
   instead of sitting there eating a sundae?   _____

2. My father says that Senator Raines is a true statesman
   and a man of great statue.   _____

3. I know it is a long ways to travel, Cecilia, but going to   _____
   Glacier Bay is a very unique experience.   _____

4. My sewing teacher taught me to place the pattern on the
   fabric thusly and then pin it neatly in place.   _____

5. Although timid and unassuming, Mrs. Tyler is a woman of
   high principals.   _____

6. Elise says that she has lost her allusions about Bradley,   _____
   and she pretends that she has all ready forgotten him.   _____

7. The fellow who ran past us just now probably don't   _____
   realize that he almost knocked you down.   _____

8. Everyday I expect to get an answer to my job application,   _____
   but I guess that the company must be disinterested in my   _____
   working there.   _____

9. The plane is due at twelve noon, and we can't hardly wait   _____
   for it to arrive with our four cousins aboard.   _____

10. Quite a few students attended Dr. Erwin's lecture on   _____
    Henry James, but I couldn't go, due to a sore throat.   _____

11. Some people enjoy the cold weather of winter, but I'll
be glad when it's over with.

_____

12. Most of the pupils at our university come from within
the state.

_____

13. This is such a good dinner; in fact, I'd say it's fantastic.

_____

_____

14. Johnny fell off of his bicycle going down that steep hill;
hopefully he hasn't any busted bones.

_____

_____

_____

15. Janet was so mean to me the last time I saw her that I'm
apt to take a while to get over my resentment.

_____

_____

16. Your going to be surprised, Tillie, when you hear whose
coming to dinner with us tonight.

_____

_____

17. The tabby cat sat licking it's chops as I poured warm
milk into the bowl.

_____

18. Its not like you, Jonathan, to flaunt the rules of ethical
conduct.

_____

_____

19. Although some people don't care for this type art, the
trustees of the museum want this painting hanged in a
prominent position.

_____

_____

20. It's me that Lucy is trying to convince to go skating with
her.

_____

_____

23

Building a Vocabulary

As you know from your own experience, one of your greatest needs for successful composition is to improve your vocabulary. One of the best ways to build a vocabulary, of course, is always to look up in a dictionary the meanings of unfamiliar words which you hear spoken or come across in your reading. This chapter on vocabulary will provide you with a minimal body of information concerning word formation and the derivations of the various words which comprise the English language. For a more intensified study of all aspects of this fascinating subject, including ways to strengthen your own vocabulary, consult and use frequently a book devoted exclusively to this purpose.

Learning the derivation of a word will fix in your mind the meaning and spelling of that word. Since the largest part of our English vocabulary comes from three main sources—the Anglo-Saxon, the Greek, and the Latin languages—a knowledge of commonly used prefixes, roots, and suffixes from these languages will prove very useful.

A **prefix** is a short element, a syllable or syllables, that comes before the main part of the word, which is the **root**. A **suffix** is added to the end of the word. Thus the word *hypodermic* has *hypo-*, meaning "under," as its *prefix*; *derm*, meaning "skin," as its *root*; and *-ic*, meaning "having to do with," as its *suffix*. You see that the *prefix* and *suffix* of a word modify the meaning of the *root*. The word, then, *hypodermic,* when used as an adjective, means "having to do with something under the skin."

There are actually more words of classical origin, i.e., Greek and Latin, than of Anglo-Saxon in our language; however, we use the Anglo-Saxon words much more frequently in every sentence that we write or speak. For instance, the Anglo-Saxon prefixes *un-* (not) and *for-* (from) are found in many of our words, such as *unfair* and *forbid*. The Anglo-Saxon root word *hlaf* (loaf) gives us the word *lord*, a lord being a loafkeeper or warden (*hlaf-weard*). The root word *god* (God) gives us *goodbye*, a contraction of *God be with ye*. Anglo-Saxon suffixes such as *-ish* (having the qualities of) and *-ly* (like) are seen in many words such as *foolish* and *courtly*.

If you combine the Greeek root *tele*, meaning "at a distance," with *graph* (writing), *phone* (sound), *scope* (seeing), *pathy* (feeling), you have *telegraph* (writing at a distance), *telephone* (sound at a distance), *telescope* (seeing at a distance), *telepathy* (feeling at a distance).

The Latin root *duc* is seen in such words as *adduce, aqueduct, conduce, conduct, induce, produce, reduce, seduce, conductor, ducal,* and *ductile.* If you know that *duc* means "to lead," and if you know the meanings of the prefixes and suffixes combined with it, you can make out the meanings of most of these words.

Each prefix, root, and suffix that you learn may lead to a knowledge of many new words or give a clearer understanding of many you already know. Therefore, a list of some of the most common prefixes, roots, and suffixes is given below. Look up others in your dictionary, or as suggested earlier, get a good vocabulary text book and use it often.

23a   Prefixes

Prefixes Showing Number or Amount

BI– (*bis–*) two	*(bi)*annual, *(bis)*sextile
CENT– (*centi–*) hundred	*(cent)*enarian, *(centi)*pede
DEC– (*deca–*) ten	*(dec)*ade, *(Deca)*logue
HEMI– half	*(hemi)*sphere, *(hemi)*stich
MILLI– (*mille–*) thousand	*(milli)*on, *(mille)*nnium
MULTI– many, much	*(multi)*form, *(multi)*graph
MON– (*mono–*) one	*(mono)*gyny, *(mono)*tone
OCTA– (*octo–*) eight	*(octa)*ve, *(octo)*pus
PAN– all	*(pan)*acea, *(pan)*demonium, *(pan)*orama
PENTA– five	*(penta)*gon, *(Penta)*teuch
POLY– much, many	*(poly)*glot, *(poly)*chrome
PROT– (*proto–*) first	*(prot)*agonist, *(proto)*type
SEMI– half	*(semi)*circle, *(semi)*final
TRI– three	*(tri)*angle, *(tri)*ad
UNI– one	*(uni)*fy, *(uni)*cameral

Prefixes Showing Relationship in Place and Time

AB– (*a–, abs–*) from, away from	*(a)*vert, *(ab)*sent, *(abs)*tract
AD– (*ac–, af–, al–, ag–, an–, ap–, ar–, as–, at–*) to, at	*(ad)*mit, *(ac)*cede, *(af)*fect, *(al)*lude, *(ag)*gregate, *(an)*nounce, *(ap)*pear, *(ar)*rive, *(as)*sume, *(at)*tain
AMB– (*ambi–*) around, both	*(ambi)*dextrous, *(ambi)*guous
ANTE– before	*(ante)*cedent, *(ante)*date
ANTI– (*ant–*) against	*(anti)*thesis, *(ant)*agonist
CATA– away, against, down	*(cata)*clysm, *(cata)*strophe
CIRCUM– around, about	*(circum)*scribe, *(circum)*stance
CON– (*com–, col–, cor–*) with, together, at the same time	*(con)*tract, *(com)*pete, *(col)*league, *(cor)*relate
CONTRA– (*counter–*) opposite, against	*(contra)*dict, *(counter)*mand
DE– from, away from, down	*(de)*pend, *(de)*form, *(de)*tract
DIA– through, across	*(dia)*gram, *(dia)*meter
DIS– (*di–, dif–*) off, away from	*(dis)*tract, *(di)*verge, *(dif)*fuse
EN– (*em–, in-*) in, into	*(en)*counter, *(em)*brace, *(in)*duct
EPI– on, over, among, outside	*(epi)*dermis, *(epi)*demic
EX– (*e–, ec–, ef–*) out of, from	*(ex)*pel, *(e)*lect, *(ec)*centric, *(ef)*face

EXTRA–(*extro–*) outside, beyond	*(extra)*mural, *(extro)*vert
HYPO– under	*(hypo)*dermic, *(hypo)*crite
INTER– among, between, within	*(inter)*fere, *(inter)*rupt
INTRO– (*intra–*) within	*(intro)*spection, *(intra)*mura!
OB– (*oc–, of–, op–*) against, to, before toward	*(ob)*ject, *(oc)*casion, *(of)*fer, *(op)*press
PER– through, by	*(per)*ceiver, *(per)*ennial
PERI– around, about	*(peri)*meter, *(peri)*odical
POST– after	*(post)*script, *(post)*erity
PRE– before	*(pre)*cedent, *(pre)*decessor
PRO– before in time or position	*(pro)*logue, *(pro)*bate
RETRO– back, backward	*(retro)*gress, *(retro)*spect
SE– aside, apart	*(se)*clude, *(se)*duce
SUB– (*suc–, suf–, sug–, sum–, sup–, sus–*) under, below	*(sub)*scribe, *(suc)*cumb, *(suf)*fer, *(sug)*gest, *(sum)*mon, *(sup)*pose, *(sus)*pect
SUPER– (*sur–*) above, over	*(super)*sede, *(super)*b, *(sur)*pass
TRANS– (*tra–, traf–, tres–*) across	*(trans)*port, *(tra)*vesty, *(traf)*fic, *(tres)*pass
ULTRA– beyond	*(ultra)*marine, *(ultra)*modern

Prefixes Showing Negation

A– (*an–*) without	*(an)*onymous, *(a)*theist
IN– (*ig–, im–, il–, ir–*) not	*(in)*accurate, *(ig)*nore, *(im)*pair, *(il)*legal, *(ir)*responsible
NON– not	*(non)*essential, *(non)*entity
UN– not	*(un)*tidy, *(un)*happy

23b Greek Roots

ARCH	chief, rule	*(arch)*bishop, an*(archy)*, mon*(archy)*
AUTO	self	*(auto)*graph, *(auto)*mobile, *(auto)*matic
BIO	life	*(bio)*logy, *(bio)*graphy, *(bio)*chemistry
CAU(S)T	burn	*(caust)*ic, holo*(caust)*, *(caut)*erize
CHRON(O)	time	*(chron)*icle, *(chron)*ic, *(chrono)*logy
COSM(O)	order, arrangement	*(cosm)*os, *(cosm)*ic, *(cosmo)*graphy
CRIT	judge, discern	*(crit)*ic, *(crit)*erion
DEM(O)	people	*(demo)*crat, *(demo)*cracy, *(dem)*agogue
DERM	skin	epi*(dermis)*, *(derm)*a, pachy*(derm)*, *(derm)*ophobe
DYN(A) (M)	power	*(dynam)*ic, *(dynam)*o, *(dyn)*asty
GRAPH	write	auto*(graph)*, *(graph)*ic, geo*(graphy)*
HIPPO	horse	*(hippo)*potamus, *(hippo)*drome
HYDR(O)	water	*(hydr)*ant, *(hydr)*a, *(hydro)*gen
LOG(Y), LOGUE	saying, science	*(log)*ic, bio*(logy)*, eu*(logy)*, dia*(logue)*
MET(E)R	measure	thermo*(meter)*, speedo*(meter)*, *(metr)*ic
MICRO	small	*(micro)*be, *(micro)*scope, *(micro)*cosm
MOR(O)	fool	*(moro)*n, sopho*(more)*
NYM	name	ano*(nym)*ous, pseudo*(nym)*
PATH	experience, suffer	a*(path)*y, sym*(path)*y, *(path)*os

PED	child	*(ped)*agogue, *(ped)*ant, *(ped)*iatrician
PHIL	love	*(phil)*antrophy, *(phil)*osophy, *(phil)*ander
PHON(O)	sound	*(phono)*graph, *(phon)*etic, *(phono)*gram
PSYCH(O)	mind, soul	*(psycho)*logy, *(psych)*ic, *(Psych)*e
SOPH	wisdom	philo*(sopher)*, *(soph)*ist, *(soph)*istication
THEO	God	*(theo)*logy, *(theo)*sophy, *(theo)*cratic
THERM	heat	*(therm)*ostat, *(therm)*ometer, *(therm)*os

23c Latin Roots

AM	love	*(am)*ity, *(am)*orist, *(am)*orous
ANIM	breath, soul, spirit	*(anim)*al, *(anim)*ate, un*(anim)*ous
AQU(A)	water	*(aqu)*educt, *(aqua)*tic, *(aqua)*rium
AUD	hear	*(aud)*itor, *(aud)*ience, *(aud)*itorium
CAPIT	head	*(capit)*al, *(capit)*ate, *(capit)*alize
CAP(T), CEP(T), CIP(T)	take	*(cap)*tive, pre*(cept)*, pre*(cip)*itate
CED, CESS	go, yield	ante*(ced)*ent, con*(cede)*, ex*(cess)*ive
CENT	hundred	*(cent)*ury, *(cent)*urion, per*(cent)*(age)
CER(N), CRI(M,T), CRE(M,T)	separate, judge, choose	dis*(cern)*, *(crim)*inal, dis*(crete)*
CRED	believe, trust	*(cred)*it, in*(cred)*ible, *(cred)*ulity
CLAR	clear, bright	*(clar)*ity, *(clar)*ify, de*(clar)*ation
CORD	heart	dis*(cord)*, con*(cord)*, *(cord)*ial
CORP(OR)	body, substance	*(corpor)*al, *(corp)*se, *(corp)*ulent
DON	give	*(don)*or, *(don)*ate
DOM(IN)	tame, subdue	*(domin)*ant, *(domin)*ate, *(domin)*ion
DORM	sleep	*(dorm)*ant, *(dorm)*itory, *(dorm)*ient
DUC	lead	con*(duc)*t, *(duc)*tile, aque*(duc)*t
FER	bear	in*(fer)*ence, *(fer)*tile, re*(fer)*
FORT	strong	*(fort)*ress, *(fort)*e, *(fort)*itude
FRAG, FRING FRACT	break	*(frag)*ile, in*(fring)*e, *(fract)*ure
GEN	beget, origin	en*(gen)*der, con*(gen)*ital, *(gen)*-eration
JAC(T), JEC(T)	cast	e*(jac)*ulate, pro*(ject)*, e*(ject)*
LATE	carry	col*(late)*, vacil*(late)*, re*(late)*
MI(SS,T)	send	dis*(miss)*, *(miss)*ionary, re*(mit)*
NOMIN, NOMEN	name	*(nomin)*ate, *(nomen)*clature
NOV	new	*(nov)*el, *(nov)*ice, in*(nov)*ation
PED	foot	*(ped)*al, centi*(pede)*, *(ped)*estrian
PLEN, PLET	full	*(plen)*ty, *(plen)*itude, re*(plete)*
PORT	bear	*(port)*er, de*(port)*, im*(port)*ance
POTENT	able, powerful	*(potent)*, *(potent)*ial, *(potent)*ate
SECT	cut	dis*(sect)*, in*(sect)*, *(sect)*ion

23d Suffixes

NOUN SUFFIXES

1. *Suffixes Denoting an Agent*

   —ANT (*–ent*) one who, that which   ten*(ant)*, ag*(ent)*
   —AR (*–er*) one who   schol*(ar)*, farm*(er)*
   —ARD (*–art*) one who (often deprecative) cow*(ard)*, bragg*(art)*
   —EER one who   privat*(eer)*, auction*(eer)*
   —ESS a woman who   waitr*(ess)*, seamstr*(ess)*
   —IER (*–yer*) one who   cash*(ier)*, law*(yer)*
   —IST one who   novel*(ist)*, Commun*(ist)*
   —OR one who, that which   act*(or)*, tract*(or)*
   —STER one who, that which   young*(ster)*, road*(ster)*

2. *Suffix Denoting the Receiver of an Action*

   —EE one who is the object of some action   appoint*(ee)*, divorc*(ee)*

3. *Suffixes Denoting Smallness or Diminutiveness*

   —CULE (*–cle*)   mole*(cule)*, ventri*(cle)*
   —ETTE   din*(ette)*, cigar*(ette)*
   —LET   ring*(let)*, brace*(let)*
   —LING   duck*(ling)*, prince*(ling)*

4. *Suffixes Denoting Place*

   —ARY indicating location or repository   diction*(ary)*, api*(ary)*
   —ERY place or establishment   bak*(ery)*, nunn*(ery)*
   —ORY (*–arium, –orium*) place for, concerned
       with   dormit*(ory)*, audit*(orium)*

5. *Suffixes Denoting Act, State, Quality,*
   or Condition

   —ACY denoting quality, state   accur*(acy)*, delic*(acy)*
   —AL pertaining to action   refus*(al)*, deni*(al)*
   —ANCE (*–ancy*) denoting action or state   brilli*(ance)*, buoy*(ancy)*
   —ATION denoting result   migr*(ation)*, el*(ation)*
   —DOM denoting a general condition   wis*(dom)*, bore*(dom)*
   —ENCE (*–ency*) state, quality of   abstin*(ence)*, consist*(ency)*
   —ERY denoting quality, action   fool*(ery)*, prud*(ery)*
   —HOOD state, quality   knight*(hood)*, false*(hood)*
   —ICE condition or quality   serv*(ice)*, just*(ice)*
   —ION (*–sion*) state or condition   un*(ion)*, ten*(sion)*
   —ISM denoting action, state, or condition bapt*(ism)*, plagiar*(ism)*
   —ITY (*–ety*) action, state, or condition joll*(ity)*, gai*(ety)*
   —MENT action or state resulting from   punish*(ment)*, frag*(ment)*

—NESS quality, state of   good*(ness)*, prepared*(ness)*
—OR denoting action, state, or quality   hon*(or)*, lab*(or)*
—TH pertaining to condition, state, or action   warm*(th)*, steal*(th)*
—URE denoting action, result, or instrument   legislat*(ure)*, pleas*(ure)*

ADJECTIVE SUFFIXES

—ABLE (*–ible, –ile*) capable of being   lov*(able)*, ed*(ible)*, contract*(ile)*
—AC relating to, like   elegi*(ac)*, cardi*(ac)*
—ACIOUS inclined to   pugn*(acious)*, aud*(acious)*
—AL pertaining to   radic*(al)*, cordi*(al)*
—AN pertaining to   sylv*(an)*, urb*(an)*
—ANT (*–ent*) inclined to   pleas*(ant)*, converg*(ent)*
—AR pertaining to   sol*(ar)*, regul*(ar)*
—ARY pertaining to   contr*(ary)*, revolution*(ary)*
—ATIVE inclined to   demonstr*(ative)*, talk*(ative)*
—FUL full of   joy*(ful)*, pain*(ful)*
—IC (*–ical*) pertaining to   volcan*(ic)*, angel*(ical)*
—ISH like, relating to, being   devil*(ish)*, boy*(ish)*
—IVE inclined to, having the nature of   elus*(ive)*, nat*(ive)*
—LESS without, unable to be   piti*(less)*, resist*(less)*
—OSE full of   bellic*(ose)*, mor*(ose)*
—OUS full of   pi*(ous)*, fam*(ous)*
—ULENT (*–olent*) full of   fraud*(ulent)*, vi*(olent)*

VERB SUFFIXES

The following verb suffixes usually mean "to make" (to become, to increase, etc.).

—ATE   toler*(ate)*, vener*(ate)*
—EN   madd*(en)*, wid*(en)*
—FY   magni*(fy)*, beauti*(fy)*
—IZE (*–ise*)   colon*(ize)*, exerc*(ise)*

Exercise 93	**WORD ANALYSIS: PREFIXES**

Break the following English words into their parts, and give the literal meaning of each part as derived from its source. Consult the lists of prefixes and roots given on previous pages. Use your dictionary if you find a part not given in these lists. Be able to use each word in a sentence.

WORD	PREFIX (and literal meaning)	ROOT (and literal meaning)	MEANING OF WHOLE WORD
unicorn	*uni-, one*	*-corn, a horn*	*one-horned*
1. abnormal			
2. admire			
3. anticipate			
4. befriend			
5. biceps			
6. catalog			
7. coherent			
8. controversy			
9. decide			

WORD	PREFIX (and literal meaning)	ROOT (and literal meaning)	MEANING OF WHOLE WORD
10. diagram	_____	_____	_____
	_____	_____	_____
11. dismiss	_____	_____	_____
	_____	_____	_____
12. energy	_____	_____	_____
	_____	_____	_____
13. epitaph	_____	_____	_____
	_____	_____	_____
14. euphemism	_____	_____	_____
	_____	_____	_____
15. excellent	_____	_____	_____
	_____	_____	_____
16. introduce	_____	_____	_____
	_____	_____	_____
17. kilometer	_____	_____	_____
	_____	_____	_____
18. mistake	_____	_____	_____
	_____	_____	_____
19. multiple	_____	_____	_____
	_____	_____	_____
20. obtain	_____	_____	_____
	_____	_____	_____

WORD	PREFIX (and literal meaning)	ROOT (and literal meaning)	MEANING OF WHOLE WORD
21. paragraph			
22. postscript			
23. predict			
24. progress			
25. reflect			
26. semiannual			
27. supervise			
28. synthesis			
29. tricycle			
30. unwise			

Exercise 94 | WORD ANALYSIS: SUFFIXES

Break the following English words into their parts, and give the literal meaning of each part as derived from its source. Consult the lists of suffixes and roots given on previous pages. Use your dictionary if you find a part not given in these lists. Be able to use each word in a sentence.

WORD	ROOT (and literal meaning)	SUFFIX (and literal meaning)	MEANING OF WHOLE WORD
wonderful	*wonder-, a marvel*	*-ful, full of*	*causing wonder; marvelous*
1. acceptable			
2. active			
3. artistic			
4. avowal			
5. careless			
6. cashier			
7. childish			
8. confusion			

WORD	ROOT (and literal meaning)	SUFFIX (and literal meaning)	MEANING OF WHOLE WORD
9. contentment			
10. density			
11. dentist			
12. dependence			
13. dutiful			
14. freedom			
15. friendship			
16. furious			
17. harmonize			
18. heroism			
19. icy			

WORD	ROOT (and literal meaning)	SUFFIX (and literal meaning)	MEANING OF WHOLE WORD
20. inventor	_____	_____	_____
	_____	_____	_____
21. laggard	_____	_____	_____
	_____	_____	_____
22. laundress	_____	_____	_____
	_____	_____	_____
23. lavatory	_____	_____	_____
	_____	_____	_____
24. piratical	_____	_____	_____
	_____	_____	_____
25. practical	_____	_____	_____
	_____	_____	_____
26. primary	_____	_____	_____
	_____	_____	_____
27. privacy	_____	_____	_____
	_____	_____	_____
28. tenacious	_____	_____	_____
	_____	_____	_____
29. terrify	_____	_____	_____
	_____	_____	_____
30. youngster	_____	_____	_____
	_____	_____	_____

| Exercise 95 | WORD ANALYSIS: ROOTS |

For each root listd below write the meaning and at least three words containing the root. Do not use the same word with two roots. If the root given is not listed on the previous pages, look it up in your dictionary, which is also the best source for finding the words you need. Remember that some words containing these roots will have prefixes.

ROOT	MEANING	WORDS CONTAINING ROOT
sense, sent	*feel*	*sensitive, sensual, sentimental*
1. am(are)		
2. aster, astr		
3. bibl(ia)		
4. cent		
5. clam		
6. clud, claud, clus		
7. doc(ere)		
8. dom(in)		
9. geo		
10. grad, gress		
11. hosp(es)		
12. mechan(e)		
13. mega		
14. memor		
15. micro		
16. phon(o)		
17. sequ(i), secut		

ROOT	MEANING	WORDS CONTAINING ROOT
18. uti(l)	_____	_____
19. vol	_____	_____
20. vox, vocis	_____	_____

| Exercise 96 | **VOCABULARY: PREFIXES AND SUFFIXES** |

A. Underline the prefix in each of the following words, give its meaning, and use the word in a sentence so as to show the meaning of the prefix.

	MEANING OF PREFIX	**SENTENCE**
_chrono_logical	time	George, please name the presidents of the United States in chronological order.
1. circum-ference		
2. convention		
3. dissolve		
4. foremost		
5. nonsense		
6. precede		
7. semicircle		
8. superlative		

	MEANING OF PREFIX	SENTENCE
9. <u>trans</u>- portation	_____	_____
	_____	_____
10. <u>tri</u>ple	_____	_____
	_____	_____

B. In the following list of words underline each suffix, give its meaning, and use the word in a sentence.

	MEANING OF SUFFIX	SENTENCE
power<u>ful</u>	*full of*	*A good swimmer must have powerful arms and legs.*
	_____	_____
1. accur<u>acy</u>	_____	_____
	_____	_____
2. back<u>ward</u>	_____	_____
	_____	_____
3. commun<u>ism</u>	_____	_____
	_____	_____
4. curi<u>ous</u>	_____	_____
	_____	_____
5. despic<u>able</u>	_____	_____
	_____	_____
6. govern<u>ment</u>	_____	_____
	_____	_____

	MEANING OF SUFFIX	SENTENCE
7. malignant	_____	_____
	_____	_____
8. manager	_____	_____
	_____	_____
9. necessary	_____	_____
	_____	_____
10. winsome	_____	_____
	_____	_____

Exercise 97 | VOCABULARY: LATIN AND GREEK ROOTS

A. Use the derivatives of **duc**, meaning "lead," necessary to complete the following statements. (In this and the following exercises, remember that these roots may be found in words that contain prefixes.)

1. A tube, channel, or canal through which a gas or liquid moves is known as a _____.

2. When one lessens something in size, weight, amount, or value, he _____ it.

3. Something made by either nature or human art or industry is called a _____ .

4. A person who is a leader, guide, or manager, especially the director of an orchestra, is a

   _____ .

5. To lead to a given place, to add as a new feature, or to present persons to each other is
   the act of _____.

B. Use the derivatives of **vert**, meaning "turn," necessary to complete the following statements.

1. A person whose interest is more in himself than in his environment or in other people is
   an _____ .

2. When one turns something upside down, he _____.

3. _____ is a sensation of dizziness in which an individual feels that he or his
   surroundings are whirling about sickeningly.

4. One person's account of an incident which he reports or describes from only one point of
   view is his _____ .

5. An automobile with a top that can be folded back to change it into a topless car is a

   _____ .

C. Use the derivatives of **fin**, meaning "end," necessary to complete the following statements.

1. The end of something, such as the last chapter in a book or an examination at the end of
   the school term, is frequently described as _____.

2. To bring to an end or complete some task or activity is to _____ it.

3. The _____ of an entertainment or performance is its last scene or feature.

4. Something that is so small that it cannot be measured may may be described as being

   _____ .

5. Something that is of superior quality, i.e., something that has been finished and per-
fected, is often described as _____ .

D. Use the derivatives of **met(e)r**, meaning "measure," necessary to complete the following
sentences.

1. The regular rhythmic quality of verse which follows a specific pattern of stressed and un-
stressed syllables is called _____ .

2. A _____ is a clockwork device with an inverted pendulum, beating time
at a determined rate and helping a musician maintain regular tempo while playing.

3. The measurement of the range and power of one's eyesight is the science of _____ .

4. The decimal system of weights and measures in which the gram, the meter, and the liter
are basic units of weight, length, and capacity is known as the _____ system.

5. The straight line which passes through the center of a circle or sphere from one side to
the other is the _____ .

24

Spelling

Spelling is an important aspect of written communication. Instructors seldom have the opportunity, however, to spend adequate classroom time on the subject. The responsibility for the mastery of spelling, therefore, rests almost solely on the individual student.

Here are a few practical suggestions on how to approach the problem of spelling:

1. Always use the dictionary when you are in doubt about the spelling of a word.

2. If there is a rule applicable to the type of words which you misspell, learn that rule.

3. Employ any "tricks" which might assist you in remembering the spelling of particular words that give you trouble. If, for example, you confuse the meaning and hence the spelling of *statue* and *stature,* remember that the longer word refers to bodily "longness." Certain troublesome words can be spelled correctly if you will remember their prefixes (as in *dis/appoint*) or their suffixes (as in *cool/ly*). Also it might help you to remember that there are only three *-ceed* words: *exceed, proceed,* and *succeed.*

4. Keep a list of the words which you misspell. In writing down these words, observe their syllabication and any peculiarities of construction. Try to "see" — that is, to have a mental picture of — these words.

5. Practice the correct pronunciation of troublesome words. Misspelling is often the result of mispronunciation.

Of the many rules governing spelling four are particularly useful since they are widely applicable. Study these four rules carefully.

24a Final *e*

Drop the final *e* before a suffix beginning with a vowel (*-ing, -ous,* etc.) but retain the final *e* before a suffix beginning with a consonant (*-ment, -ly,* etc.):

    Final *e* dropped: come + ing = coming
                         fame + ous = famous

love + able = lovable
guide + ance = guidance

Final *e* retained: move + ment = movement
fate + ful = fateful
sole + ly = solely

EXCEPTIONS: Acknowledge, acknowledgment; abridge, abridgment; judge, judgment; dye, dyeing; singe, singeing; hoe, hoeing; mile, mileage; due, duly; awe, awful; whole, wholly. The final **e** is retained after **c** or **g** when the suffix begins with **a** or **o**: peace, peaceable; courage, courageous.

24b Final Consonant

Double a final consonant before a suffix beginning with a vowel if (1) the word is of one syllable or is accented on the last syllable and (2) the final consonant is preceded by a single vowel:

Word of one syllable: stop + ed = stopped

Word in which the accent falls on the last syllable: occur + ence = occurrence

Word in which the accent does not fall on the last syllable: differ + ence = difference

24c *ei* and *ie*

When **ei** and **ie** have the long **ee** sound (as in *keep*), use **i** before **e** except after **c**. (The word *lice* will aid you in remembering this rule; **i** follows **l** and all other consonants except **c**, while **e** follows **c**.)

ie	*ei* (after *c*)
chief	ceiling
field	receive
niece	deceive
siege	conceit

EXCEPTIONS (grouped to form a sentence): Neither financier seized either species of weird leisure.

24d Final *y*

In words ending in *y* preceded by a consonant, change the *y* to *i* before any suffix except one beginning with *i.*

Suffix beginning with a letter other than *i*:

fly + es = flies
ally + es = allies
easy + ly = easily
mercy + ful = merciful
study + ous = studious

Suffix beginning with *i*:

fly + ing = flying
study + ing = studying

24e Spelling List

The following list is made up of approximately 450 frequently misspelled words. Since these are commonly used words, you should learn to spell all of them after you have mastered the words on your individual list.

absence	audience	competent	dining
academic	autumn	competition	diphtheria
accept	auxiliary	complement	disappear
accidentally	awkward	completely	disappoint
accommodate	bankruptcy	compliment	disastrous
accumulate	barbarous	compulsory	discipline
accustomed	becoming	confident	discussion
acknowledge	beginning	congratulate	disease
acquaintance	believe	connoisseur	dissatisfied
across	beneficial	conqueror	dissipate
address	benefited	conscience	distribute
advantage	brilliant	conscientious	divine
aggravate	Britain	conscious	division
allege	buoyant	contemptible	dormitories
all right	bureau	continuous	drudgery
altogether	business	convenient	dual
always	cafeteria	coolly	duchess
amateur	calendar	council	duel
among	camouflage	counsel	dyeing
amount	candidate	courteous	dying
analysis	captain	criticism	ecstasy
angel	carburetor	curiosity	efficiency
anonymous	carriage	curriculum	eighth
anxiety	cavalry	dealt	eligible
any more	ceiling	deceit	eliminate
apology	cemetery	decide	embarrassed
apparatus	certain	defendant	eminent
apparent	changeable	definite	emphasize
appearance	characteristic	dependent	enthusiastic
appreciate	chauffeur	descend	environment
appropriate	choose	descent	equipped
arctic	chosen	describe	equivalent
argument	clothes	description	erroneous
arithmetic	colloquial	desert	especially
around	colonel	desirable	exaggerate
arrangement	column	despair	excellent
ascend	coming	desperate	except
assassin	commission	dessert	exercise
association	committee	dictionary	exhaust
athletics	comparative	dietitian	exhilaration
attendance	compel	difference	existence
attractive	compelled	dilapidated	expel

expelled	immediately	momentous	permanent
experience	incidentally	morale	permissible
explanation	independence	mortgage	perseverance
extraordinary	indispensable	murmur	persistent
familiar	inevitable	muscle	personal
fascinate	infinite	mysterious	personnel
February	influential	naturally	perspiration
finally	innocence	necessary	persuade
financial	instance	nevertheless	physically
financier	instant	nickel	physician
forehead	intellectual	niece	picnicking
foreign	intelligence	ninety	piece
foreword	intentionally	ninth	pleasant
forfeit	interested	noticeable	politician
formally	irrevelant	notoriety	politics
formerly	irresistible	nowadays	politicking
forth	its	nucleus	possession
forty	it's	obedience	possible
fourth	judgment	obstacle	practically
fraternity	kindergarten	occasion	precede
friend	knowledge	occasionally	preference
fulfill	laboratory	occurrence	preferred
fundamental	led	o'clock	prejudice
futile	legitimate	off	preparation
furniture	leisure	omission	prevalent
gauge	library	omitted	principal
generally	likable	operate	principle
genius	literature	opinion	privilege
government	livelihood	opportunity	probably
grammar	loose	optimism	procedure
granddaughter	lose	organization	professor
grandeur	lovable	original	prominent
grievance	magazine	outrageous	pronunciation
guarantee	maintain	overrun	propaganda
handkerchief	maintenance	paid	psychology
harass	maneuver	pamphlet	publicly
having	manual	parallel	purchase
height	manufacture	paralysis	pursue
hindrance	mathematics	paralyzed	quantity
hitchhike	meant	parliament	quarter
hoping	medicine	particularly	questionnaire
hygiene	mediocre	partner	quiet
hypocrisy	miniature	passed	quite
illusion	mirror	past	quiz
imaginary	mischievous	pastime	quizzes
imitation	misspell	perform	realize

really	seize	stretch	unnecessary
recognize	sense	studying	until
recommend	sentence	superintendent	unusual
region	separate	supersede	using
reign	sergeant	surprise	usually
relevant	severely	susceptible	vaccine
religious	sheriff	syllable	vacuum
remembrance	shining	symmetry	valuable
repetition	shriek	temperature	vegetable
representative	siege	tendency	vengeance
resistance	significant	their	vigilance
respectfully	similar	thorough	vigorous
respectively	sincerely	too	village
restaurant	sophomore	tournament	villain
rhetoric	source	tragedy	weather
rheumatism	speak	transferred	Wednesday
ridiculous	specimen	tremendous	weird
sacrifice	speech	truly	whether
sacrilegious	stationary	Tuesday	who's
salable	stationery	twelfth	whose
salary	statue	tying	women
sandwich	stature	tyranny	writing
schedule	statute	unanimous	written
science	strength	undoubtedly	
secretary	strenuous	universally	

| Exercise 98 | SPELLING |

A. Combine the specified suffix with each of the following words and write the correct form in the space provided.

EXAMPLE: hope + ing   _____*hoping*_____

1. marry + age   _____

2. carry + ed   _____

3. menace + ing   _____

4. finance + ial   _____

5. tendency + s   _____

6. judge + ment   _____

7. ninety + eth   _____

8. equip + ed   _____

9. expel + ed   _____

10. recognize + able _____

11. hop + ed   _____

12. approve + al   _____

13. beauty + fy   _____

14. demonstrate + ive _____

15. offer + ed   _____

16. benefit + ed   _____

17. public + ly   _____

18. deny + al   _____

19. amiable + ly   _____

20. control + ing _____

21. migrate + ion _____

22. try + ed _____

23. please + ant _____

24. forgot + en _____

25. mad + en _____

26. obligate + ion _____

27. journey + s _____

28. lonely + ness _____

29. country + s _____

30. fury + ous _____

B. Supply either *ei* or *ie* in each of the following words. Then write the correct form in the space provided.

EXAMPLE: h *ei* ght _____*height*_____

1. shr___k _____   11. f___gn _____

2. fr___ndly _____   12. pr___st _____

3. n___ghbor _____   13. w___ght _____

4. l___sure _____   14. conc___t _____

5. f___ndish _____   15. s___ze _____

6. h___ress _____   16. c___ling _____

7. sl___gh _____   17. fr___ght _____

8. forf___t _____   18. l___utenant _____

9. gr___f _____   19. w___ner _____

10. ach___ve _____   20. s___ge _____

Exercise 99 | SPELLING

If there is a misspelled word in any line of five words given below, underline it and write it correctly at the right. If all five words are correctly spelled, write **C** in the blank.

EXAMPLE: disappoint, elegible, courteous, chosen, except   *eligible*

1. cemetery, dilapadated, arctic, bureau, divine   _____

2. conscious, vigilence, transferred, written, tying   _____

3. siege, villain, permanant, grammar, fulfill   _____

4. sense, unecessary, tragedy, thorough, ninety   _____

5. nucleus, pleasant, facinate, generally, amateur   _____

6. harass, pursue, publically, nowadays, genius   _____

7. strenuous, unanimous, syllable, recommend, salable   _____

8. sacreligious, similar, innocence, led, eighth   _____

9. procedure, parliament, strength, mirrow, muscle   _____

10. psychology, mispell, mysterious, schedule, deceit   _____

11. apology, carriage, chauffeur, coolly, alledge   _____

12. criticism, dissipate, auxilary, dining, likable   _____

13. vacuum, hankerchief, purchase, having, foreword   _____

14. sincerly, symmetry, unusual, valuable, sandwich   _____

15. brilliant, carberator, drudgery, absence, angel   _____

16. awkward, ecstasy, erroneous, beginning, definate   _____

17. address, alright, eminent, diphtheria, supersede   _____

18. privilege, temperature, sergeant, severely, personnel _____

19. sentence, gauge, grandeur, seperate, lovable _____

20. pamphlet, quanity, nickel, mortgage, hindrance _____

Exercise 100	SPELLING

Underline any word which is misspelled. Then write it correctly at the right. If a sentence contains no misspelled word, write **C** in the blank.

EXAMPLE: Don't you think that Terry <u>exagerated</u> his story about being lost in the woods?   *exaggerated*

1. It seemed to Pat that there apology was insincere. _____

2. It was no easy job keeping twenty people quiet so that Janie would be really suprised at the party. _____

3. Our cat is no longer the loveable kitten she once was. _____

4. "I suppose it's all right to reply to this questionaire, but I refuse to give my age," said Aunt Gertrude. _____

5. The accomodations at this hotel are rather poor, but its convenient location is desirable. _____

6. Alicia says that mathamatics is no problem. _____

7. Jake is hoping that it will be permissable for him to dance with the duchess at the Valentine Ball in February. _____

8. The actions of the assasin were definitely those of a psychotic individual. _____

9. Mr. Pimm tells me that his grandaughter is a sophomore at the university and that your wife is one of her professors. _____

10. With the housing industry paralyzed, Mr. Franklin's filing for bankrupcy was almost inevitable. _____

11. When the calvary rode up with banners flying and bugles sounding, every little boy in the audience cheered loudly. _____

12. The sherriff of our county told Hetty that the mysterious occurrence she had described was probably imaginary. _____

13. The man at the appliance store reminded me that the pamplet of
    instructions that came with the food processor is indispensable.   _____

14. Amelia and Doris have benefitted enormously from their daily
    exercise class.   _____

15. On his latest trip to Britian Mike was able to purchase a piece of
    porcelain that was made during the reign of Henry VIII.   _____

16. Melinda, you're a perfect angle to help me hem this full skirt,
    especially when you are undoubtedly pressed for time.   _____

17. Mr. Locklear was in dispair over his son's mischievous ways, and he
    was particularly embarrassed at the boy's latest scrape.   _____

18. John, if you would elimanate some of your bad eating habits,
    such as having two desserts, you could get back to the size you
    formerly were.   _____

19. Roger was finally willing to acknowledge that he found Matt's
    presence a hinderance, not a help.   _____

20. As the defendent saw the jury filing into the courtroom, he knew
    immediately that the verdict was "Guilty."   _____

21. If you are comming to harass me about cleaning up my room,
    Julia, I recommend that you go away.   _____

22. I believe that the mother of the groom will preceed the mother of
    the bride in entering the church.   _____

23. Have you seen the minature poodle that the Martins gave Serena
    for her ninth birthday?   _____

24. Does that sociologist really believe that a person's early enviroment
    is irrelevant to the emotional problems of adulthood?   _____

25. The two roads run paralell for several miles, eventually curving off
    in divergent directions.   _____

TEST ON LESSONS 1-7

A. In each of the following sentences underline the subject once and the verb twice; then circle the complement (or complements). On the first line at the right tell whether the verb is transitive active **(TA)**, transitive passive **(TP)**, or intransitive **(I)**. On the second line tell whether the complement is a direct object **(DO)**, an indirect object **(IO)**, a predicate nominative **(PN)**, a predicate adjective **(PA)**, an objective complement **(OC)**, or a retained object **(RO)**. Note that not all sentences have complements.

1. Foreigners are touring America in increasing numbers.   _____ _____

2. Lonnie's muscles ached from chopping wood.   _____ _____

3. The full moon cast a silvery reflection on the water.   _____ _____

4. Mother sent me a box of homemade cookies.   _____ _____

5. Wes was fortunate to get a job for the summer.   _____ _____

6. There on the stair stood Emily.   _____ _____

7. The restaurant around the corner burned last night.   _____ _____

8. I was asked a difficult question by my teacher.   _____ _____

9. The research results are quite surprising.   _____ _____

10. The hockey team elected Marshall captain and Mike co-captain.   _____ _____

B. What part of speech is each of the following underscored words?

1. in in the first sentence above   _____

2. wood in the second sentence above   _____

3. silvery in the third sentence above   _____

4. homemade in the fourth sentence above   _____

5. Wes in the fifth sentence above   _____

6. There in the sixth sentence above   _____

7. around in the seventh sentence above   _____

8. I in the eighth sentence above   _____

9. quite in the ninth sentence above   _____

10. and in the tenth sentence above   _____

C. In each of the sentences below identify the *italicized* expression by writing one of the following numbers in the space at the right:

1 if it is a *prepositional phrase,*   6 if it is an *absolute phrase,*
2 if it is a *participial phrase,*   7 if it is a *noun clause,*
3 if it is a *gerund phrase,*   8 if it is an *adjective clause,*
4 if it is an *infinitive phrase,*   9 if it is an *adverbial clause.*
5 if it is an *appositive phrase,*

1. I have two reports to prepare *for my accounting class.* _____

2. I enjoyed *reading A Tale of Two Cities.* _____

3. Jessie telephoned last night and said *that she needed some money.* _____

4. Will you be ready *to leave on time today?* _____

5. *Eating out* has become quite expensive for a family. _____

6. *If you eat that cake,* you will never lose weight. _____

7. Recently we visited Sea Island, *which is off the coast of Georgia.* _____

8. Donna, *my sister's roommate,* is from Australia. _____

9. *Having explained his problem,* Joe asked for Marsha's help. _____

10. *The class being over,* we all rushed to the cafeteria. _____

D. Underline the dependent clause (or clauses) in each of the following sentences. In the first space at the right tell whether the clause is a noun clause **(N)**, an adjective clause **(Adj)**, or an adverbial clause **(Adv)**. In the second space tell how the noun clause is used (that is, whether it is a *subject, direct object,* etc.), or what the adjective or adverbial clause modifies.

1. Critics of the decision say that sufficient planning was lacking. _____ _____

2. Can you recommend someone who would be a dependable babysitter? _____ _____

3. The consensus of the faculty was that no major changes in curriculum should be made. _____ _____

4. While we were in class, someone left a bag of candy in our room. _____ _____

5. Although I would like to read Walker Percy's latest book, I have not had time. _____ _____

6. Why everyone was so excited was a mystery to me. _____ _____

7. This room will be cooler if you close the blinds. _____ _____

8. Don't you know that she is an honorable person? _____ _____

9. Can you remember the house where you lived as a child? _____ _____

10. Although Carl spoke eloquently, he spoke too long. _____ _____

E. In the following sentences insert all necessary commas and semicolons. Rewrite sentence fragments in such a way as to make complete sentences. If a sentence is correct, mark it **C.**

1. I never did understand his attitude but I always liked him.

2. Because Amy had no afternoon classes she took a part-time job.

3. Mr. Ray, whose first name is Billy.

4. You won't get the scholarship unless you apply for it at once.

5. If Mr. Ward goes to London next month Mrs. Ward will go with him.

6. Before you go please mow the lawn I don't have time.

7. My mother who was born in Indiana has lived in Alabama for many years.

8. Angie ran out of gas while she was on her way to the grocery store.

9. Energy independence is necessary to economic recovery therefore everyone should practice conservation.

10. When you finish college what are you planning to do?

TEST ON LESSONS 8–18

Correct all errors in the following sentences. Errors may be crossed out and corrections written above the sentence. A misplaced element may be underscored and its proper place in the sentence indicated by a caret (∧). In some cases the entire sentence will have to be rewritten. If a sentence is correct, write **C**.

1. The jogger's hair was damp, frizzy, and she had tied it back with a scarlet ribbon.

2. I believe that you hanged the umbrella on the coatrack in the lobby.

3. From the bridge we had a clear view of the tanker laying at anchor.

4. I dropped your clothes by the laundry, and I went to the library, and then I met Maude for lunch.

5. Everyone has their own estimate of the size of the crowd at a political rally.

6. Mr. Scranton has sold more policies than any insurance agent in town.

7. In the morning either Bess or I are going to take Tony to the airport.

8. To pack a suit and enough shirts, another suitcase is going to be necessary.

9. While sitting in the sun, my hair dried slowly.

10. Carlos was so sleepy last night that he only typed half of his research paper.

11. Celeste has a better grasp of statistics than me.

12. I would make banana pudding, but we ate all of them last night.

13. Trudy is studious, conscientious, and **who is also** clever.

14. Once trained, Mitzi hopes to show her spaniel in New York.

15. I believe that the typewriter case is **setting** on the other side of the desk.

16. **Whom** do you think will represent the Republicans in the race for governor?

17. My father was paged at the football game, which certainly surprised him.

18. The children caught the bus to go to the Christmas parade, which stops at our corner every twenty minutes.

19. Because stamp collecting is his hobby, I know that he will be pleased with these from Brazil.

20. His costume calls for a Panama hat, a black string tie, and a white linen suit.

21. John and I had dinner at Harvey's, and we saw John's friend Barton, and John introduced me to him.

22. **Because Dad had built** a fire pleased all of us who had been shoveling snow.

23. Melissa **sure** was glad that she had found a summer job at Green Falls.

24. A year ago Mr. Bladen planned to **have begun** raising horses.

25. Kurt can speak German as well if not better than our instructor.

26. The watercolors were painted by art students hanging in the administration building.

27. Murphy is one of those baseball fans who never misses a home game.

28. Because the thermometer reads ninety-five degrees is the reason you feel hot.

29. I cannot find the tape or the scissors, which means I won't wrap this package today.

30. In the bottom of Sue's tote bag were a pack of chewing gum, candy bar, and a pair of sunglasses.

31. If I was you, I'd put the begonias in a sunny window.

32. Neither Grandmother nor Aunt Libby ever remember to wind the clock.

33. Last Sunday the Rankins asked Paul and I to ride up to the mountains with them.

34. About four o'clock is when we usually drop by Sadie's Ice Cream Shop.

35. Who do you think can refinish the table and chairs for us?

36. After eating lunch, our bus left the main highway and travelled on a narrow road that runs along the coast.

37. Today's humidity is less than yesterday.

38. A breakdown of these figures are available in Mr. Baxter's office.

39. Marsha doesn't remember if her recipe for onion soup calls for six or eight onions.

40. Before waxing your car, be sure to thoroughly dry it.

41. With the prospect of a trip to Hawaii, who wouldn't feel good?

42. The trees along Monroe Avenue sure have grown in the last year or two.

43. Do you remember the year when the cable was first lain across the Atlantic?

44. The sidewalk looks icy, so do walk careful.

45. My subject will require more research than Gage.

46. The breakfast dishes had been washed, and lunch had been planned, and all of us set out for the beach.

47. After a swim we gathered up our belongings, which we had laid near a sand dune.

48. The dispatcher said that the train passed through Leesville every day at noon.

49. Joyce wishes that she was able to study ballet as well as piano.

50. I could tell by the voice that it was not him who called.

TEST ON LESSONS 19–24

A. In the following sentences insert all necessary punctuation marks, and correct all errors of mechanics.

1. Honestly Judy I didn't know that you had ever lived in detroit.

2. The Atlanta Constitution has changed it's format and now carries a political opinion column on the front page.

3. The ex mayor of our city has announced that he will run for an alderman's post; the present alderman has decided to retire.

4. This winters weather has been terrible for the north and I hear that another snowstorm is headed toward Maine and Massachusetts this week.

5. Remember to take your raincoat called Mother its supposed to rain this afternoon.

6. The baby said Sally is ready for her nap.

7. Whenever I re-read Huckleberry Finn I enjoy it all over again.

8. This falllike weather is a pleasant relief lets go for a hike up Stone Mountain.

9. The French term chaise longue is often mispronounced.

10. Heres a list for those who are going on the field trip it includes the following field glasses hiking boots windbreaker and sandwiches for lunch.

11. Is this copy of Nicholas Nickleby your's Suzanne?

12. My Mother is planning a trip to St. Louis while she is there she will stay at Franklin's and Olivia's house.

13. I wonder whose going to stay with the baby while Martha is in London maybe her mother in law will be able to come.

14. Nan's youngest brother Kevin is a self taught guitarist but he is a better musician than many who have had lessons.

15. My english teacher has assigned us Browning's poem My last duchess for tomorrow.

B. After each of the following groups of words indicate the level of usage of the *italicized* word(s), using the following abbreviations: **A** for archaic, **D** for dialectal, **I** for informal (colloquial), and **S** for slang. Use your dictionary for this test.

1. You *goofed* when you didn't baste the hem before stitching it.   *S*

2. Little Robbie is the *least* one of the Smiths' children.   _____

3. Tom got the *brush-off* from Audrey.   _____

4. Roger is a perpetual *sorehead.*   _____

5. Omar the poet said that "wilderness is Paradise *enow.*"   _____

6. We're headed for the *shindig* over at the Thompsons'.   _____

7. The newspaper says that the escaped convict is a three-time *loser.*   _____

8. Our old cat is a haughty *critter.*   _____

9. Jane was *shook up* at failing the history test.   _____

10. *Wherefore* are you angry with me?   _____

C. The following section of the test is based on the Glossary of Faulty Diction. Cross out all the errors or colloquialisms and write the preferred forms above each sentence.

1. If you will loan me your portable typewriter, Caroline, I will be able to finish my term paper.

2. Jerome said that he had less guests at his party than he had expected; I guess some people were worried about the weather.

3. The McPhersons immigrated from Scotland in 1946.

4. Lavinia seems muchly enthused about her prospective trip to Hawaii.

5. The government official says that the media is to blame for the unpopularity of the administration program.

6. The continuous rain storms that occurred again and again last week have left our streams very flooded.

7. It is hard to determine if I should go on that new crash diet I've heard about.

8. Don't you think that Beverly was kind of mean to refuse a date with Ed?

9. If you would work hard like your brother does, Gary, you could make all A's too.

10. I use to could make good spaghetti sauce, but it has been a right long time since I have tried.

11. The beautiful pink rose that Mr. Darden has entered in the flower show is more perfect than his entry for last year.

12. The reason I want to ride to Athens with you is because I have a close friend who lives there.

13. Mother almost cried when Ruthie accidently broke her antique Waterford decanter.

14. Mr. Mayfield told the university president that he is an alumni and wants to attend his class reunion.

15. We had to miss the entire first act of *La Bohème* due to a flat tire on the way.

D. Give the meaning of each of the following prefixes or roots. Then write two words containing each prefix or root.

1. *ad* _____

    (1)_____ (2)_____

2. *cur(r), curs* _____

    (1)_____ (2)_____

3. *derm* _____

    (1)_____ (2)_____

4. *dia-* _____

    (1)_____ (2)_____

5. *inter-* _____

    (1)_____ (2)_____

6. *loc* _____

    (1)_____ (2)_____

7. *man(u)* _____

    (1)_____ (2)_____

8. *pend, pens* _____

    (1)_____ (2)_____

9. *rupt* _____

    (1)_____ (2)_____

10. *sub-* _____

    (1)_____ (2)_____

E. If there is a misspelled word in any line of five words given below, write it correctly in the space at the right. If all five words are spelled correctly, write **C** in the space.

1. committee, cemetary, quarter, difference, especially   _____

2. dessert, eligible, writing, strenuous, dispair   _____

3. emphasize, conscious, twelfth, captain, camoflage   _____

4. conscience, disipline, Tuesday, vengeance, thorough   _____

5. secretary, repetition, ecstacy, confident, choose   _____

6. curriculum, connoisseur, delapidated, colonel, arctic   _____

7. piece, mortgage, nucleus, kindergarden, source   _____

8. obstacle, parliament, parallel, unanimous, lovable   _____

9. superintendant, until, seize, optimism, livelihood   _____

10. propaganda, greivance, grammar, surprise, syllable   _____

11. preferred, privilege, nowadays, irrevelant, judgment   _____

12. anxiety, fascinate, maintenance, harass, minature   _____

13. height, generally, forty, guage, fulfill   _____

14. column, curiosity, exaggerate, beginning, restaraunt   _____

15. dealt, continuous, academic, compell, argument   _____

ACHIEVEMENT TEST

A. In the following sentences identify the part of speech of each *italicized* word by writing one of the following numbers in the space at the right:

1	if it is a *noun,*	**5**	if it is an *adverb,*
2	if it is a *pronoun,*	**6**	if it is a *preposition,*
3	if it is a *verb,*	**7**	if it is a *conjunction,*
4	if it is an *adjective,*	**8**	if it is an *interjection.*

1. *Oh,* I wish that you would come to California with me. _____
2. *Neither* you *nor* I will be able to read three novels by Monday. _____
3. Opera is becoming increasingly popular *in* the United States. _____
4. During the last fifty years *much* progress has been made in understanding the formation of the stars. _____
5. Eugene O'Neill's instinct for theater *was nurtured* by his parents. _____
6. My mother had a *talent* for squeezing a dime. _____
7. Astronomers *discovered* quasars in the 1960's. _____
8. The senior class made a *very* generous donation to the school's scholarship fund. _____
9. He does an excellent job of planning and cooking the evening meals *almost* every day. _____
10. *Everyone* has gone to the basketball game. _____
11. Tommy took first place in the fishing contest *with* his ten-pound bass. _____
12. The bank served cookies and punch at *its* grand opening. _____
13. Dick loved to go to the airport to watch the big *jet* planes take off. _____
14. Everyone *except* Nancy planned to attend the concert. _____
15. Marty cut *her* hand while slicing vegetables. _____
16. I will send *whoever* comes home first. _____
17. A mother's pride swept over her *as* she watched her son walking toward her. _____
18. The boys walked single file down the narrow *forest* path. _____
19. The water was *too* cold for swimming. _____
20. The old, dilapidated truck *sputtered* and stopped. _____
21. I had rubber *heels* put on my shoes. _____
22. Hal found it very *difficult* to stay awake on the afternoon bus. _____
23. While we were snowbound, we sat before the fire *and* toasted marshmallows. _____
24. Most *of* us are fascinated by science fiction. _____
25. *Rarely* has anything influenced so many people as television. _____

B. Each of the following sentences either contains an error in grammar or is correct. Indicate the error or the correctness by writing one of the following numbers in the space at the right:

1 if the *case of the pronoun is incorrect,*
2 if the *subject and the verb do not agree,*
3 if a *pronoun and its antecedent do not agree,*
4 if an *adjective or adverb is used incorrectly,*
5 if the *sentence is correct.*

26. The media can speak for itself. _____

27. You did good on your final essay. _____

28. If they would arrive on time, they could finish on time. _____

29. Bertha as well as her two sisters are going to Canada this year. _____

30. Neither of the restaurants wanted to close their doors because of the snow. _____

31. They invited both Rosa and I to their party. _____

32. Each of the pies is cut into six pieces. _____

33. I sure hope to see you and your family this summer. _____

34. Each of the states made their own plans for the celebration. _____

35. One should vote for whomever is best qualified. _____

36. Despite staying in bed all day Friday, I still feel badly. _____

37. My father as well as my mother are enthusiastic about contract bridge. _____

38. Appearing calmly, Mary Jane stepped from the wrecked car. _____

39. The commission has announced its decision regarding the zoning dispute. _____

40. Otis has often discussed his interest in Japan with Craig and I. _____

41. If you want a real good quiche, go to Shreve's. _____

42. Neither my brother nor I are interested in investing in that company. _____

43. In spite of the thunder storm, my old collie slept sound all night. _____

44. In this class everybody is required to order their own copy of the *Wall Street Journal.* _____

45. I don't understand why neither tea nor coffee are on the menu. _____

46. At lunch the guest speaker will sit between Edgar and her. _____

47. Mr. Noyes is one of those persons who prefers trains to planes. _____

48. We appreciated you giving us a ride to the bus stop. _____

49. Not one of the birch trees has shed their leaves. _____

50. At each of our places was a note pad and pencil. _____

C. Each of the following sentences either contains an error in sentence structure or is correct. Indicate the error or correctness by writing one of the following numbers in the space at the right:

1 if the sentence contains a *dangling modifier,*
2 if the sentence contains a *misplaced modifier,*
3 if the sentence contains a *faulty reference of a pronoun,*
4 if the sentence contains *faulty parallelism,*
5 if the sentence is *correct.*

51. After opening the back door, the kitchen cooled quickly. _____
52. The electrician only worked a few minutes to fix the light switch. _____
53. The morning was bright, cool, and it was perfect for the wedding. _____
54. The beautician told Mildred that she really should spend more time at the shop. _____
55. Diane is a good sport and who can laugh at herself. _____
56. Having read until two in the morning, the words began to run together. _____
57. To find out the time, one should either turn on the radio or tune in Channel 10. _____
58. Clifford called to ask us to have breakfast with him during lunch. _____
59. The Wadsworths hardly have any jonquils in their yard this spring. _____
60. The director asked that the scene be shot again, which certainly annoyed the actress. _____
61. Our committee found it difficult to completely justify tearing down the building. _____
62. Those sunflowers are as tall if not taller than any I've ever seen. _____
63. If one can read, you will have no difficulty following this recipe. _____
64. Grandfather always has and probably always will subscribe to the *Chronicle.* _____
65. When riding through the park, the bright yellow of the marigolds caught our attention at once. _____
66. Adams assured me that he would be on time; however, this seems unlikely. _____
67. Generally speaking, the first test from an instructor is the most difficult one to take. _____
68. By the time I got to the party, the Scott twins had nearly eaten all the refreshments. _____
69. While watching the basketball game, my coat was stolen from the rack in the gym. _____
70. Everyone crowded around Marty to warmly congratulate her on her tennis victory. _____
71. The coach having called for time out, our team huddled briefly for a conference. _____
72. My sister Frances is working in New York this summer, which is a good opportunity for her to learn about city life. _____
73. Theodore told me that he had read an interesting story about Abraham Lincoln's life last spring. _____
74. Hoke says that farming is a wonderful way of life, but Louis says that he can't imagine being one. _____
75. The woman who was sweeping vigorously moved along the walkway. _____

D. Each of the following sentences contains an error in punctuation or mechanics, or is correct. Indicate the error or the correctness by writing one of the following numbers in the space at the right:

    1 if a *comma* has been omitted,
    2 if a *semicolon* has been omitted,
    3 if an *apostrophe* has been omitted,
    4 if *quotation marks* have been omitted,
    5 if the sentence is *correct.*

76. Mr. Fuller who was born in Alaska has always wanted to return there for a visit. _____

77. January 30 1982 was the hundredth anniversary of Franklin D. Roosevelt's birth. _____

78. John's oldest brother Eugene is going to be married in June. _____

79. I took the roast from the freezer to defrost then I started making a lemon chiffon pie. _____

80. Wanting to show his appreciation David sent Mrs. Canby a dozen red roses. _____

81. Wanting always to have one's own way is a selfish approach to life. _____

82. Ruths new silk blouse was imported from China. _____

83. I can't believe that the sun would burn you in just one hour, exclaimed Mike. _____

84. The last three digits in my telephone number are *8*s. _____

85. Without Ernie Morris couldn't find his way back to the cabin. _____

86. The boat left Cologne at five o'clock the passengers who were left behind had to catch the train to Dusseldorf. _____

87. A friend of mine a mystery novelist will speak to our amateur writers' club tomorrow night. _____

88. One of Father's favorites has always been Edgar Allan Poe's story The Gold Bug. _____

89. The man wearing the gray flannel suit is Mr. Bartley's nephew. _____

90. Wishing I were a million miles away I climbed the diving tower and looked fearfully at the water far below. _____

91. My cousin Penelope has always been such a good cook that I wish she would write a cookbook. _____

92. The recipe for the chicken casserole we had at dinner last night is Penelopes. _____

93. James cordially invited me to join them at their table I had no choice but to accept: _____

94. Frankly Nancy I prefer your blue dress to that purple one. _____

95. When whipping cream always be sure that it is thoroughly chilled. _____

96. It's about time for me to give the puppy its dinner. _____

97. My twin brother Joseph is two inches shorter than I. _____

98. Hoagie Carmichael, the composer of the song Stardust, was born in Indiana. _____

99. From the mountain top we could see the whole countryside; below the roads looked like narrow ribbons. _____

100. Yours is the first application we have had for this job I think your promptness will be in your favor. _____

Index

Absolute phrase, 68–69
Adjectives
  comparison of, 155–156
  defined, 3
  demonstrative, 3
  indefinite, 3
  interrogative, 3
  possessive, 143
  predicate, 31, 153–154
  proper, 4
  use of, 153–156
Adverbs
  conjunctive, 11, 84
  defined, 10
  use of, 153–156
Agreement
  of pronoun and antecedent, 125–126
  of subject and verb, 111–114
Ambiguous modifiers, 192
Apostrophe, 247–248
Appositive phrase, 69
Articles, 3

Brackets, 231

Capital letters, 245–246
Case
  nominative, 141
  objective, 142
  of pronouns, 141–143
  possessive, 143
Clauses, 83–85, 93–96
  adjective, 94–95
  adverbial, 95–96
  dangling, 181
  dependent, 93–96
  independent, 83–85
  noun, 93–94
Colon, 228–229
Comma splice, 84–85
Commas, 226–228
  with dependent clauses, 94–95
  with independent clauses, 83–85
  with phrases, 68–69
Complements, 30–32
Complex sentence, 96
Compound sentence, 96
Compound-complex sentence, 96
Conjugation of verbs, 5–8
Conjunctions
  coordinating, 11
  correlative, 11, 200

defined, 11
  subordinating, 11, 210
Connotation, 280–281

Dangling modifiers, 181–182
Dash, 229
Diction, 277–289
  glossary of faulty, 281–289
Dictionary, use of the, 261–264
Direct object, 31

Euphemisms, 280
Exclamation mark, 225-226

Gerund, 53–55
Gerund phrase, 67–68
  dangling, 181
Glossary of faulty diction, 281–289
Greek roots, 309, 311–312

Hyphen, 248–250

Idiom, 280
Illogical comparisons and
  mixed constructions, 217–219
Indirect object, 31
Infinitive, 55
  split, 193
Infinitive phrase, 68
  dangling, 181
Interjection, 11
Italics, 246–247

Latin roots, 309–310, 312
Lie, lay, 164–165

Mechanics, 245–250
Mixed or confused constructions,
  217–219
Modifiers
  ambiguous, 192
  dangling, 181–182
  misplaced, 191–193
Mood, 6–9, 167
  imperative, 9
  indicative, 6–8
  subjunctive, 9, 167